C

Programming

For Problem Solving

First Edition

By Hemant Jain and Sukhendra Singh

C programming for problem solving.

Hemant Jain & Sukhendra Singh

ACKNOWLEDGEMENT

The authors are very grateful to GOD ALMIGHTY for his grace and blessing.

We would like to express profound gratitude to our friends for their invaluable encouragement, supervision, and useful suggestion throughout this book writing work. Their support and continuous guidance enable me to complete our work successfully.

Hemant Jain and Sukhendra Singh

Table of Contents

Table of Contents

CHAPTER 1: INTRODUCTION TO COMPUTER SYSTEM

Computer

A computer is a programmable electronic device designed to provide various services. It stores, retrieves and processes data efficiently. A computer receives data and instructions through "Input Devices" that get processed in the Central Processing Unit (CPU) and the result is displayed to "Output Devices."

The computer is a combination of Hardware and Software. Both Hardware and Software are equally important for the functioning of Computers.

Hardware

Hardware is a physical component of a computer like Processor, Memory, Mouse, Keyboard, Printer, Monitor etc.

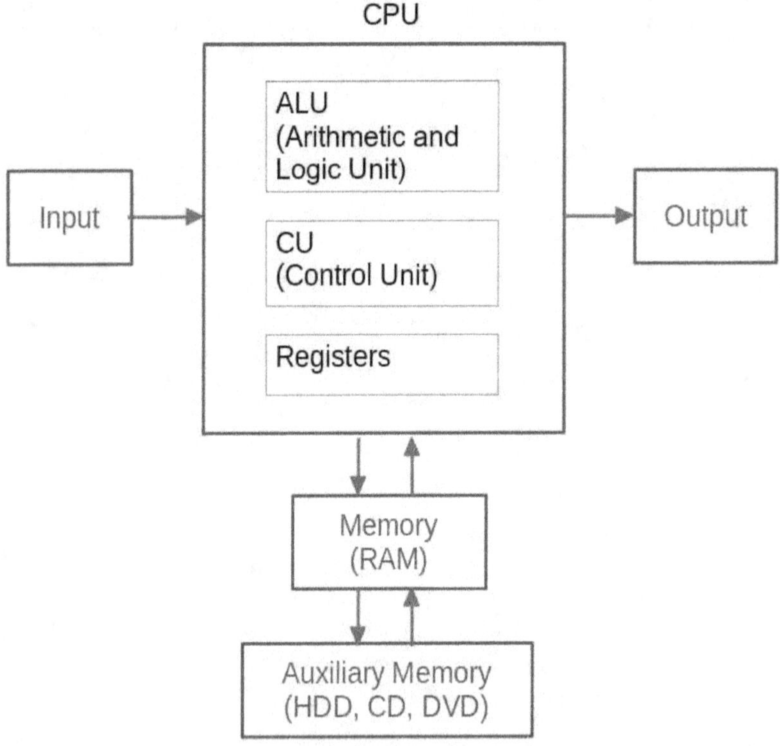

Functional Components of a Computer

Components of Computer are:
1. Input Devices
2. Output Devices
3. Processor / CPU (Central Processing Unit)
4. Memory / RAM (Random Access Memory, Non-persistent storage)
5. Storage or Auxiliary Memory (Persistent storage)

Input Devices: These devices are used to input data and instructions into the computer. E.g. Keyboard, Mouse etc.

CPU (Central Processing Unit): It is responsible for processing data and instructions. It receives data from input devices. It processes the data and stores the output or display to the output devices.

The Central Processing Unit is divided into three sections:
- ALU (Arithmetic & Logical Unit): It is responsible for performing various arithmetic operations like addition, subtraction, division, multiplication etc.
- CU (Control Unit): It is responsible for coordinating and controlling data in and out of the CPU. It controls the ALU, Memory Registers and also Input / Output Devices.
- Memory Registers: It is Non-persistent / temporary storage in the CPU. These are used to store data that is directly used by the CPU.

Output Devices: It is used to display the result to the user. The common output devices are Monitor, Printer, etc.

Memory / RAM: It is the memory attached to the CPU and is used to store data and instructions. When a program is executed its data is loaded into the memory and remains in the memory till the program end. Memory is also referred to as Main Memory, Primary Memory or RAM (Random access memory).

Storage or Auxiliary Memory: It is the persistent storage of data in which the data resides even if we switch off the computer. For example: Hard-drives, CD, DVD etc.

Lets understand the whole process by an example. Let's suppose you had clicked a text file MyFile.doc then the input device is mouse. Then then the file is brought to the Memory from the Auxiliary memory i.e. Hard drive. The program which can open files with ".doc" extension i.e. some word processor is also loaded to the Memory. Finally the file is displayed to the monitor which is the output device.

Generations of Computer

First Generation:

The period of the first generation: 1946-1959.
Core Technology: Vacuum tube-based.
Use Machine code as the programming language.

Advantage:
- Could perform various operations in milliseconds.

Disadvantages:
- Very big in size, weight in tons.
- Very costly.
- Not efficient.
- Huge electricity consumption.
- Punch cards and magnetic tapes are used to take input.

Second Generation

The period of the second generation: 1959-1965.
Core Technology: Transistor-based.
Assembly language and high-level programming languages like FORTRAN, COBOL were used.

Advantages:
- Quite small compared with the first generations.
- Low cost compared with the first generations.

Disadvantages:
- Still produces a lot of heat. So a cooling system is required.
- Very limited usage
- Still, punch cards are used to take input.

Third Generation

The period of the third generation: 1965-1971.
Core Technology: Integrated Circuit (IC).
High-level languages like FORTRAN-II TO IV, COBOL, PASCAL, BASIC etc. were used.

Advantages:
- Smaller than the second generation.
- Cheaper than the second generation.
- The mouse and keyboard are used to take input.
- Fast and reliable.
- Storage capacity is increased.
- Computational time is reduced from microseconds to nanoseconds.

Disadvantages:
- Still, a cooling system is required.
- IC chips are difficult to make.

Fourth Generation

The period of the fourth generation: 1971-1980.
Core Technology: VLSI (Very Large Scale Integrated) microprocessor.
High-level languages like C, C++ etc. were used.

Advantages:
- Smaller in size compared to the third generation.
- All types of high-level languages are used.
- Faster than the previous generation.
- Less heat generated.

Disadvantages:
- VLSI chips design and fabrication is complex.

Fifth Generation

The period of fifth-generation: 1980-onwards.
Core Technology: ULSI (Ultra Large Scale Integration) microprocessor and Artificial Intelligence.
All the high-level languages like C and C++, Java, .Net, etc. are used.

Advantages:
- Very light and handy.
- Reliable and work faster.
- All high-level languages can be used.

Disadvantages:
- ULSI chip design and fabrication is very complex.

Generation of Programming Language

A **First-generation (programming) language (1GL)** is a machine-level programming language that is used to program first-generation computers.

A **Second-generation programming language (2GL)** is Assembly languages.

A **Third-generation programming language (3GL)** is much more machine-independent and more programmer-friendly. The most popular general-purpose languages today are 3GL, such as C, C++, C#, Java, BASIC, etc.

A **Fourth-generation programming language (4GL)** is such a language whose statements are similar to the statements of the English language. 4GL languages are used to solve very specific problems. 4GL languages may include support for Database management, report generation, mathematical optimization, GUI development, or web development. E.g. SQL, R, etc.

A **Fifth-generation programming language (5GL)** is any programming language to solve the problem based on constraints and logic, rather than using an algorithm written by a programmer. 5GL is designed to make the computer solve a given problem without the programmer. E.g. OPS5, Mercury, etc.

Software

The software consists of various types of programs that control the operation of computers. The software is further divided into System Software, Utility Software, and Application Software.

System Software

System Software is the software that directly controls and utilizes computer hardware. These programs help in running application programs. System software directs the computer what to do, when to do and how to do.

System software can be further categorized into:
1. Operating System
2. Device Driver
3. Language Processors

Operating System

An **Operating system** is a software that provides an interface to the user to use computer hardware. It is a set of programs that control and supervise the computer hardware, software resources and also provide services to application software and the users. Process Management, Memory Management, Device Management, and File management are key functions of the Operating System. A computer system is of no use without an Operating System. When a computer is switched on the Operating System is the first program that is loaded to its memory.

Examples of Operating Systems used are Linux, Windows, Unix, etc.

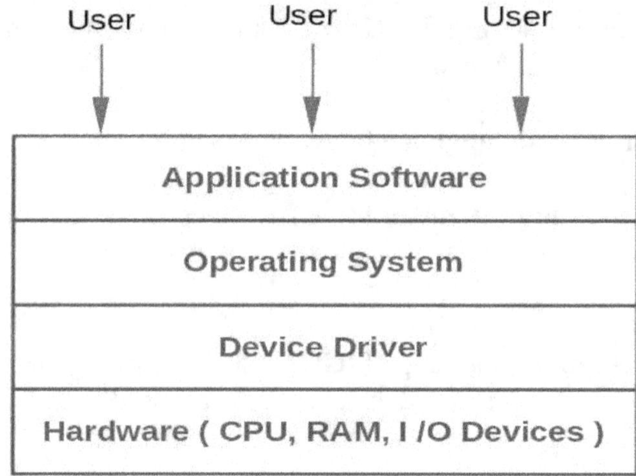

Functions of Operating System:
1. **Processor Management**: It deals with the management of the Central Processing Unit or CPU. The operating system performs the allotment of CPU time to various processes.
2. **Memory Management**: The operating system loads a program into memory when it needs to be executed and removes the program from memory when it is no longer needed.
3. **Device Management**: The operating system helps in communication between various types of hardware.
4. **File Management**: The operating system manages the files, folders, and directory structures of the computer. The operating system file manager is used to create, edit, copy, move, and delete files.

Device Driver

A device driver is a program that controls a particular device. Each device like a keyboard, mouse, printer, etc. need their driver to work. The device driver acts as a translator between the operating system and the device connected to the computer.

Language Processors

The computer can understand only instructions in machine code, i.e. in the form of 0s and 1s. It is very difficult to write computer programs directly in machine code. The programs are written mostly in high-level languages, i.e. C, C++, Python, etc. A program written in any high-level programming language is called the Source Program or Source Code.

The source code cannot be executed directly by the computer. The source code must be converted into machine language to be executed.

Language Processors are translator software that is used to translate the program written in a high-level language (or Assembly language) into machine level language. The language processors are of three types- Assembler, Compiler, and Interpreter.

Assembler

The Assembler is used to translate the program written in Assembly language into machine level language or machine code. The input of Assembler is a source program that contains assembly language instructions. The output generated by the assembler is the machine code that can be executed by the computer.

Compiler

The compiler is used to translate the high-level languages source program as a whole into machine level language. Some of the examples are C and C++ compilers. The source code is translated to object code successfully if it is free of errors. If there are any errors in the source code, the compiler specifies the errors at the end of compilation with line numbers. The errors must be removed before the compiler can successfully recompile the source code.

Difference between Assembler and Compiler.

Assembler	Compiler
Assembler converts, assembly language code into machine code.	The compiler converts source code written in higher-level language into machine level language.
Input is Assembly code	Input is Source code in some higher language.
GAS, GNU is an example of Assembler	C, C++, Java compilers are examples of compilers.

Interpreter

The interpreter is a language processor that translates a single statement of a source program into machine level language and executes it immediately before moving on to the next line. If there is an error in the statement the interpreter terminates its translating process at that statement and displays an error message. Only after removal of the error, the interpreter moves on to the next line for execution.

Difference between Compiler and Interpreter

Compiler	Interpreter
The compiler scans the whole program and translates it into machine code at once.	The interpreter translates just one statement of the program at a time into machine code.
Overall execution is fast	Overall execution is slow
A compiler creates an intermediary object code.	It does not create object code.
The program does not require translation / compilation every time you run the program.	Programs require translation every-time you run the program.
A compiler generates the error message only after it scans the complete program.	Keep translating the program until the first error is found.
The compiler is used by programming languages like C, C++, Java, C# etc.	Interpreters are used by programming languages like Python, Ruby, etc.

Linker

A linker combines one or more object files and possibly some library to create an executable.

Loader

A loader reads the executable code into memory and tries to run the program.

Difference between Linker and Loader

Linker	Loader
It generates executable files.	It loads the executable file into the main memory.
It takes input as object code and generates executables.	It takes executable code generated by linker as input.
It combines various object code into one single executable.	It allocates the address to an executable into the main memory.

Diagram Representing Linker and Loader.

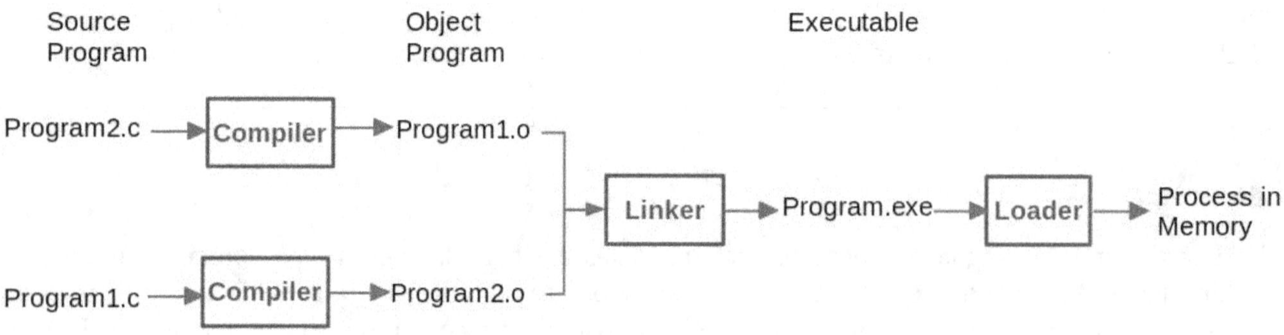

Stages of Compilation and Execution

1. Preprocessor: C programs are passed to preprocessor to resolve preprocessor directives and include files in the program.
2. Compiler: Compiler converts C program into machine language. In this step, an object file is created.
3. Linker: Linker combines various object files and libraries to form an executable.
4. Loader: Loader loads the executable file into the main memory.

Utility Software

Utility software provides certain tasks that help to manage, maintain, and control computer resources. The utility software is used to keep the computer system running smoothly. Examples of utility programs are antivirus software, backup software, etc. Antivirus software helps to protect computers from viruses and other harmful programs. Backup software helps in the creation of backup of the files on your computer. Hard-drives are used for storage; they are robust but can fail or crash. So backup software is used to create copies of the most important files in some external drive.

Application Software

Application software is used to solve a particular problem or perform some specific task.

Few examples of application software:
1. Microsoft Office
2. Photoshop
3. Music Players
4. Games

Number Systems

Number Systems are the way of representing numbers.

The most frequently used Number Systems are:
1. Decimal: It is a base 10 number system whose digits are 0, 1, 2, 3, 4, 5, 6, 7, 8, 9
   e.g. $(124)_{10}$, $(111)_{10}$
2. Binary: It is a base 2 number system whose digits are 0 and 1
   e.g. $(1010)_2$, $(111)_2$
3. Octal: It is a base 8 number system whose digits are 0, 1, 2, 3, 4, 5, 6, 7
   e.g. $(167)_8$, $(234)_8$
4. HexaDecimal: It is a base 16 number system whose digits are 0, 1, 2, 3, 4, 5, 6, 7, 8, 9, A, B, C, D, E, F
   e.g. $(2AF)_{16}$, $(14E)_{16}$

   Note: In hexadecimal number system A, B, C, D, E, F are corresponding to 10, 11, 12, 13, 14, 15

Example: which of the number system representation is invalid?
1. $(123)_{10}$
2. $(101)_2$
3. $(138)_8$
4. $(ABC)_{16}$

The solution is $(138)_8$ is invalid since the octal value should have digits from 0 to 7. So digit 8 in the number makes it invalid.

Conversion of Number Systems
1. Binary to Octal
2. Binary to Decimal
3. Binary to Hexadecimal
4. Octal to Binary
5. Octal to Decimal
6. Octal to Hexadecimal
7. Decimal to Binary
8. Decimal to Octal
9. Decimal to Hexadecimal
10. Hexadecimal to Binary
11. Hexadecimal to Octal
12. Hexadecimal to Decimal

Octal to Binary

Three digits of binary are corresponding to one digit of Octal. Or each digit of octal corresponding to 3 digits of binary

Table for converting Binary to Octal

Binary	Octal
0 0 0	0
0 0 1	1
0 1 0	2
0 1 1	3
1 0 0	4
1 0 1	5
1 1 0	6
1 1 1	7

Example 1.1: Convert $(567)_8$ to $()_2$?
5 = 101
6 = 110
7 = 111
So answer is $(101110111)_2$

Example 1.2: Convert $(23.4)_8$ to $()_2$?
The solution will be $(010011.100)_2$ or we can ignore the last zeroes and the final answer will be $(10011.1)_2$

Note: You don't have to make a table each time you want to make a conversion.
You need to find factors of 4, 2, and 1 in the number.
For example, 5 is made of 4 and 1 so the binary code will be 101
Similarly, 6 is made of 4 and 2 so the binary code will be 110
Similarly, 7 is made of 4, 2, and 1 so the binary code will be 111

Binary to Octal

Each octal digit corresponds to 3 binary digits. We do a grouping of 3 digits to convert from binary to octal.

Example 1.3: Convert $(10011)_2$ to $()_8$
10 011

Note: Extra zeroes can be added if required.
010 011
2 3
Answer is $(23)_8$

Example 1.4: Convert $(11.1)_2$ to $()_8$
11.1
011 . 100
3.4
Answer is $(3.4)_8$

Note: Extra zeroes can be added on the left for the whole part and on the right for fractional parts.

Hexadecimal to Binary

Four digits of Binary are corresponding to one digit of Hexadecimal. Or each digit of Hexadecimal corresponding to 4 digits of Binary

Table for converting Binary to Hexadecimal

Binary	Hexadecimal
0 0 0 0	0
0 0 0 1	1
0 0 1 0	2
0 0 1 1	3
0 1 0 0	4
0 1 0 1	5
0 1 1 0	6
0 1 1 1	7

1 0 0 0	8
1 0 0 1	9
1 0 1 0	10 => A
1 0 1 1	11 => B
1 1 0 0	12 => C
1 1 0 1	13 => D
1 1 1 0	14 => E
1 1 1 1	15 => F

Example 1.5: Convert $(A6)_{16}$ to $()_2$

A = 10 = 1010

6 = 0110

Answer will be $(1010\ 0110)_2$

Note: You don't need to make a table each time you do some conversion to Hexadecimal.

Find factors of 8,4,2 and 1

So A which is 10 is made of 8 and 2, so the corresponding binary code will be 1010

Similarly, C which is 12 is made of 8 and 4, so the corresponding binary code will be 1100

Similarly, D which is 13 is made of 8, 4, and 1, so the corresponding binary code will be 1101

Binary to Hexadecimal

Each hexadecimal digit corresponds to 4 binary digits. So to convert binary to hexadecimal we will do a grouping of 4 binary digits. We will add extra zeros if required to the number to make a group of 4 digits.

Example 1.6: Concert $(1111110)_2$ to $()_{16}$

111 0110 is the same as 0111 1110

Answer is 7E

Example 1.7: Convert $(11.11)_2$ to $()_{16}$

0011 . 1100

Answer is 3.C

Note: After adding the required zeroes we need to calculate the value "1100" is 8+4 = 12 and the digit of hexadecimal will be C. If the calculated value is between 10 to 15 then the corresponding digit A to F will be replaced.

Octal to Hexadecimal

There is no direct conversion from Octal to Hexadecimal; we need to convert Octal to Binary and then from Binary to Hexadecimal.

Example 1.8: Convert $(75.2)_8$ to $()_{16}$.

$(111\ 101\ .\ 010)_2$

Now we need to make a grouping of 4
11 1101 . 0100
Add the required number of zeroes to make a grouping of 4
0011 1101 . 0100
Answer is $(3D.4)_{16}$

Note: You don't need to make a complete table to solve one conversion if the value calculated is less than or equal to 9 then it is the value if the calculated value is greater than 9 then it will be between A to F. For example 1101 the value will be 8+4+1 so 13 and 13 is D.

Hexadecimal to Octal

There is no direct conversion from Hexadecimal to Octal we need to convert Hexadecimal to Binary and then from Binary to Octal.

Example 1.9: Convert $(3D.4)_{16}$ to $()_8$.
$(0011\ 1101 . 0100)_2$
Now we need to make a grouping of 3
00 111 101 . 010 0
Add the required number of zeroes to make a grouping of 3. Also ignoring the most left group of zeroes in the whole number and ignoring the most right zeroes in the fractional part.
111 101 . 010
Answer is $(75.2)_8$

Decimal to Binary

Decimal to binary is converted using division by 2 methods for the whole part. And multiplication by 2 methods for the fractional part.

Example 1.10: Convert $(200)_{10}$ to $()_2$

	Quotient	Reminder
2	200	
2	100	0
2	50	0
2	25	0
2	12	1
2	6	0
2	3	0
2	1	1
	0	1

All the reminder in reverse order: 11001000
Answer is $(11001000)_2$
We can check that the binary number is correct $2^7 + 2^6 + 2^3 = 128 + 64 + 8 = 200$

For converting fractional decimals to binary we need to multiply the fractional part till we get zero fractional part or we get repetition in number.

Example 1.11: Convert $(.125)_{10}$ to $()_2$

Fractional * 2	Value	Integral Value
.125 * 2	.250	0
.23 * 2	.5	0
.5 * 2	1.0	1
0		

Answer is $(.001)_2$

Example 1.12: Convert $(12.125)_{10}$ to $()_2$

For converting a number with both fractional and integral parts find the binary equivalent for both and then add them.

Finding integral part 12 binary equivalent

	Quotient	Reminder
2	12	
2	6	0
2	3	0
2	1	1
	0	1

All the reminder in reverse order: 1100
The binary representation of integral part $(1100)_2$
the fractional part solution as given above $(.125)_{10}$ is $(.001)_2$
So the answer is $(1100.001)_2$

Decimal to Octal

Decimal to octal are converted using division by 8 method for integral part. And multiplication by 8 methods for the fractional part.

Example 1.13: Convert $(200)_{10}$ to $()_8$

	Quotient	Reminder
8	200	
8	25	0
8	3	1
	0	3

All the reminder in reverse order: 310
Answer is $(310)_8$
We can check that the octal number is correct: $8^2*3 + 8 = 64*3+8 = 192 + 8 = 200$

Example 1.14: Convert $(.125)_{10}$ to $()_8$

Fractional * 8	Value	Integral Value
.125 * 8	1.000	1
0		

Answer is $(.1)_8$

Example 1.15: Convert $(200.125)_{10}$ to $()_8$
For converting a number with both fractional and integral parts find the octal equivalent for both and then add them.
The octal equivalent can be found as given in previous problems. So the solution will be $(310.1)_8$

Decimal to Hexadecimal

Decimal to hexadecimal is converted using division by 16 methods for an integral part. And multiplication by 16 methods for the fractional part.

Example 1.16: Convert $(200)_{10}$ to $()_{16}$

	Quotient	Reminder
16	200	
16	12	8
	0	12 => C

All the reminders in reverse order: C8. Answer is $(C8)_{16}$
We can check that the octal number is correct: $12*16 + 8 = 192 + 8 = 200$

Example 1.17: Convert $(.125)_{10}$ to $()_{16}$

Fractional * 16	Value	Integral Value
.125 * 16	2.000	2
0		

Answer is $(.2)_{16}$

Example 1.18: Convert $(200.125)_{10}$ to $()_{16}$
For converting a number with both fractional and integral parts find the hexadecimal equivalent for both and then add them. The octal equivalent can be found as given in previous problems. So the solution will be $(C8.2)_{16}$

Binary to Decimal

Example 1.19: Convert $(11001000)_2$ to $()_{10}$
$1*2^7+1*2^6+1*2^3 = 128 + 64 + 8 = 200$
Answer is $(200)_{10}$

Example 1.20: Convert $(.001)_2$ to $()_{10}$
$1*2^{-3} = 1 * 1/8 = 1/8 = 0.125$
Answer is $(.125)_{10}$

Note: In the case of fractional and integral parts we need to calculate them separately and then adding both will produce the final result.

Octal to Decimal

Example 1.21: Convert $(310)_8$ to $()_{10}$
$3* 8^2 + 1* 8 = 3 * 64 + 1 * 8 = 192 + 8 = 200$
Answer is $(200)_{10}$

Example 1.22: Convert $(.1)_8$ to $()_{10}$
$1*8^{-1} = 1 * 1/8 = 1/8 = 0.125$
Answer is $(.125)_{10}$

Hexadecimal to Decimal

Example 1.23: Convert $(C8)_{16}$ to $()_{10}$
$C * 16^1 + 8 = 12 * 16 + 8 = 192 + 8 = 200$
Answer is $(200)_{10}$

Example 1.24: Convert $(.2)_{16}$ to $()_{10}$
$2*16^{-1} = 2 * 1/16 = 1/8 = 0.125$
Answer is $(.125)_{10}$

Questions & Answers

Question 1: Define the concept of Modular programming?
Answer: Modular programming is the process of dividing a computer program into separate sub-programs. A module is a separate software program. It can often be developed and tested separately before integrated to firm the complete application.

When the program or software is big and contains thousands or millions of lines of code. Then functionality is divided into various modules that are developed and tested separately. Finally when all the modules or sub-programs are developed and tested. Then they are integrated to form the final program.

Each module has a separate API and separate feature set which helps in dividing the project among various teams that can work on separate modules.

Question 2: Describe the Top-down development approach.
Answer: In a computer program the program is divided into sub-programs called modules. In the top-down approach, the main program is developed first and then stubs of subprograms are called from the main program. Stubs are just placeholders of the actual sub-program; they just implement an interface but do not contain any real code inside them. The interface is the argument list and the return type of a program. Slowly these stubs will be replaced by the actual implementation of the sub-program.

Question 3: Describe the Bottom-Up development approach.
Answer: In a computer program the program is divided into sub-program called modules. In the bottom up approach first, the sub-programs are implemented then the main program is implemented which will further call the sub-program.

Question 4: Name a few Compilers of C language.
Answer: Few compilers of C language are:
- Microsoft Visual Studio.
- GCC
- Xcode
- Clang

Question 5: Why do we need a programming language?
Answer: We want the computer to perform some task then we need to provide it with instructions which are unambiguous and clear. The computers can not use natural languages like 'English' because they are ambiguous. So programming languages are created to provide unambiguous instructions to the computer.

Exercise

1. What is a Computer? Draw a block diagram of a Computer and explain each of its components.

2. What is an Operating System? What are the various types of operations performed by an Operating System?

3. Describe Compiler, Interpreter, and Assembler. Name anyone compiler used in C Programming.

4. Write the difference among Compiler, Interpreter, and Assembler.

5. Describe Linker and Loader. Write the difference between the linker and loader.

6. Point out the characteristics of a good programming language.

7. What are the stages of translation of a C program to its machine code?

8. Convert $(.3)_{10}$ and $(.5)_{10}$ into binary.

9. Convert $(10111011)_2$ to decimal and hexadecimal number system

10. Convert the following:
    1. $(0110110.1100)_2 = (\ )_8$
    2. $(74.67)_{10} = (\ )_{16}$
    3. $(AB.CD)_{16} = (\ )_8$
    4. $(EFE.45)_{16} = (\ )_2$
    5. $(576.4)_{10} = (\ )_6$

6. $(1234.7)_8 = (\ )_{16}$
7. $(334.43)_8 = (\ )_2$

Hints:

$(0110110.1100)_2 = (0\ 110\ 110.110\ 0)_2 = (66.6)_8$

$(74.67)_{10} = (4A.AB85)_{16}$

$(AB.CD)_{16} = (253.632)_8$

$(EFE.45)_{16} = (1110\ 1111\ 1110.0100\ 0101)_2$

$(576.4)_{10} = (2400.22)_6$

$(1234.7)_8 = (29C.E)_{16}$

$(334.43)_8 = (011\ 011\ 100.100\ 011)_2$

Algorithm

An algorithm is a finite set of unambiguous steps or instructions to solve a given problem.

An algorithm must have the following criteria or characteristics:
1. **Well defined Input**: Zero or more inputs are provided. Input should be well defined.
2. **Well defined Output**: Every algorithm must give at least one output. The output should be well defined.
3. **Unambiguous**: Each instruction is clear and unambiguous.
4. **Finiteness**: Every algorithm should terminate after a finite number of steps.
5. **Effectiveness**: The output of the algorithm should be correct.

Example 2.1: Write an algorithm to print "Hello, World!".

Step 1: Start
Step 2: **Print** "Hello, World!"
Step 3: Stop

Example 2.2: Write an algorithm to add two numbers.

Step 1: Start
Step 2: Take two numbers and store them in **variable** A and B
Step 3: Add value stored in A and B and store the sum in **variable** S
Step 4: **Print** value stored in S
Step 5: Stop

Example 2.3: Write an algorithm to find the area of a rectangle.

Step 1: Start
Step 2: Take length and breadth and store them in **variable** L and B
Step 3: Multiply by L and B and store its product in **variable** Area
Step 4: **Print** value stored in Area
Step 5: Stop

Example 2.4: Write an algorithm to compute an average of three numbers.

Step 1: Start
Step 2: Take three numbers and store them in **variable** A, B and C
Step 3: Add value stored in A, B and C and store the sum in **variable** S
Step 4: Find average by dividing S by 3 and store the value in **variable** Avg
Step 5: **The print** value stored in Avg
Step 6: Stop

Example 2.5: Write an algorithm to check whether a person is Minor or Major.

Step 1: Start
Step 2: Take age of person and store it in **variable** Age
Step 3: **If** Age >= 18 **then go-to** step 4 **else go-to** step 5
Step 4: **Print** "Is a Major" and **go-to** step 6
Step 5: **Print** "Is a Minor"
Step 6: Stop

Example 2.6: Write an algorithm to check whether a given number is +ve, -ve or zero.

Step 1: Start
Step 2: Take a number and store it in **variable** N.
Step 3: **If** value stored in N > 0, **then go-to** step 5 **else go-to** step 4
Step 4: **If** value stored in N < 0, **then go-to** step 6 **else go-to** step 7
Step 5: **Print** "Given number is +ve" and **go-to** step 8
Step 6: **Print** "Given number is -ve" and **go-to** step 8
Step 7: **Print** "Given number is zero"
Step 8: Stop

Example 2.7: Write an algorithm to check whether a given number is +ve, -ve or zero.

Step 1: Start
Step 2: Take a number and store it in **variable** N.
Step 3: **If** (N%2) == 0, **then go-to** step 4 **else go-to** step 5
Step 4: **Print** "Given number is even" and **go-to** step 6
Step 5: **Print** "Given number is odd" and **go-to** step 6
Step 6: Stop

Example 2.8: Write an algorithm to find the largest of three numbers.

Step 1: Start
Step 2: Take three numbers and store them in **variable** A, B and C
Step 3: **If** A > B **then go-to** step 4 **else go-to** step 7
Step 4: **If** A > C **then go-to** step 5 **else go-to** step 6
Step 5: **Print** "Largest value is A" **go-to s**tep 10
Step 6: **Print** "Largest value is C" **go-to** step 10
Step 7: **If** B > C **then go-to** step 8 **else go-to** step 9
Step 8: **Print** "Largest value is A" **go-to s**tep 10
Step 9: **Print** "Largest value is C" **go-to** step 10
Step 10: Stop

Flow Chart

A Flow-Chart is a pictorial representation of an algorithm. In a Flow-Chart various steps of the algorithm are represented using different shapes.

Various shapes of Flow-Chart:

Symbol	Function
(ellipse)	Start / Stop
(arrow)	Flow of Control
(parallelogram)	Input / Output
(rectangle)	Processing
(diamond)	Decision Box
(circle)	Connector

Example 2.9: Draw a Flow-Chart to print "Hello, World!".
Step 1: Start
Step 2: **Print** "Hello, World!"
Step 3: Stop

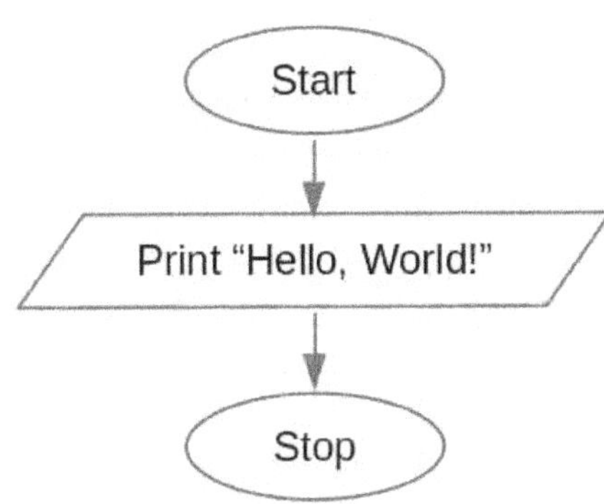

Example 2.10: Draw a Flow-Chart to add two numbers.
Step 1: Start
Step 2: Take two numbers and store them in **variable** A and B
Step 3: Add value stored in A and B and store the sum in **variable** S
Step 4: **Print** value stored in S
Step 5: Stop

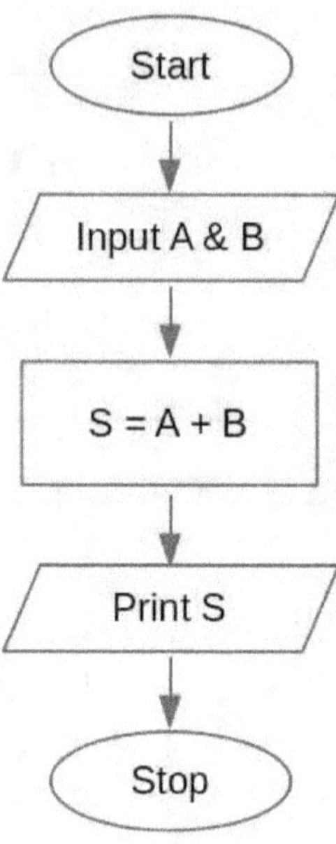

Example 2.11: Draw a Flow-Chart to find the area of a rectangle.
Step 1: Start
Step 2: Take length and breadth and store them in **variable** L and B
Step 3: Multiply by L and B and store its product in **variable** A
Step 4: **Print** value stored in A
Step 5: Stop

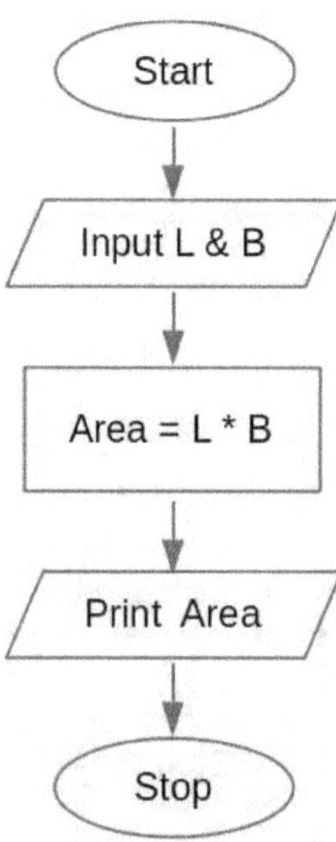

Example 2.12: Draw a Flow-Chart to compute an average of three numbers.
Step 1: Start
Step 2: Take three numbers and store them in **variable** A, B and C
Step 3: Add value stored in A, B and C and store the sum in **variable** S
Step 4: Find average by dividing S by 3 and store the value in **variable** Avg
Step 5: **Print** value stored in Avg
Step 6: Stop

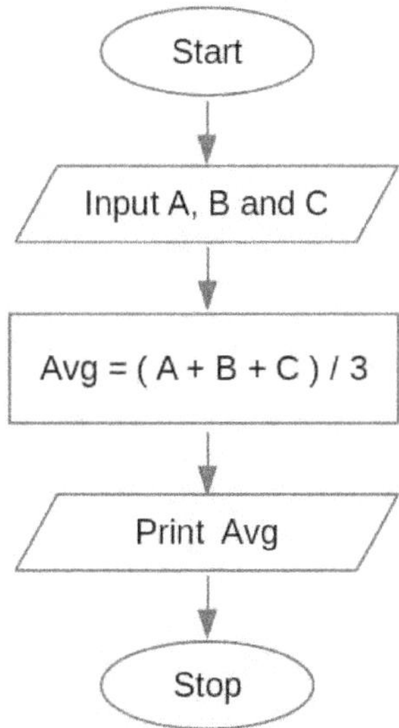

Example 2.13: Draw a Flow-Chart to check whether a person is Minor or Major.
Step 1: Start
Step 2: Take age of person and store it in **variable** Age
Step 3: **If** Age >= 18 **then go-to** step 4 **else go-to** step 5
Step 4: **Print** "Is a Major" and **go-to** step 6
Step 5: **Print** "Is a Minor"
Step 6: Stop

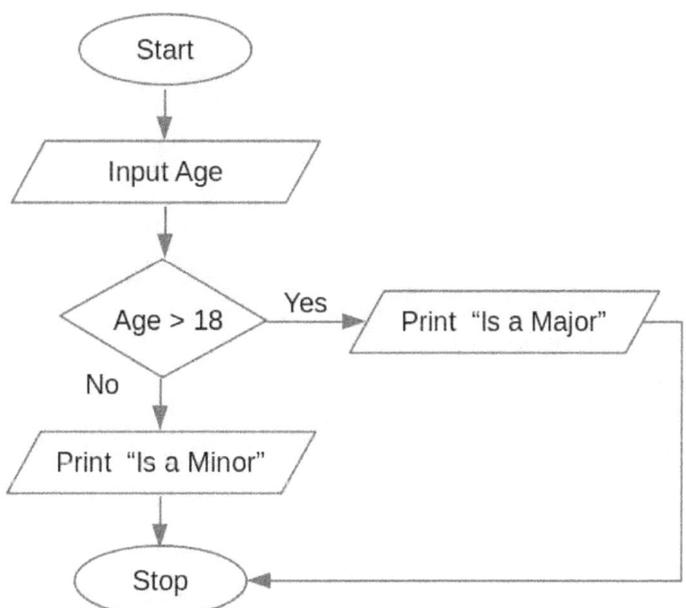

Example 2.14: Draw a Flow-Chart to check whether a given number is +ve, -ve or zero.

Step 1: Start
Step 2: Take a number and store it in **variable** N.
Step 3: **If** value stored in N > 0, **then go-to** step 5 **else go-to** step 4
Step 4: **If** value stored in N < 0, **then go-to** step 6 **else go-to** step 7
Step 5: **Print** "Given number is +ve" and **go-to** step 8
Step 6: **Print** "Given number is -ve" and **go-to** step 8
Step 7: **Print** "Given number is zero"
Step 8: Stop

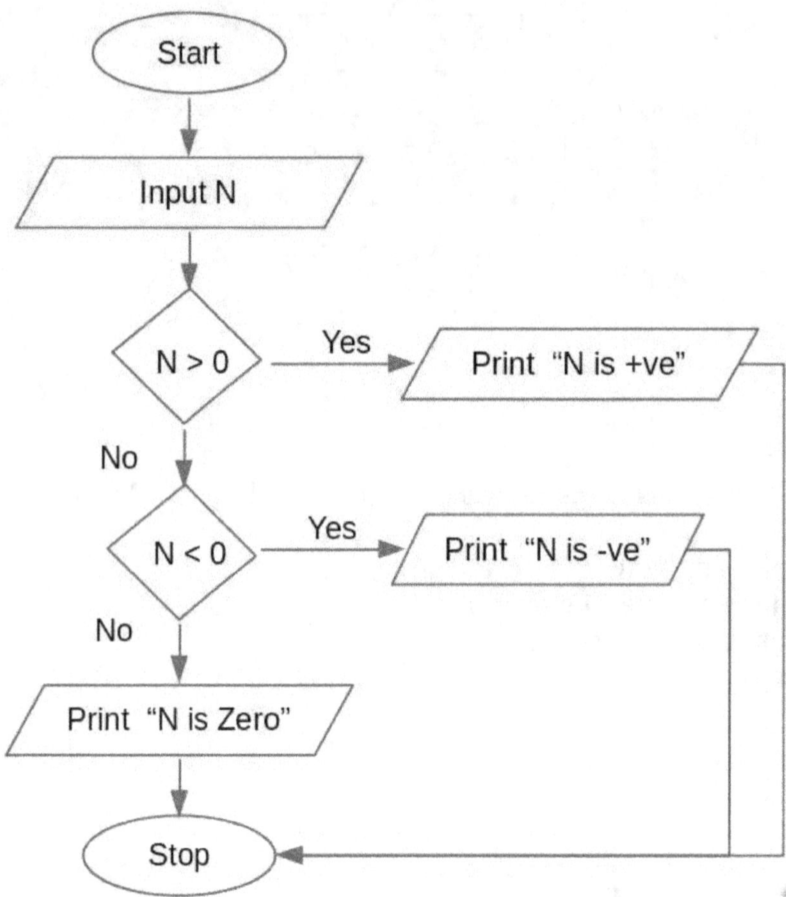

Example 2.15: Write an algorithm to check whether a given number is +ve, -ve or zero.

Step 1: Start
Step 2: Take a number and store it in **variable** N.
Step 3: **If** (N%2) == 0, **then go-to** step 4 **else go-to** step 5
Step 4: **Print** "Given number is even" and **go-to** step 6
Step 5: **Print** "Given number is odd" and **go-to** step 6
Step 6: Stop

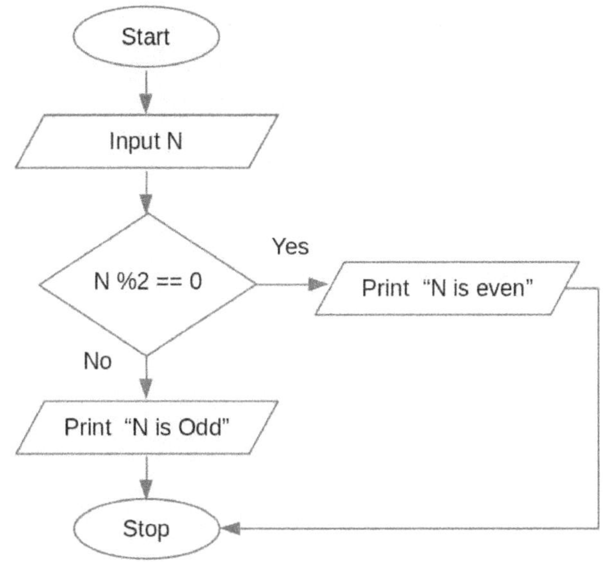

Example 2.16: Draw a Flow-Chart to find the largest of three numbers.
Step 1: Start
Step 2: Take three numbers and store them in **variable** A, B and C
Step 3: **If** A > B **then go-to** step 4 **else go-to** step 7
Step 4: **If** A > C **then go-to** step 5 **else go-to** step 6
Step 5: **Print** "Largest value is A" **go-to s**tep 10
Step 6: **Print** "Largest value is C" **go-to** step 10
Step 7: **If** B > C **then go-to** step 8 **else go-to** step 9
Step 8: **Print** "Largest value is A" **go-to s**tep 10
Step 9: **Print** "Largest value is C" **go-to** step 10
Step 10: Stop

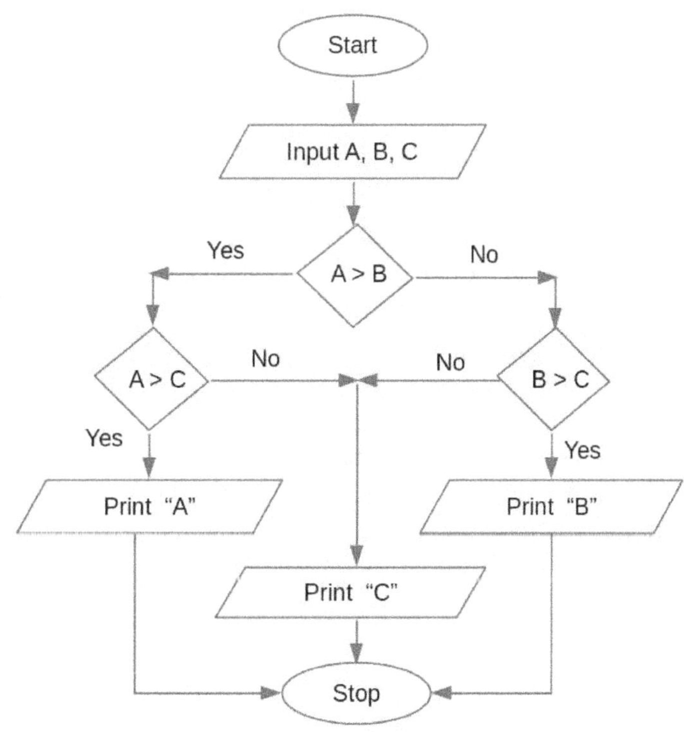

Example 2.17: Write algorithm and Flowchart for finding Area and Circumference given radius of circle.

Step 1: Start
Step 2: Take radius of circle and store them in **variable** R
Step 3: Calculate Area = 3.14 * R * R
Step 4: Calculate Circum= 2 * 3.14 * R
Step 5: **Print** value stored in Area and Circum
Step 6: Stop

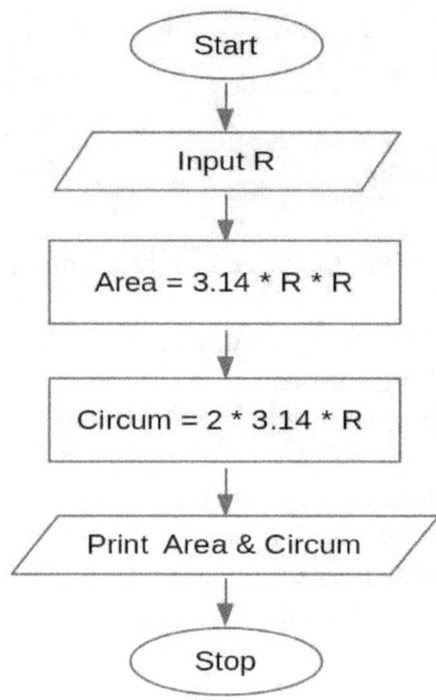

Pseudo Code

It is an informal text-based detailed design of a program that helps programmers to develop programs in some programming language. It is an intermediary between an algorithm and source code. Pseudocode can be used to write source code in any high-level language.

Example 2.18: Write an algorithm to add two numbers.

Step 1: Start
Step 2: Take two numbers and store them in **variable** A and B
Step 3: Add value stored in A and B and store the sum in **variable** S
Step 4: **Print** value stored in S
Step 5: Stop

```
FUNCTION Sum(A, B)
     S = A + B
    PRINT S
```

Example 2.19: Draw a Flow-Chart to check whether a person is Minor or Major.

Step 1: Start
Step 2: Take the age of a person and store it in **variable** Age
Step 3: **If** Age >= 18 **then go-to** step 4 **else go-to** step 5
Step 4: **Print** "Is a Major" and **go-to** step 6
Step 5: **Print** "Is a Minor"
Step 6: Stop

```
FUNCTION CheckMajorOrMinor(Age)
     IF Age > 18 than
          PRINT "Is a Major"
     ELSE
          PRINT "Is a Minor"
```

Example 2.20: Write an algorithm to find the Factorial of a number.

Step 1: Start
Step 2: Take the input number and store it in **variable** N
Step 3: **From** values N to 1, multiply each value and store in **variable** Fact
Step 4: **Print** Fact
Step 5: Stop

```
FUNCTION findFactorial(N)
     fact = 1
     FOR val = N to 1
          fact = fact * val

     PRINT fact
```

Problem Solving Methods

Problem Solving Method / Program development cycle:
- Define the problem.
- Develop an Algorithm.
- Coding.
- Testing & Debugging.

1. Define the Problem
- A clear problem statement needs to be created.
- Input and output need to be specified.
- Constraints need to be specified.

2. Develop an Algorithm
- Sequence of steps that need to be followed is specified.
- An algorithm can be created along with flowchart or pseudocode.

3. Coding
- ◆ Actual code is written using some programming language.
- ◆ Compilation of code to convert it into machine language.
- ◆ When the compiler finds an error, it prevents code conversion into machine language.

4. Testing & Debugging
- ◆ Testing is done to find if the program is performing correctly.
- ◆ If a program has errors then these errors are fixed using debugging.
- ◆ The coding, Testing, and Debugging phase is repeated until the program gives the desired outcome.

Questions & Answers

Question 1: What is the difference between Algorithm and Pseudo-Code?

Answer:

Algorithm	Pseudo Code
An algorithm is a well-defined sequence of steps to solve a particular problem.	A pseudocode is a method to represent algorithms.
Algorithms are written in natural language kind of format.	Pseudocode is written in a format that closely resembles a higher-level programming language.

Question 2: What is the difference between Algorithm, Pseudo-code, and Source Code?

Answer:

Algorithm	Pseudo Code	Source Code
An algorithm is a well-defined sequence of steps to solve a particular problem.	Pseudocode is a method of representing algorithms in a format that closely resembles high-level programming language.	It is code written by a programmer in some programming language.

e.g. Factorial of a given number.
 	
Step 1: Start
Step 2: Take the input number and store it in **variable** N
Step 3: **From** values N to 1, multiply each digit and store in **variable** Fact
Step 4: Print Fact
Step 5: Stop
	e.g. Factorial of a given number.
	
	FUNCTION findFactorial(N)
	   fact = 1
	   FOR val = N to 1
	      fact=fact * val
	
	   PRINT fact
		e.g. Factorial of a given number.
		
		int factorial(int N){
		   int fact = 1;
		   while (N > 1){
		     fact=fact*N;
		     N--;
		   }
		   return fact;
		}

Question 3: What is the difference between Pseudocode and Flowchart?

Answer: A Flow-Chart is a pictorial representation of an algorithm. In a Flow-Chart various steps of the algorithm are represented using different shapes.

For example Flow-Chart for adding two numbers.

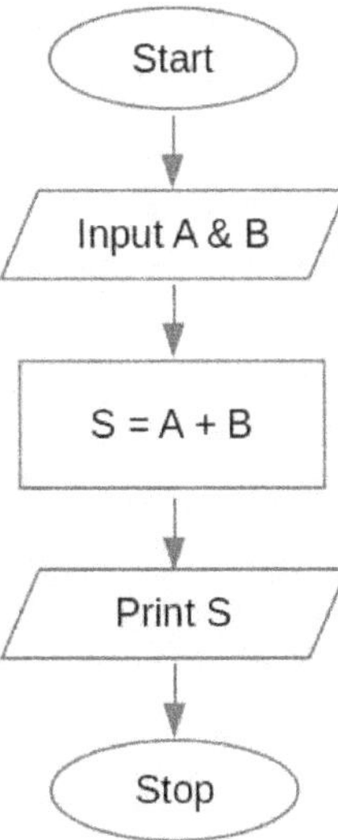

A Pseudocode is an informal text-based detailed design of a program that helps programmers to develop a program in some programming language. It is an intermediary between an algorithm and source code. Pseudocode can be used to write source code in any high-level language.

For example Pseudo-code for the addition of two numbers.
```
FUNCTION Sum(A, B)
     S = A + B
     PRINT S
```

Question 4: What is an algorithm? What are the main steps followed in the development of an algorithm? Write an algorithm for the sum of digits in a given number.

Answer: An Algorithm is a finite set of unambiguous steps or instructions to solve a given problem.

The main steps followed in the development of an algorithm are:
1. Description of problems:
   - The problem statement that needs to be solved.
   - The constraints that need to be followed while solving the problem.
   - The input is taken by the problem.
   - The expected output of the problem.

2. Designing the Algorithm.
   - Higher level algorithms which show the major steps that need to be followed.
   - The lower level algorithm which contains details about all the steps.

3. Reviewing:
    ◦   We need to work through the algorithm step-by-step to determine whether or not it will solve the given problem.

    Step 1: Start
    Step 2: Take the input number and store it in **variable** N
    Step 3: Declare a **variable** SUM = 0
    Step 4: **Repeat** step 5 and 6 **until** values N > 0,
    Step 5: Get the rightmost digit of number N by using the "%" remainder operator. And add the reminder to the SUM.
    Step 6: Divide the number by 10 using the "/" operator.
    Step 7: **Print** the value stored in SUM.
    Step 8: Stop

Exercise

1. Write an Algorithm to find a minimum of three numbers.

2. Draw a Flowchart to find a minimum of three numbers.

3. Write Pseudocode to find a minimum of three numbers.

4. Draw a Flowchart to find the factorial of a given number.

5. What do you mean by the algorithm? Explain the characteristics of algorithms.

6. How is pseudocode different from an algorithm?

7. Why is it better to conceptualize algorithm and pseudocode before writing actual source code?

8. How a pseudo code is different from the actual source code?

9. Draw a flowchart for displaying the sum of the smallest and largest numbers of three given numbers.

10. Draw the flowchart for testing for the Primality of a number.

CHAPTER 3: PROGRAMMING BASICS

Introduction

Welcome to the C language. The C language is a procedural language, which means we specify the sequence of steps that need to be followed to reach the desired output. It is as if I will do "job1" than "job2" and finally "job3" and at the end, my work is done.

C is a compiled language, which means you have to run C code through a compiler to make it understandable to your computer. Normally the C's program compilation process involves four stages, which are pre-processor, compiler, assembler, and linker. At the end, there should be a single executable file (these stages are explained in detail in the Library chapter). An executable file is run to see output.

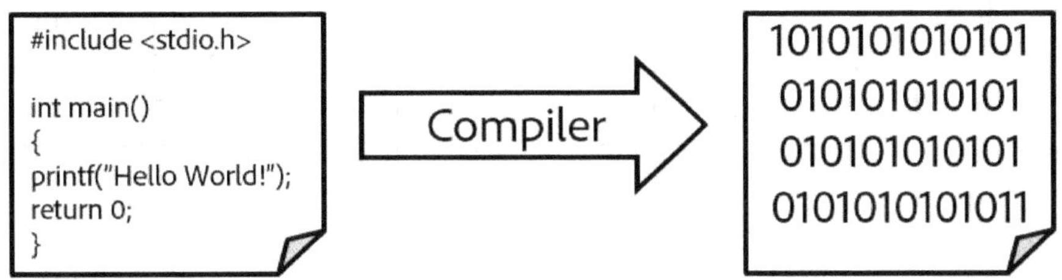

C is a general-purpose programming language, so it does not matter whether your operating system is Linux, Windows, or Mac. Before we begin this chapter, I recommend that you should get your system ready. Various IDEs (Integrated development environment) are available to compile and run C programs.

You can use CodeBlocks IDE which can be downloaded from http://www.codeblocks.org. CodeBlocks supports all the three most famous operating systems- Windows, Linux and Mac OS. If you want to use the command line you can use GCC.

Source code is provided as an argument to GCC and an executable if produced which can further be executed to see the output.

gcc hello.c -o hello.exe
In the above line, hello.c file is compiled using GCC compiler and the output is stored in a hello.exe file. You can run the hello.exe file.

./hello.exe
The output will be printed into the display.

A Simple C Program

Let's start with a very basic C program, which will print "Hello World!" to the screen. Each line of the program that does something is called a statement. Each statement ends with a semicolon ";".

Example 3.1 : hello.c

```
1.    #include <stdio.h>
2.
3.    int main()
4.    {
5.         printf("Hello world!\n");
6.         return 0;
7.    }
```

Output:

```
1.    Hello, World!
```

Analysis:

- Line 1: #include<> is used to tell the compiler which file's functions we are going to use. C language provides several files and pre-compiled code (called libraries) which contains functions/facilities that are commonly used in programming. For example, in the above program, we have included file "stdio.h", this is the file that contains the implementation of printf() function which is used to print "Hello, World!" to the standard output which is the screen. The stdio.h file is called standard input output file which contains functionality related to input and output.

- Line 3: int main(), this is the starting point of C programs. Every program has a main() function in it. The return value of main() is "int", this return value is used by the system to tell whether the program terminated normally or if some error had occurred. If the return value is zero then the program terminated successfully, otherwise, there was some error.

- Line 4 and 7: Symbol "{" is called the start of a block and Symbol "}" is called the end of a block. Every start of a block has a corresponding end of a block. The block, which is after the function name, is called the body of a function.

- Line 5: In this line, we are printing "Hello, World!" string to the screen. printf() function is defined in stdio.h file, so you need to include it before using this function.

- Line 6: This is the return statement that will return 0 to the system. Return value 0 means that the function is terminated properly.

Note: In short, every C language program which prints something to the screen and which takes input from the keyboard must always include stdio.h file.

Note: Every program starts with main() and the last statement of the main is return 0; No line after return will be executed.

Character Set

A **character set** defines the characters that can be used in programs. The *source character set* is the set of characters available for the source text. The *execution character set* is the set of characters available when executing a program.

Most ANSI-compatible C compilers accept the following ASCII characters for both source and execution character sets.

- The 26 lowercase English characters: a b c d e f g h i j k l m n o p q r s t u v w x y z

- The 26 uppercase English characters: A B C D E F G H I J K L M N O P Q R S T U V W X Y Z

- The 10 decimal digits: 0 1 2 3 4 5 6 7 8 9

- The 30 graphic characters: ! # % ^ & * ( ) - _ = + ~ ' " : ; ? / | \ { } [ ] , . < > $

- Five white space characters: Space ( ), Horizontal tab (\t), Form feed (\f), Vertical tab (\v), New-line character (\n)

ASCII Characters

ASCII value represents the characters as numbers, each letter is assigned a number from 0 to 127. For example, the ASCII value for uppercase A is 65.

Decimal	Character	Decimal	Character	Decimal	Character
0	NULL	64	@	96	`
32	SPACE	65	A	97	a
33	!	66	B	98	b
34	"	67	C	99	c
35	#	68	D	100	d
36	$	69	E	101	e
37	%	70	F	102	f
38	&	71	G	103	g
39	'	72	H	104	h
40	(	73	I	105	i
41	)	74	J	106	j
42	*	75	K	107	k
43	+	76	L	108	l
44	,	77	M	109	m
45	-	78	N	110	n
46	.	79	O	111	o
47	/	80	P	112	p
48	0	81	Q	113	q
49	1	82	R	114	r

50	2	83	S	115	s
51	3	84	T	116	t
52	4	85	U	117	u
53	5	86	V	118	v
54	6	87	W	119	w
55	7	88	X	120	x
56	8	89	Y	121	y
57	9	90	Z	122	z
58	:	91	[	123	{
59	;	92	\	124		
60	<	93	]	125	}
61	=	94	^	126	~
62	>	95	-	127	DEL
63	?				

Variable and scanf

"**Variables**" are simply storage locations for data. Same as "**printf**" is used to put the output to screen, "**scanf**" is used to give input from the keyboard. Let us look into program 1.2 where we will ask you about your age and the program will print it back on your screen. Ah! Do not worry, it does not verify if you answered correctly or not.

Example 3.2. Variable.c demonstrates variable and scanf function.

```
1.      /*
2.             Author: Hemant Jain
3.             Description: Program with printf and scanf.
4.      */
5.
6.      #include<stdio.h>
7.
8.      int main()
9.      {
10.            int age=16;
11.            printf("What is your age:: ");
12.            scanf("%d",&age);
13.            printf("You are %d Years old.", age);
14.            return 0;
15.      }
```

Output:

```
1.    What is your age:: 21
2.    You are 21 Years old.
```

Analysis:
- ◆ Line 1–4: You can put your important notes in the program. These notes are called comments. Comments are enclosed under "/*" (start of a comment) and "*/" (end of comment). Every C program should start with a comment on the Author's name and Description of the program.

Whenever you want to put some notes in the program, you can use "/*" and "*/" tags to enclose them. C compiler ignores everything inside "/*" and "*/"

- Line 10: In this line, we are declaring a variable "age" of type "int" or "integer". Then assign it a value "16". In most of the programs, we want to store some values and then use it later in the program. Therefore, we store these values in variables of different types or sizes. You can think of variables like a box that can hold things. You can store values in variables with the = sign (called the assignment operator).

- Line 11: Print to screen "What is your age":

- Line 12: This line is storing your input to age variable. scanf("%d", &age); is a function which is provided by #include<stdio.h> or stdio.h file. In this statement, "%d" is a Format specifier, which tells the compiler, what type of input you are going to provide. The format specifier always starts with the "%" sign. The program waits for the user to input some text. Make sure you enter some numbers.

- Line 13: In this line, the value stored in the "age" variable is printed to the screen with the age you had provided. In this line, there is "%d" a Format specifier that again tells the compiler what type of variable you want to have an output to the screen.

- Line 14: Return from your program.

Escape sequences in printf() function

Before we proceed further, you need to understand the escape sequence. You may want your program to output the result in a particular fashion. For example, you may want to print the details of a student in this format:

Name: Jane
Age: 25

Now hear the escape sequences come to your rescue. To print the same, this is what the C compiler would expect.

```
printf("Name: \t Jane \n");
printf("Age: \t %d \n");
```

When you are programming in C language, sometimes you need to represent a newline character, single quotation mark, a tab space, etc. For this, a character combination of the backslash, '\', represents the escape character. The characters or digits followed by escape are called "escape sequences."

The most frequently used escape sequences in printf().
```
\n    new line, go to next line
\t    horizontal tab, skip to next tab stop
\b    backspace, move the cursor left by one position
```

\r	return, move the cursor to the beginning of the current line
\\	Backslash, print backslash
\'	single quote, print single quote
\"	double quote, print double quote
\?	Question mark

Example 3.3. EscapeSequence.c

```c
1.    #include<stdio.h>
2.
3.    int main()
4.    {
5.         printf("Hello, World!\n");
6.         printf("Hello, \nWorld!\n");
7.         printf("Hello, \tWorld!\n");
8.         printf("Hello, \bWorld!\n");
9.         printf("Hello, \rWorld!\n");
10.        printf("Hello, \\World!\n");
11.        printf("Hello, \'World!\n");
12.        printf("Hello, \"World!\n");
13.        return 0;
14.   }
```

Output:

```
1.    Hello, World!
2.    Hello,
3.    World!
4.    Hello,      World!
5.    Hello, World!
6.    World!
7.    Hello, \World!
8.    Hello, 'World!
9.    Hello, "World!
```

Analysis:

- Line 5: In this line, there is one \n used. What this \n will do is make a newline after "Hello, World!" and the cursor moves to the next line. Output Line 1 is corresponding to this line.

- Line 6: In this line, there are two "\n", one in between Hello and world and one in the end. Therefore, the Output line 2 & 3 are corresponding to this line.

- Line 7: In this line, a \t is tab space. Therefore, there is a tab space in between Hello and World in the Output line 4

- Line 8: In this line, a \b is a backspace. Therefore, after writing "Hello, " to the screen the cursor will move one space back and then write "World". Thereby overwriting the last " " of "Hello, ". Output line 5 is corresponding to this line.

◆ Line 9: In this line, a \r moves the cursor to the beginning of the current line. Therefore, after writing Hello, the cursor is moved back to the beginning of the line, and then "World!" is written so "Hello, " is overwritten. Output line 6 is corresponding to this line.

◆ Line 10: In this line, a \\ is used to print \ (backslash) to the screen that is a special character. Output line 7 is corresponding to this line.

◆ Line 11: In this line, there is a \' which is used to print ' (single quote) to the screen which is a special character. Output line 8 is corresponding to this line.

◆ Line 12: In this line, there is a \\ which is used to print " (double quote) to the screen which is a special character. Output line 9 is corresponding to this line.

Reserved Keywords in C

Keywords are predefined reserved names that have special meanings for the C compiler. They cannot be used as variable names in your program. There are 32 keywords reserved for C Language.

These keywords are:

auto	break	char
case	const	continue
default	do	double
else	enum	extern
float	for	goto
if	int	long
register	return	short
signed	sizeof	static
struct	switch	typedef
union	unsigned	void
volatile	while	

We do not need to remember all of them as we will visit each of them in the coming chapters.

Identifiers

In C language identifiers are the names given to variables, constants, functions and user-defined data like structures, enums, union.

Rules for defining an Identifier are:

1. An Identifier can only have alphanumeric characters(a-z , A-Z , 0-9) and underscore(_).
2. The first character of an identifier can only contain the alphabet(a-z , A-Z) or underscore (_).
3. Identifiers are case sensitive in C. For example, **val** and **Val** are two different identifiers.
4. Keywords are not allowed to be used as Identifiers.

5. Special characters, such as semicolon (;), period (.), white-spaces, slash (/), ampersand (&) or comma(,), etc. are not permitted to be used in an Identifier.

Few valid names of Identifiers: Var, var, count, numStudents, num_students, student1

Few invalid names of Identifier
1. 1number is not a valid identifier, Rule 2.
2. Num# is not a valid identifier, Rule 1 and Rule 5.
3. Number.Student is not a valid identifier, Rule 1 and Rule 5

Data-types or Variable

A **Variable** is a memory location, which is used to store some information. You can think of variables like a box that can hold something. When we create a variable, memory is reserved for it. When you assign a value to a variable, the value is stored in that memory location. The type of variable defines its size or how big a number it can contain inside it.

```
int age;
```

In this line, a variable "age" is defined as the type "int" (integer). Therefore, a memory that is equal to 32 bits (for 32 bits System) or 64 bits (for 64-bit system) is reserved for variable "age".

```
age=20;
```

In this line, we have assigned a value of 20 to age using "=" which is an assignment operator.

Types of Variables

C language provides various types of variables, which are used to store various types of data. Below is a list of the most commonly used Data Types/Variable in C programming:

short – This data type is used to represent a short integer. "short" can also be written as "short int".
```
short input;
input = 4;
```

int – This data type is used to represent an integer.
```
int count;
count = 30;
```

float – This data type is used to represent a floating-point number with a decimal in them. Like "5.8"
```
float distance;
distance = 5.8;
```

double – This data type is used to represent double-precision floating-point numbers.
```
double money;
money = 250000000;
```

char – This data type is used to represent character. e.g. "c", "p".

```
char myChar;
myChar = "h";
```

Constant

Constant values used within a C program are known as Literals. Four types of literals are:
1. Integer literal
2. Float or real literal
3. Character literal
4. String literal

An integer literal is a numeric literal that represents integer type values.
An integer literal can be represented in the following three ways:
1. Decimal number (base 10): Decimal literal is defined using digits between 0-9. For example 123.
2. Octal number (base 8): Octal literal is prefixed with 0 followed by digits between 0-7. For example 012 (in octal)
3. Hexadecimal number (base 16): Hexadecimal literal is prefixed with 0x or 0X following hexadecimal characters (i.e. digits from 0-9 and characters from a-f or A-F). For example 0X1A

float or real literal is a float or real constant represented either using decimal, exponent, or combination of both. For example 1.2, 1.2e10

A character literal is a single character constant enclosed within a pair of single quotes. The character takes one byte of space in memory. For example 'A', 'a', '1' are character literals.

String literal represents multiple characters enclosed within double-quotes. It contains an additional null character ('\0'), which gets automatically inserted. This null character indicates the termination of the string. For example "Hello, World!"

Constants are defined using the following two ways:
1. Using the "const" keyword with the variable definition. Constant variables are just like regular variables except that their values cannot be modified after their definition.
   For example:
   ```
   const float PI = 3.14;
   ```

2. Using "#define" preprocessor directive
   For example
   ```
   #define PI 3.14
   ```

Data type Modifiers

These are the keywords used with a data type and modify the nature of data type.

Storage Modifiers "short" and "long"

These modifiers are used only with int. The modifiers define the amount of storage allocated to the variable. The amount of memory allocated is not always fixed.

However, they follow these rules.
1. short int <= int<= long int
2. float <= double <= long double

This means that a "short int" can store less than or equal to "int" and an "int" can store less than or equal to "long int".

A "float" type can store value less than or equal to "double" and a "double" can store value less than or equal to "long double".

Storage modifier "long long": The long long modifier defines that the int variable will have at least 64 bits.

Range Modifiers "unsigned" and "signed"

These modifiers are also used with "int" data type.

An "unsigned int" can store a positive number range (0 to 65536) and "signed int" can store both negative and a positive number in the range (-32768 to 32767).

The int data type is signed by default. If you just write "int" then it means "signed int".

Let us understand all these modifiers. Take an example of the age of a human.
```
int age;
```

You know that age cannot be more than 150. Scientifically it is proved that man can live at max 150 if kept in most ideal conditions. So for this, you do not need int, your work will be done with just a short or short int.
```
short age;
```

Another thing is that the age of a person cannot be negative, so age should be "unsigned short"
```
unsigned short age;
```

sizeof() Operator

sizeof() is an operator (We will read about the operator in the next section). What sizeof does that is, it will return the number of bytes some variable or data type is taking.

Example 3.4: Explaining size of various data type
```
1.    #include<stdio.h>
2.
```

```
3.    int main()
4.    {
5.        printf("sizeof(char) = %ld bytes\n", sizeof(char));
6.        printf("sizeof(short) = %ld bytes\n", sizeof(short));
7.        printf("sizeof(int) = %ld bytes\n", sizeof(int));
8.        printf("sizeof(long) = %ld bytes\n", sizeof(long));
9.        printf("sizeof(float) = %ld bytes\n", sizeof(float));
10.       printf("sizeof(double) = %ld bytes\n", sizeof(double));
11.       printf("sizeof(long double) = %ld bytes\n", sizeof(long double));
12.       printf("sizeof(long long) = %ld bytes\n", sizeof(long long));
13.       return 0;
14.   }
```

Output:
```
1.    sizeof(char) = 1 bytes
2.    sizeof(short) = 2 bytes
3.    sizeof(int) = 4 bytes
4.    sizeof(long) = 8 bytes
5.    sizeof(float) = 4 bytes
6.    sizeof(double) = 8 bytes
7.    sizeof(long double) = 16 bytes
8.    sizeof(long long) = 8 bytes
```

Analysis:
Output Line 1 to 8:This output represents that the size of char is 1 byte, the size of int is 4 bytes, the size of short is 2 bytes, and so on.

You can remember the rule given below for the size of variables:
```
1. short int <=  int<= long int
2. float <= double <= long double
```

For a 32-bit system, these values will be

Type Name	Bytes	Range of Values
int	4	-2,147,483,648 to 2,147,483,647
unsigned int	4	0 to 4,294,967,295
char	1	-128 to 127
unsigned char	1	0 to 255
short	2	-32,768 to 32,767
unsigned short	2	0 to 65,535
long	4	-2,147,483,648 to 2,147,483,647
unsigned long	4	0 to 4,294,967,295
long long	8	-9,223,372,036,854,775,808 to 9,223,372,036,854,775,807
unsigned long long	8	0 to18,446,744,073,709,551,615
float	4	3.4E +/- 38 (7 digits)
double	8	1.7E +/- 308 (15 digits)
long double	8	1.7E +/- 308 (15 digits)

printf() function writes a formatted string to the standard output (stdout) which is by default desktop screen. printf() function uses various format specifiers to print various types of data types to stdout. Different types of Format specifiers are used to print the various types of data-type to stdout. There are many format specifiers defined in C.

The most commonly used format specifiers are:
```
"%d"  Used to print int or "integers"
"%ld" Used to print long signed int or "integers"
"%c"  Used to print "char"
"%f"  Used to print "float"
"%lf" Used to print "double"
"%u"  Used to print "Unsigned int"
"%x"  Used to print "Unsigned int hexadecimal format"
"%X"  Used to print "Unsigned int hexadecimal (capital letters) format"
"%s"  Used to print "string"
"%p"  Used to print "Memory address"
"%%"  Used to print "%" sign to stdout.
```

Note: We will read about string and pointers in the coming chapters.

Example 3.5: Printing various data types using printf function.
```
1.    /*
2.         This program will demonstrate printing of
3.         Different data types to stdout using printf
4.         function defined in stdio.h
5.    */
6.
7.    #include<stdio.h>
8.
9.    int main()
10.   {
11.       char ch = 'A';
12.       int in = 10;
13.       float pi = 3.14159;
14.       double d = 123.45;
15.       char* str = "This is a String";
16.
17.       printf("Character value of ch = %c \n", ch);
18.       printf("Integer value of in = %d \n", in);
19.       printf("Float value of pi = %f \n", pi);
20.       printf("Upper case Hexadecimal value of in = %X \n", in);
21.       printf("Lower case Hexadecimal value of in = %x \n", in);
22.       printf("Lower case Octal value of in = %o \n", in);
23.       printf("Double value of d = %lf \n", d);
24.       printf("%s \n", str);
25.       printf("Address of str = %p \n", str);
26.       return 0;
```

27.   }

Output:
```
1.    Character value of ch = A
2.    Integer value of in = 10
3.    Float value of pi = 3.141590
4.    Upper case Hexadecimal value of in = A
5.    Lower case Hexadecimal value of in = a
6.    Lower case Octal value of in = 12
7.    Double value of d = 123.450000
8.    This is a String
9.    Address of str = 0x56052d636f10
```

Analysis:
- Output Line 1: This line prints the character ch which is given a value "A" Line 9
- Output Line 2, 4 and 5: These lines print the value of the variable in of type integer, hexadecimal uppercase, and hexadecimal lower case.
- Output Line 3: Print float number pi.
- Output line 6: Print the value of double d.
- Output line 7: This line prints a bunch of characters by giving it a string pointer. Will learn about it in detail in the coming chapters.
- Output line 8: This line prints the address of the pointer. We will learn about it in detail in the coming chapters.

float Precision

Precision in floating numbers takes a minimum number of characters to represent the number and the number of characters that will hold the decimal part.

Its syntax will be % minimum number of char) . (number of character in decimal part) f

Example 3.6:
```
1.    #include <stdio.h>
2.
3.    int main(){
4.        float val = 123.123;
5.        printf("%f \n", val);
6.        printf("%.2f \n", val);
7.        printf("%8.3f \n", val);
8.        return 0;
9.    }
```

Output:
```
123.123001
123.12
  123.123
```

Analysis:
- ◆ Line 5: It is normally printing the float value.
- ◆ Line 6: It prints the float value but only reserves two characters to hold the decimal part.
- ◆ Line 7: It reserves a total field of 8 characters, within the 8 characters the last 2 will hold the decimal part.

Reading data types input using scanf

scanf() function reads a formatted string from the standard input (stdin) which is by default keyboard. scanf function uses various format specifiers to take input from various types of data types.

Different types of Format Specifier are used to read the various types of data-type from stdin (keyboard).

Most commonly used format specifiers are:
```
"%d"  Used to read "int" or "integers"
"%ld" Used to read "long int" or "long integers"
"%c"  Used to read "char"
"%f"  Used to read "float"
"%lf" Used to read "double"
"%u"  Used to read "Unsigned int"
"%x"  Used to read "Unsigned int hexadecimal format"
"%X"  Used to read "Unsigned int hexadecimal (capital letters) format"
"%s"  Used to read "string"
```

Example 3.7: Demonstrating scanf function
```
1.      /*
2.          This program will demonstrate reading of
3.             Different data types from stdin using scanf
4.             Function defined in stdio.h
5.      */
6.
7.      #include<stdio.h>
8.
9.      int main()
10.     {
11.
12.         int age;
13.         double income;
14.         char name[50];
15.         printf("Enter your name:: ");
16.         scanf("%s",name);
17.         printf("Enter your age:: ");
18.         scanf("%d", &age);
19.         printf("Enter your income:: ");
20.         scanf("%lf", &income);
21.         printf("Well Hello: %s. \n", name);
22.         printf("You are %d years old. \n", age);
```

```
23.        printf("Your income is %lf. \n", income);
24.        return 0;
25.   }
```

Output:
```
1.    Enter your name:: Hemant
2.    Enter your age:: 31
3.    Enter your income:: 10000000
4.    Well Hello: Hemant.
5.    You are 31 years old.
6.    Your income is 10000000.000000.
```

Analysis:
- Line 8-10: In these lines, we have declared three variables, age is declared of type int. Income is declared of type double and the name is a char array having the capacity to store 50 chars.
- Line 11-12: Line 11 prints "Enter your name:", and in the program will wait at line 12. Once we have entered a string, the scanf function will store that string in the name char array.
- Line 14: The program will wait for the user to enter the value to the age variable. Once the user enters a value, that value is stored in an age variable.
- Line 16: Similarly, income value, that is entered, is stored in an income variable.
- Line 17-19: Finally, the value stored in name, age and income are printed to the screen.

Example 3.8: Write a function to add two numbers.
```c
#include <stdio.h>

int main()
{
    int a, b, sum;
    printf("Enter two numbers:: ");
    scanf("%d %d", &a, &b);
    sum = a+b;
    printf("The sum is %d ", sum);
    return 0;
}
```

Output:
```
Enter two numbers: 2 3
The sum is 5
```

Analysis: Three variables a, b & sum are declared. Function scanf() is used to input values of a & b. Value stored in a & b is added and stored in variable sum. Finally the sum value is printed to the screen.

Example 3.9: Write a function to find an average of 3 numbers.
```c
#include <stdio.h>
int main()
{
    float a, b, c, sum, avg;
```

```c
    printf("Enter three numbers:: ");
    scanf("%f %f %f", &a, &b, &c);
    sum = a+b+c;
    avg = sum/3;
    printf("The average is %f", avg);
}
```

Output:
```
Enter three numbers:: 2 3 1
The average is 2.000000
```

Analysis: Three variables a, b, c, sum and avg are declared of type float. Function scanf() is used to input values of a, b & c. Value stored in a, b & c is added and stored in variable sum. Average is calculated and stored in avg. Finally avg value is printed to the screen.

Errors / What can go wrong?

It is most important to understand what types of errors we can get while writing programs. Below some of the basic mistakes that we can make are enumerated along with their corrections.

There are three types of errors:
1. **Compile time error**: Compile time errors occur when we violate the syntax rules of a programming language. These types of errors are detected by the compiler.
2. **Runtime Error**: Error which occurs when the program is executed. The compiler can't detect such errors. Various types of crashes or segmentation faults are observed because of such errors.
3. **Logical Error**: When the logic of the program has some mistake. This error is hardest to find and because of this, the wrong output is observed.

Examples of Compilation errors:
1. Missing Semicolon ";" at the end of statements.
2. Missing Parenthesis "}".
3. Using an Undeclared variable or using it without declaring a variable.
4. Meaningless statements, for example, writing "While" in place of "while". C language is case sensitive so it will report errors.

Examples of Runtime Errors:
1. Divide by Zero
2. The memory allocation function is not able to allocate memory.
3. Trying to read a file which does not exist
4. Memory errors like
   a) Uninitialized memory read
   b) Array bound read/write
   c) Beyond stack read/write
   d) Null pointer read/write
   e) Invalid pointer read/write
   f) Free memory read/write

g) Memory leak
h) Freeing non-heap memory
i) Freeing unallocated memory

Note: We will read about Memory Errors and File Handling in the coming chapters.

Examples of Logical Errors:
1. Wrong logic used in a program leads to unexpected output.
2. The wrong formula is used to calculate something.
3. Statements after the return statement.

Difference between Compile-time error and Run-time error.

Compile-time error	Run-time error
These are the syntax errors that are detected by the compiler.	These are the errors that are not detected by the compiler. They are observed when the program executes.
These errors prevent the code from being compiled properly.	They prevent the code from complete execution.
Compilers find error locations so these types of errors are easy to fix.	Manual code review is the only way to find such errors.
E.g. Missing Parentheses, Missing Semicolon, Misspelled keyword or identifier etc.	E.g. Divide-by-Zero error, Memory error like Segmentation fault, etc.

Basic Mistake 1: Missing Semicolon

Remember that every statement should end with a ";" (semicolon). So what if you miss one then the compiler will flag the point where we had missed the ";".

Example 3.10: Error1.c demonstrates error messages when ";" is missing.
```
1.    /*You missed the line ending;*/
2.    #include<stdio.h>
3.
4.    int main()
5.    {
6.        printf("C is Simple!")
7.        return 0;
8.    }
```

Error:
```
1.    error1.c||In function 'main':|
2.    error1.c|7|error: expected ';' before 'return'|
3.    Build failed: 1 error(s), 0 warning(s) (0 minute(s), 0 second(s))
```

Analysis:
- Error Line 1: It says that "In function 'main'" , which means there is something wrong in the main function.

◆ Error Line 2: "error1.c|7|error: expected ';' before 'return'|" It says that in the 7th line of your function there is a problem. The problem is "parse error" which is before the "return" statement, so just look there you will come to know that you had missed a ";" (Semicolon). This compiler is smart so it explicitly says "error: expected ';' before 'return'"

◆ Error Line 3: It shows that the build failed and there is one error.

Basic Mistake 2: Variable Undefined

Remember that every variable needs to be defined before using it. A memory location needs to be reserved before storing some value to it or reading from it.

Example 3.11: Error2.c demonstrates error messages when a variable is not defined.
```
1.    /* You missed declaring variable i */
2.    #include<stdio.h>
3.
4.    int main()
5.    {
6.        i=10;
7.        printf("Value of i is: %d", i);
8.        return 0;
9.    }
```

Error:
```
1.    error2.c||In function 'main':|
2.    error2.c|6|error: 'i' undeclared (first use in this function)|
3.    error2.c|6|note: each undeclared identifier is reported only once for
      each function it appears in|
```

Analysis: Error Line 2: This line clearly says "5.c:6: error: 'i' undeclared (first use in this function) ". This statement is clear. It says that the 'i' is undeclared, which means that we forgot to declare 'i'. Besides, the compiler does not know the data type of 'i'. So you must have forgotten something like "int i;"

Basic Mistake 3: Uninitialized variable

Every local variable needs to be assigned. When a local variable is created, it contains some random or garbage value that depends on your system condition. All the errors that we have discussed before were "Compile-time error" as the compiler catches them. However, this error is a "logical error" which means the compiler is not going to tell you that you have missed something. We will look into logical errors in the coming chapters.

Example 3.12: Error3.c demonstrates Logical Error when a variable is not defined.
```
1.    #include<stdio.h>
2.
```

```
3.     int main()
4.     {
5.         int age;
6.         printf("Your Age is: %d", age);
7.         return 0;
8.     }
```

Output:
```
1.     Your Age is: 0
```

Analysis: Output Line 1: There is no error and we got the output. However, what is this number 0? Well, it is a garbage value so it can be anything depending on your computer state. Well, in "int Age;" computers reserve memory for the variable "Age". The compiler leaves the bits of memory untouched. Therefore, what number is there is Garbage / Junk value. This is a logical error, so the computer is not going to give any error. You look into the output and then figure out that "Oh, I missed" the initialization of the variable "Age".

Type Qualifiers

A Quantifier is used to qualify or modify the properties of variables in some ways. There are two types of quantifiers "const" and "volatile".

Constants

The const type qualifier declares that the variable value cannot be modified if once declared. The compiler will make sure that you are not allowed to modify the value of the const variable in your program. const is resolved at compile time and they do not have any performance penalty.

For example:
```
const float PI=3.14;
```

In this example, PI is a constant whose value will not change and it will remain 3.14.

Another way of defining constants is by using #define pre-processor (we will read about this in the preprocessor chapter).

```
#define PI 3.14159
```

The compiler does many optimizations with const. Each reference of the const variable is replaced by their value. If the compiler can determine that they cannot be referenced from a different compilation unit, or that your code is not using the address of the const variable, it is free to optimize it away

volatile

The volatile type qualifier declares an item whose value can be changed by something beyond the control of the program in which it appears, such as a concurrently executing thread. Since it can be changed beyond the control of the program, the value of a variable must always be read from memory rather than from a register.

The syntax is:
```
volatile data-type variable-name;
```

Solved Examples

Problem 3.1: Write a C program to count bits set in an integer?

Example 3.13:
```c
int bitCount(int num)
{
        int ctr=0;
        for(;num!=0;num>>=1)
        {
                if(num&1)
                {
                        ctr++;
                }
        }
        printf("\n Number of bits set in %d = %d\n", num, ctr);
        return ctr;
}
```

Problem 3.2: What will be the output of the below program?
```c
int main()
{
    int a = 300, b, c;
    if (a >= 400)
        b = 300;
    c = 200;
    printf("\n%d %d", b, c);
}
```

Solution: Since a = 300. So the condition a>400 is false and b will not get initialized. So the variable b contains garbage value and c is initialized to 200.

the output will be some garbage value followed by a space followed by 200.
<garbage value> 200

Problem 3.3: Write a program to reverse the bits of an integer.

Example 3.14:
```c
unsigned int reverseBits( unsigned int num)
{
        unsigned int temp = 0;
        int i;
```

```c
for (i = (sizeof(num)*8-1); i; i--)
{
        temp = temp | (num & 1);
        temp <<= 1;
        num >>= 1;
}

temp = temp | (num & 1);
return temp;
}
```

Summary

1. Constants are fixed and their value will never change.
2. The volatile modifier tells the compiler that the value of a variable may change at any time from external influences
3. #include<stdio.h>: The file, which contains scanf() and printf() kind of functions, which are used in input and output.
4. main(): Main is the starting point of your program.
5. printf(): function used to print output to the screen.
6. scanf(): function used to take user input.
7. Keywords: predefined reserved names which can't be used as variables
8. We have read about variables and various types of variables.
9. Storage modifier and Range modifier of the variable.
10. sizeof() operator.
11. Const keyword should be used whenever we know that the value of the variable is not going to change.
12. Errors in C language are classified under three categories:
13. Compiler errors: Those errors which are detected by the compiler and because of which compiler stops compilation
14. Linker error: Those errors, which are generated by the linker, mainly because of some unresolved dependencies.
15. Logical errors: These errors are generated because of the mistake in logical thinking of the programmer. No error message is generated in this kind of error, but because of this, we do not get the desired output. These errors are corrected by line-by-line analysis of the execution of a program. Debuggers like GDB are used to find logical errors.

Questions & Answers

Question 1: What will happen when I use some reserved keyword as a variable?
Answer: The compiler will give an error.

Question 2: What is the difference between a statement and a block?
Answer: A statement is a single C expression terminated with a semicolon ";". A block is a group of statements which are enclosed in curly-braces "{" and "}".

Question 3: What is the loss if we use a large double variable to store everything?
Answer: We should not use a very large size variable to store small data in this case we are wasting space. In addition, we should not use a very small variable to store large value, it will lead to overflow of value.

Question 4: What type of constant should I use the **const** keyword or #define?
Answer: Always prefer const keyword to #define. #define is a preprocessor directive so it will replace the entire occurrence with a value. Therefore, it is dumb and the compiler will never see the #defines as they are replaced. Therefore, since the compiler cannot see it you cannot debug it. On the other hand, using const keywords makes the code clearer and we can debug it.

Note: In the preprocessor chapter, we will read the uses of #define. Try to use the **const** keyword in all the other places.

Question 5: Define the various data-types used in C with examples.
Answer: various types of data-type provided by C programming language are:

> **short** – This data type is used to represent a short integer. "short" can also be written as "short int".
> ```
> short input = 4;
> ```
>
> **int** – This data type is used to represent an integer.
> ```
> int count = 30;
> ```
>
> **float** – This data type is used to represent a floating-point number with a decimal in them. Like "5.8"
> ```
> float distance = 5.8;
> ```
>
> **double** – This data type is used to represent double-precision floating-point numbers.
> ```
> double money = 250000000;
> ```
>
> **char** – This data type is used to represent the character. e.g. "c", "p".
> ```
> char myChar = "h";
> ```

Question 6: Explain the basic structure of the C Program.
Answer:
```
#include <stdio.h>

int main()
{
    printf("Hello world!\n");
    return 0;
}
```

The structure of a C program is as follows:
1. Inclusion of Header Files.
2. Main Method which is the starting point of C program.
3. Body of the main method.

4. Various statements inside the main method.
5. Return Statement.

Question 7: Distinguish between int main() and void main()?
Answer: int main(): This prototype refers to the main function in a C program that returns an integer value. The return value is the exit code of the program that defines if the program is completed successfully or not. In case of successful execution, 0 is returned. Else any other value is returned. This format is now the standard ANSI format in C programming.
void main(): This prototype refers to the main function in a C program that does not return any value.

Question 8: Write short notes on High level and low-level languages.
Answer:
Higher level languages are programming languages in which programs are written are easily understood by the programmer. Ex. Java, C, C++, Python.

Low-level languages are programming languages that are very difficult to write and understand by a programmer. These languages are very close to machines. Ex. Binary language, Assembly language.

Question 9: What is the use of exit() function.
Answer: The exit() function is used to terminate the execution of a program. The exit code "0" indicates that the program terminated without any error but other values indicate that the program terminated with an error. This exit() function is defined in stdio.h file.

Exercise

1. Write a simple program that will print your name to the screen.

2. Write a program that will print your name under ""(double quote).

3. What is the difference between keyword and variable?

4. What are storage modifiers and what is its effect on variables?

5. What is the use of unsigned keywords?

6. What are the rules for naming valid identifiers in C?

7. Draw the Skeleton of a C program.

8. What are the different examples of runtime errors?

9. Why are comments used in a programming language

10. What are the different format specifiers available in C?

CHAPTER 4: ARITHMETIC EXPRESSION AND PRECEDENCE

Operators

C programming language provides several operators to perform different kinds of operations. There are five kinds of operators Arithmetic, Assignment, Logical, Bitwise, and Miscellaneous. Most operators are binary which means they take two operands. There are unary and ternary operators as well.

```
int i=1;
int j=2;
print("result of i + j is %d", i+j);
```

This program will print

```
The result of i + j is 3
```

In this program, i and j are operands upon which the operator is applied. Besides, the + sign is an operator that is called an addition operator. + (addition operator) is a binary operator that takes two operands and produces one result which is value 3 in the above case.

Arithmetic Operators

Arithmetic operators are used to perform arithmetic / mathematical operations on operands.

They are applied to only integer or float kinds of operands. Among this Modulus Operator is applied only over integral operands.

Operator	Symbol	Description
Addition	+	Perform the addition of two operands.
Subtraction	-	Subtract the second operand from first.
Multiplication	*	Multiple two operands.
Division	/	Divide the first operand with the second operand.
Modulus/remainder	%	Find the modulus of the second over the first.

Let us consider two integers A = 10, B = 5

Operator	Syntax	Result
Addition	A + B	15
Subtraction	A - B	5
Multiplication	A * B	50
Division	A / B	2
Modulus/ remainder	A % B	0

Example 4.1: Demonstrate various Arithmetic Operators

```c
1.      #include<stdio.h>
2.
3.      int main()
4.      {
5.          int i=10;
6.          int j=5;
7.          int value;
8.
9.          value = i + j;
10.         printf(" i + j = %d \n", value);
11.         value = i - j;
12.         printf(" i - j = %d \n", value);
13.         value = i * j;
14.         printf(" i * j = %d \n", value);
15.         value = i / j;
16.         printf(" i / j = %d \n", value);
17.         value = i % j;
18.         printf(" i %% j = %d \n", value);
19.
20.         return 0;
21.     }
```

Output:

```
1.     i + j = 15
2.     i - j = 5
3.     i * j = 50
4.     i / j = 2
5.     i % j = 0
```

Analysis:

- Line 9 & 10: In these lines, "+" addition operator is used and the result can be seen in Output line 1
- Line 11 & 12: In these lines, "-" subtraction operator is used and the result can be seen in Output line 2
- Line 13 & 14: In these lines, "*" multiplication operator is used and the result can be seen in Output line 3
- Line 15 & 16: In these lines, "/" division operator is used and the result can be seen in Output line 4
- Line 17 & 18: In these lines, "%" modulus or remainder operator is used and the result can be seen in Output line 5

If an integer is divided by another integer, then the result will also be an integer. So what will happen when the division is not perfect? Consider the below case, what value is stored in the result variable.

Example 4.2: Truncation / Floor value in integer division.

```c
1.      #include<stdio.h>
2.
```

```c
3.     int main()
4.     {
5.         int i=11;
6.         int j=5;
7.         int result;
8.
9.         result = i / j;
10.        printf(" i / j = %d \n", result);
11.
12.        return 0;
13.    }
```

Output:
```
1.    i / j = 2
```

Analysis: The value stored in the result will be a floor value of 11 / 5. floor (11/5) == floor(2.2) == 2. Therefore, the value stored in the result is 2. If we want the decimal value too, then we need to make the division operation of type float and store result in float type. The next program will demonstrate this.

Example 4.3: Preventing truncation by using floating-point division.
```c
1.     #include<stdio.h>
2.
3.     int main()
4.     {
5.         int i=11;
6.         int j=5;
7.         float result;
8.
9.         result = (float)i / j;
10.        printf(" i / j = %f \n", result);
11.
12.        return 0;
13.    }
```

Output:
```
1.    i / j = 2.200000
```

Analysis:
- Line 7:Variable result is declared of type float so that it can store float value 2.2
- Line 9:Variable "i" is cast to float using "(float)" cast so that the division operation is float type.
- Line 10:Print the output to the standard output using a %f type specifier to print the float type result variable.

The other options can be
```c
float result=i;
result=result / j;
printf(" i / j = %f \n", result);
```

Assignment Operators

Assignment operators are used in assigning some value to variables. The various variants of assignment operator are:

Operator	Symbol	Description
Assignment	=	Assignment operator, Assigns values from right side operands to left side operand e.g. A = B, Value stored in B will be stored in A
Assignment Add	+=	Add & Assignment operator, It adds the right operand to the left operand and assigns the sum to the left operand. e.g. A+= B, is equivalent to A = A + B
Assignment Subtract	-=	Subtract & Assignment operator, It subtract the right operand form the left operand and assign the difference to the left operand. e.g. A-= B, is equivalent to A = A - B
Assignment Multiply	*=	Multiply & Assignment operator, It multiplies the right operand and the left operand and assigns the product to the left operand. e.g. A*= B, is equivalent to A = A * B
Assignment Divide	/=	Divide & Assignment operator, It divides the right operand by the left operand and assigns the result to the left operand. e.g. A/= B, is equivalent to A = A / B
Assignment Modulus	%=	Modulus & Assignment operator, Find module of left operand by right operand and assign result to left operand. e.g. A %= B is equivalent to A = A % B
Assignment Left shift	<<=	Left Shift & Assignment operator, Left shift the left operand right operand number of times and assign the result to the left operand. e.g. A <<= B is equivalent to A = A << B

Assignment Right shift	>>=	Right Shift & Assignment operator, Right shift the left operand right operand number of times and assign the result to the left operand. e.g. A >>= B is equivalent to A = A >>B
Assignment Bitwise AND	&=	Bitwise AND Assignment operator, Find bitwise AND between two operands and assign the result to the left operand. e.g. A &= B is equivalent to A = A & B
Assignment Bitwise exclusive OR (XOR)	^=	Bitwise XOR Assignment operator,, Find bitwise XOR between two operands and assign the result to the left operand. e.g. A ^= B is equivalent to A = A ^ B
Assignment Bitwise OR	|=	Bitwise OR Assignment operator, , Find bitwise OR between two operands and assign the result to the left operand. e.g. A |= B is equivalent to A = A | B

"=" Assignment operator is used to assign some value to a variable.

```
int i=10;
```

"+=" Add is used to add some value to the variable.

```
i += 5;
```

The value of i is increased by 5 and then assigns it back to i.

Logical & Relational Operators

Relational operators are used for comparison of the values of two operands. The logical operator is also called Boolean operators because their result is either true / 1 or false / 0. All these operators are binary except! (Not) which is a unary operator.

In C programming language value "0" is considered as False any other value (negative or positive other than zero) is considered as True. The logical operator returns 0 if the condition is False and return 1 if the condition is True.

The various logical operators are:

Operator	Symbol	Description
Equal	==	If both the operands are the same then return 1 else return 0
Not	!	Reverse the value of the operand. If the operand is 0 then it will make it 1. If the operand is other then zero it will make it 0.
Not equal	!=	If both the operands are unequal then return 1 else return 0.
Greater than	>	If the first operand is greater then second then return 1 else return 0.
Less than	<	If the first operand is less than the second operand then return 1 else return 0.
Greater than or equal	>=	If the first operand is greater than or equal to the second operand then return 1 else return 0
Less than or equal	<=	If the first operand is less then or equal to the second operand then return 1 else return 0
And	&&	If both the conditions are true then return 1 else return 0
Or	||	If anyone of the conditions is true then return 1 else return 0.

Let us suppose A = 10 and B = 5

Operator	Symbol	Result
Equal	A == B	0
Not equal	A != B	1
Greater than	A > B	1
Less than	A < B	0
Greater than or equal	A >= B	1
Less than or equal	A <= B	0
Not	! (A <= B)	1
And	(A > B) && (A < B)	0
Or	(A > B) || (A < B)	1

Truth table for Logical "And" operators

Expression A	Expression B	A && B
True	True	True or 1
True	False	False or 0
False	True	False or 0
False	False	False or 0

Example 4.4:

```c
int main()
{
    int a = 1, b = 2, c = 3, d;
    d = b && a < b && c < b;
    printf("Value of d:: %d ", d);
}
```

Output:
```
Value of d:: 0
```

Analysis: An operator is evaluated from left to right. If the operand at the left is False then it will not look for the right operand and will return False. If the operand at the left is True then it will evaluate the operand at the right.

In the above expression "b && a < b && c < b", b's value is 2 so it is True, then a < b is also True at the end c < b is false so the overall expression will be False or 0. The result 0 will be stored in d and displayed.

Truth table for Logical Or operators

Expression A	Expression B	A ‖ B
True	True	True or 1
True	False	True or 1
False	True	True or 1
False	False	False or 0

Note: C language 0 is treated as False and 1 is treated as True.

Example 4.5:
```c
int main()
{
    int a = 1, b = 2, c = 3, d;
    d = a == b || a < b || b < c;
    printf("Value of d:: %d ", d);
}
```

Output:
```
Value of d:: 1
```

Analysis:
Our operator is evaluated from left to right. If the operand at the left is True then it will not look for the right operand and will return True. If the operand at the left is False then it will evaluate the operand at the right. In the above expression "a == b || a < b || b < c", a == b is False, then a < b is True so the evaluation process will stop here and True or 1 is returned. Finally the value of d is 1.

Bitwise Operators

As the name suggests bitwise operators are applied to bits that are a binary representation of a number. For example, "2" is "10" in binary.

Operator	Symbol	Function
AND (Binary operator)	&	Take two numbers as operands and apply AND on every bit of the two numbers. The result of AND is 1 only if both bits are 1.
OR (Binary operator)	|	Take two numbers as operands and apply OR on every bit of the two numbers. The result of OR is 1 if any of the two bits is 1.

XOR (Binary operator) or Exclusive OR	∧	Take two numbers as operands and apply XOR on every bit of the two numbers. The result of XOR is 1 if the two bits are different.
ONE's Complement	~	Inverts all bits of the given number.
Left Shift	<<	Takes two numbers, left shifts the bits of the first operand, the second operand number of times.
Right Shift	>>	Takes two numbers, right shifts the bits of the first operand, the second operand number of times.

Let us understand all these bitwise operators with an example.

The & operator

The bitwise AND (&) operator takes two operands and does AND operation on each bit of the two numbers. The result of AND is 1 if both the bits are 1 otherwise 0.

Truth table for AND
```
1 & 1 = 1
1 & 0 = 0
0 & 1 = 0
0 & 0 = 0
```

For example: A=12 and B=10. So in binary A=1100 and B=1010
A & B == 1000 (Binary) == 8 (Decimal)

The | operator

The bitwise OR (|) operator takes two operands and does OR operation on each bit of the two numbers. The result of OR is 1 if any of the bits are 1 and 0 if both the bits are 0.

As we remember the basic | OR gate rule.
```
1 | 1 = 1
1 | 0 = 1
0 | 1 = 1
0 | 0 = 0
```

For example A=12 and B=10. So in binary A=1100 and B=1010
A | B == 1110 (Binary) == 14 (Decimal)

The ∧ operator

The bitwise XOR(∧) operator takes two operands and does XOR operation on each bit of the two numbers. The result of XOR is 1 if the two bits are different.

As we remember the basic ^ XOR gate rule.

```
1 ^ 1 = 0
1 ^ 0 = 1
0 ^ 1 = 1
0 ^ 0 = 0
```

For example: A=12 and B=10. So in binary A=1100 and B=1010
A ^ B == 0110 (Binary) == 6 (Decimal)

There are three unary bitwise operators to shift value, right or left. Let us assume A = 2 (Decimal) = 0000 0010 (binary) considering A is just 1 byte to explain this concept.

The ~ operator

The bitwise NOT(~) operator takes one number and inverted all bits of it.

As we remember, the basic ~ NOT gate rule.

```
~1  = 0
~0 = 1
```

~A == ~ (0000 0010) == 1111 1101 (Binary) = 253 (Decimal)
The thing to notice here, is that, each bit is reversed. Moreover, the final value is not important because it will depend on the integer length in your system so if you will run this program this value will be different.

The << shift left operator

The left shift operator (<<) takes two numbers, The first operands bits are shifted in the left. The value of the second operand is the number of shifts.
        Let us suppose A is 2 and its binary equivalent is 0010, A<<1 is equal to 100 which is equal to 4 in decimal. We can give the number of shifts with the << operator. So A<<2 is equal to 8 in decimal. So A<<N will shift the value of A, N number of times on the left. If this shifting reaches the maximum limit then the value is truncated.

```
int a=10;
int b;
b = a << 8 * sizeof(int);
```

In this example, the value of A is truncated. No matter what is stored in A, B will always be 0.

The >> shift right operator

The right shift operator (>>) takes two numbers, The first operands bits are shifted in the right. The second operand is the number of shifts.

Let us suppose A is 2 and its binary equivalent is 0010, A>>1 is equal to 1 which is equal to 1 in decimal. We can give the number of shifts with the << operator. So A>>N will shift A value N number of times.

Miscellaneous Operators

There are some operators, which are special in their work.

Operator	Symbol	Description
Sizeof Operator	sizeof()	It returns the size of the variable in bytes. E.g. sizeof(a), where a is an integer, will give 4
Address Operator	&	It returns the address of a variable. E.g. &a will give the actual address of a. Will talk about it later in the pointers chapter.
Indirection Operator	*	Pointer to a variable or indirection operator. E.g. *(pointer) operator is used in two ways. First "int *a;" In this "a" is declared as a pointer to int. Second *a is used to get the value stored in a. We will talk about it later in the pointers chapter.
Conditional Operator	?:	Conditional Expression. This is a ternary operator as it takes three values. It is used as below. If Condition is true? Then value X: Otherwise, value Y E.g. a= (b)? 0 : 1; In the above example, depending upon the value of b if positive, then a will be 0 otherwise a will be 1.

Problem: Write a program to find larger among the two variables using ternary operator ?:.

Example 4.6:
```
1.      int main()
2.      {
3.          int a, b, c;
4.          printf("Enter the two variables:: ");
5.          scanf("%d%d", &a, &b);
6.          c = a>b?a:b;
7.          printf("Larger value is:: %d", c);
8.      }
```

Output:
```
1.      Enter the two variables:: 10 11
2.      Larger value is:: 11
```

Analysis:
In line 6: The ternary operator checks the condition a>b if the condition is true then c will take the value of variable a. And if the condition a>b is false then c will take the value of variable b. Since the input values are 10 & 11. 10>11 is false so the value 11 is assigned to c.

Increment and Decrement Operator

The increment operator ++ increases the value of a variable by 1. Similarly, the decrement operator - - is decreasing the value of the variable by 1.

If ++ operator is used as a prefix of a variable like ++a. The value of the variable is incremented by 1, then return the value of the variable.

If ++ operator is used as a postfix of a variable like a + +. The value of the variable is returned first then it is incremented by 1.

Example 4.7:

```
1.    int main()
2.    {
3.         int a = 1, b, c;
4.         b = ++a;
5.         c = a++;
6.         printf("Value of b = %d, c = %d", b, c);
7.    }
```

Output:

```
1.    Value of b = 2, c = 2
```

Analysis:
- In line 4 the value of a is incremented and then it is assigned to variable b.
- In like 5 the value of a is assigned to variable c then it is incremented by one.
- The value stored in b and c is printed to the screen.

The decrement operator - - is decreasing the value of the variable by 1.

If -- operator is used as a prefix of variable like --a. The value of the variable is decremented by 1, then returns the value of the variable.

If -- operator is used as a postfix of variable like a--. The value of the variable is returned first then it is decremented by 1.

Example 4.8:

```
1.    int main()
2.    {
3.         int a = 3, b, c;
4.         b = --a;
5.         c = a--;
6.         printf("Value of b = %d, c = %d", b, c);
7.    }
```

Output:

```
1.    Value of b = 2, c = 2
```

Analysis:
- In line 4 the value of a is decremented and then it is assigned to variable b.
- In like 5 the value of a is assigned to variable c then it is decremented by one.
- The value stored in b and c are printed to the screen.

Operator Precedence & Associativity

Precedence Rules

The precedence rules of a language specify which operator is evaluated first when two operators with different precedence are adjacent in an expression.

Associativity Rules

The associativity rules of a language specify which operator is evaluated first when two operators with the same precedence are adjacent in an expression. It can be either left-to-right or right-to-left.

This table will list C operators in decreasing order of precedence (highest to lowest).

Operator	Description	Associativity
( )	Parentheses (function call)	
[ ]	Brackets (array subscript)	Left-to-right
.	Member selection via object name	
->	Member selection via pointer	
++ --	Postfix increment/decrement	
++ -+	Prefix increment/decrement	Right-to-left
!	Unary plus/minus Logical	
~	Negation/bitwise complement	
(type)	Cast	
*	Dereference	
&	Address (of operand)	
sizeof	Determine size in bytes	
* / %	Multiplication/division/ Modulus	Left-to-right
+ -	Addition/subtraction	Left-to-right
<<	Bitwise shift left,	Left-to-right
>>	Bitwise shift right	

<=	Relational less than or equal to	Left-to-right
>=	Relational greater than or equal to	
== !=	Relational is equal to/ is not equal to	Left-to-right
&	Bitwise AND	Left-to-right
^	Bitwise exclusive OR	Left-to-right
|	Bitwise inclusive OR	Left-to-right
&&	Logical AND	Left-to-right
||	Logical OR	Left-to-right
? :	Ternary conditional	Right-to-left
=	Assignment	Right-to-left
+=	Assignment Addition	
-=	Assignment Subtraction	
*=	Assignment Multiplication	
/=	Assignment Division	
%=	Assignment Modulus	
&=	Assignment Bitwise	
^=	Assignment Bitwise ex- OR	
|=	Assignment Bitwise OR	
<<=	Assignment Bitwise shift left	
>>=	Assignment Bitwise shift right	
,	Comma (separate expressions)	Left-to-right

Type Conversion and Type Casting

Type conversion is converting one data-type to another data-type.
There are two types of type conversion:
- **Implicitly / automatically** Type conversion
- **Explicit** type conversion or Type Casting.

Implicit Type Conversion is converting one data-type to another automatically by the compiler.
The two conditions for Implicit Type Conversion are:
1. The two data-types are compatible with each other.
2. The destination type must be larger than the source type else data loss will happen.

All the data types of the variables are upgraded to the largest data type.
bool -> char -> short int -> int -> long -> long long -> float -> double -> long double

```
int a =10;
float b;
b = a;
```

Explicit Type Conversion or Type casting is the conversion of one data-type to another data-type explicitly by the programmer using casting.

Syntax:
```
(type) expression
```

```
int a;
float b=10;
a = (int)b;
```

Implicit Type Conversion	Explicit Type Conversion / Type Casting
Conversion of one data-type to another done automatically by the compiler.	One data-type is assigned to another by using a casting operator.
Type conversion is only performed when two data types are compatible.	Type casting can be applied to two incompatible data types.
No operator is required	Casting operator '( )' is required.
The destination data type must be larger than the source datatype.	No such size restrictions.

Example:
    int a =10;
    float b;
    b = a;
	Example:
	    int a;
	    float b=10;
	    a = (int)b;

Example 4.9:
```
int main()
{
    int a = 11;
    float b = a / 2;
    printf("%f", b);
}
```

Output:
```
5.000000
```

Analysis: When a 2 both the values are integer so integral division happens. Integral division 11/2 is 5

Example 4.10:
```
int main()
{
    int a = 11;
    float b ;
```

```c
        b = a / 2.0;
        printf("%f", b);
}
```

Output:
```
5.500000
```

Analysis: The value of a is converted to float before dividing it with 2.0 which is float. Finally, the value 5.5 is assigned to the variable b of type float.

Solved Example

Problem 1: Write a program of swapping values of two numbers using a third variable.

Example 4.11:
```c
1.    int main()
2.    {
3.        int a;
4.        int b;
5.        int c;
6.        printf("Input two values: ");
7.        scanf("%d%d", &a, &b);
8.        c = a;
9.        a = b;
10.       b = c;
11.
12.       printf("Values stored in a & b are: %d & %d", a, b);
13.   }
```

Output:
```
Input two values: 12 13
Values stored in a & b are: 13 & 12
```

Analysis: The value of the first variable a is stored in variable c. The value of variable b is copied to a. Then the value stored in variable c is copied to b. So both the variable values are swapped.

Problem 2: Write a program of swapping values of two numbers without using a third variable.

Example 4.12:
```c
1.    int main()
2.    {
3.        int a;
4.        int b;
5.        printf("Input two values: ");
6.        scanf("%d%d", &a, &b);
7.        a = a + b;
8.        b = a - b;
9.        a = a - b;
```

```
10.        printf("Values stored in a & b are : %d & %d", a, b);
11.    }
```

Output:
```
Input two values: 10 11
Values stored in a & b are : 11 & 10
```

Analysis: Two input values are stored in variables a & b. Then the sum of a & b is stored in a. If we subtract the value of b from the sum stored in a and store the value in b. Then b will have "sum – b" or "a + b -b" or "a" stored inside it. Now if we further subtract value stored in b from sum and store inside "a" then values are replaced.

a = 10
b= 11
a = a + b = 10 + 11 = 21
b = a – b = 21 – 11 = 10
a = a – b = 21 – 10 = 11

Problem 3: Write a program to find simple interest given principal, rate, and time.

Example 4.13:
```
1.    int main()
2.    {
3.         float p, r, t, si;
4.         printf("Input Principal, rate and time: ");
5.         scanf("%f%f%f", &p, &r, &t);
6.         si = (p * r * t)/100;
7.         printf("Simple interest is : %f ", si);
8.    }
```

Output:
```
Input Principal, rate and time: 4000 10 5
Simple interest is : 2000.00000
```

Analysis: Input is taken and stored in variables p, r and t. All variables are of type float so that fractional calculation is possible. Simple interest is calculated using formula si = (p*r*t)/100 and stored inside variable si. Finally, simple interest is printed to the screen.

Problem 4: Write a program to find compound interest given principal, rate, and time.

Example 4.14:
```
#include<stdio.h>
#include<math.h>

int main()
{
    float p, r, t, ci, a;
    printf("Input Principal, rate and time: ");
```

```c
    scanf("%f%f%f", &p, &r, &t);
    a = p * pow(1 + r/100, t);
    ci = a - p;
    printf("Compound interest is : %f ", ci);
}
```

Output:
```
Input Principal, rate and time: 100 10 10
Compound interest is: 159.374298
```

Analysis: Input is taken and stored in variables p, r, and t. Simple interest is calculated and stored inside variable si. Finally, simple interest is printed to the screen.

Problem 5: Solve the expression based on operator precedence.
1. 9*5+3
    45+3
    48
    Analysis: * has higher precedence than +

2. 1+2*3/6-4
    1+6/6-4
    1+1-4
    2-4
    -2
    Analysis: * and / have higher precedence than + and minus. Associativity of * and / is from left-to-right and associativity of + and – is also left-to-right.

Problem 6: Find output of the below program.
```c
int main()
{
    float a=1, b=2, c=3, d=4, e=6, f;
    f = a+b*c/e-d;
    printf("The result of expression is %f", f);
}
```

Output:
```
The result of the expression is -2.000000
```

Problem 7: Write a program to find if a given integer is a power of 2.

Example 4.15:
```c
int is2Pow(int num)
{
    return (!(num & (num - 1)) && num) ? 1 : 0;
}
```

Problem 8: WAP that accepts the temperature in Centigrade and converts into Fahrenheit using the formula C/5=(F-32)/9.

Example 4.16:
```c
int main()
{
    float c;
    printf("Enter the temperature in Centigrade:: ");
    scanf("%f", &c);
    printf("Fahrenheit value:: %.2f", (c/5)*9 + 32);
}
```

Output:
```
Enter the temperature in Centigrade:: 32
Fahrenheit value:: 89.60
```

Problem 9: WAP that accepts the marks of 5 subjects and finds the sum and percentage marks obtained by the student.

Example 4.17:
```c
int main()
{
    int a, b, c, d, e;
    float sum, percentage;

    printf("Enter the marks of first subject:: ");
    scanf("%d", &a);
    printf("Enter the marks of second subject:: ");
    scanf("%d", &b);
    printf("Enter the marks of third subject:: ");
    scanf("%d", &c);
    printf("Enter the marks of fourth subject:: ");
    scanf("%d", &d);
    printf("Enter the marks of fifth subject:: ");
    scanf("%d", &e);

    sum = a+b+c+d+e;
    percentage = (sum /500)*100;
    printf("Sum is %f and Percentage is %.2f", sum, percentage);
}
```

Output:
```
Enter the marks of first subject:: 89
Enter the marks of first subject:: 98
Enter the marks of first subject:: 100
Enter the marks of first subject:: 88
Enter the marks of first subject:: 99
Sum is 474.000000 and Percentage is 94.80
```

Question 1: Is ++i faster than i++?
Answer: Compiler should generate equal assembly code for i++, ++I, I = i+1. The compiler is responsible for doing such optimization. Well, the actual answer will depend on how this feature is implemented in the compiler.

Exercise

1. Write a program which will have variables a=2, b=4, c=8 and d=4 and then calculate the function
   x = (a * b) (c-d) and then finally print the value of x using printf().

2. Write a program which takes input variables a, b, c and d using scanf(), and then finally calculate the function x = (a * b)(c-d) and then finally print the value of x using printf().

3. What is short-circuiting in C expressions?
   It means that when we have multiple expression which is made of multiple parts using || or &&. The expression is evaluated from left to right. So the condition, when the value of the left side of || or && determines the result and the right side of expression is not evaluated, this condition is called short-circuiting the C expression.

   When the left side of || is true, then the whole expression is true.
   When the left side of && is false, then the whole expression is false.

4. Do we have a Boolean data type in C?
   Answer: No, C does not have a Boolean data type. We can use int, char, enums and #defines to do the same. Inside all the conditional statements like if, for, while etc. 0 is considered as false and any other value is considered as true.

   Similarly, we can use
   ```
   #define FALSE 0
   #define TRUE 1
   ```

   Alternatively, we can use enums like
   ```
   enum bool
   {
        False=0,
        True
   };
   ```

5. Write a function that rounds off a float to integer int round (float).

   Hint: we always get a roof of the float value when we cast it to an int. Think what will happen when we add 0.5 to a float value.

6. Function to find out the minimum number of bits needed to represent a number in binary. For example, 2 = 10 requires 2 bits, 10 = 1010 requires 4 bits.

   Hint: Use >> operator, until we get zero value.

7. Given 2 integers A and B, find the no. of bits that need to be flipped in A to get B.

   Hint: xor A and B and then count the number of bits in the result.

8. Write a program, which will tell if a machine is 32bit or 64 bit.

   Hint: - use sizeof() operator over an int and if return 4 then the system is 32bit if return 8 then the system is 64bits.

9. What is the role of precedence and associativity of an operator?

10. Suggest a better way to determine if a given integer is a power of 2.

11. When is type casting required in programming?

12. Write the increasing order of precedence of common operators available in C.

CHAPTER 5: CONDITIONAL BRANCHING

Introduction

There are many situations in which we want to execute some block of code only if some condition is true otherwise don't execute that piece of code. This decision-making is done using "if-condition" and "switch-case".

if condition

If the condition consists of a Boolean condition followed by one or more statements. It allows you to take different paths of logic, depending on a given Boolean condition.

Syntax of If the condition
```
if (boolean_expression)
{
     // statements
}
```

Flow Diagram:

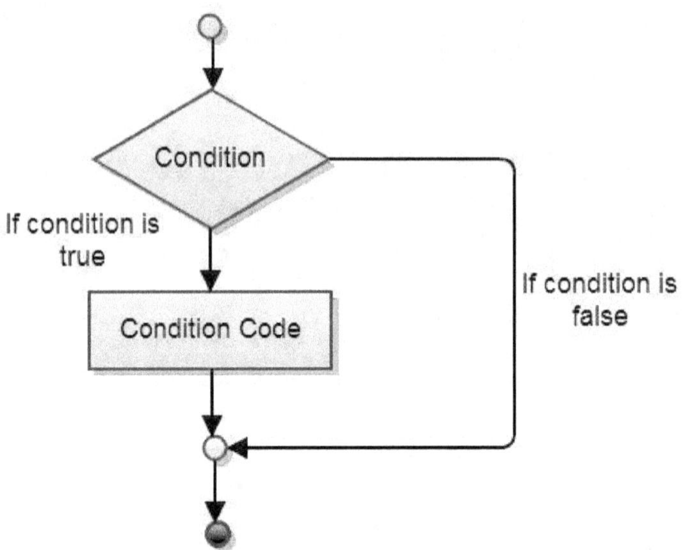

IF condition control flow

Example 5.1: If condition
```
1.    /* using "if" for decision making */
2.    #include<stdio.h>
3.
4.    int main()
5.    {
6.         int num;
7.         printf("Enter the value::");
8.         scanf("%d",&num);
```

```
9.          if(num>0)
10.             printf("Number is positive");
11.         return 0;
12.   }
```

Output:
```
1.    Enter the value::10
2.    Number is positive
```

Analysis:
- Line 6-8: The name is an integer and you are supposed to give a value to it. Let us suppose the value given is 10.
- Line 9: In this line, there is an if-condition which is checking that the value of num is greater than 0 or not. Since we have entered 10 then this condition is true.
- Line 10: Since the above condition was true this line "num is positive" will be printed otherwise this line will not be printed to the screen.

if-else condition

If the statement can follow by else statements and an optional else statement which is executed when the Boolean condition is false.

Syntax of If-Else condition:
```
if(boolean_expression)
{
     /* if condition statements, boolean condition true */
}
else
{
     /* else condition statements, boolean condition false*/
}
```

Flow Diagram:

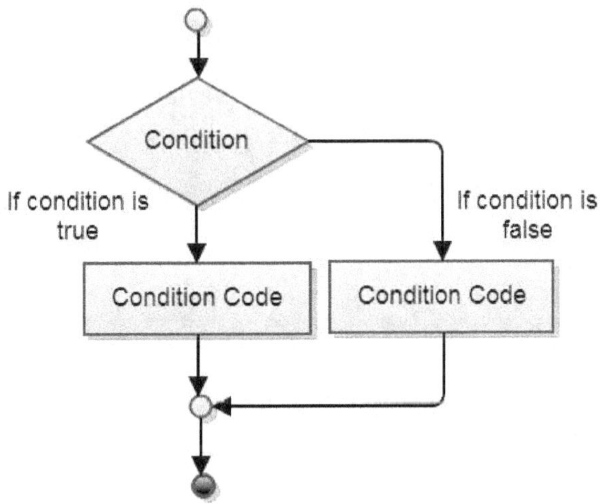

Example 5.2: If-Else condition

```
1.    /* using "if" for decision making */
2.    #include<stdio.h>
3.
4.    int main()
5.    {
6.        int num;
7.        printf("Enter the value:: ");
8.        scanf("%d",&num);
9.        if(num>0)
10.           printf("Number is positive");
11.       else
12.           print(" Number is negative or zero");
13.       return 0;
14.   }
```

Output:

```
1.    Enter the value:: -10
2.    Number is negative
```

Analysis:

- Line 9: In this line there is an if-condition which is checking that the value of num is greater than 0 or not. Since we have entered -10 then this condition is false.
- Line 12: Since the above condition is false the statement in the else block will be executed. Then we have seen the output "num is negative".

Note: If-else can be nested which means there can be any number of if statement under one if block. It applies to the other block.

Note: C does not have a Boolean type so 0 is considered as false and anything else is true.

switch-Case statement

In a Switch-Case statement, a variable is tested for equality against a list of values. Each value is called a case and is associated with a block of code. When the variable that is passed to the switch is having the same value as that of the case, that particular block of the case is executed.

Syntax of Switch statement:

```
switch(expression)
{
    case FirstConstant:
    {
        statement(s);
        break; /* optional */
    }
    case SecondConstant:
    {
```

```
        statement(s);
        break; /* optional */
    }
    default: /* optional */
    {
        statement(s);
    }
}
```

In this syntax, the expression is the variable that is passed to the switch statement and is compared against various constants. If it is equal to anyone of the constants, then that particular case block will be executed. If no match is found, then the default block is called. Every case code block is ended with a break, which terminates the switch and the flow of control jumps to the next line of the switch statement.

Flow Diagram:

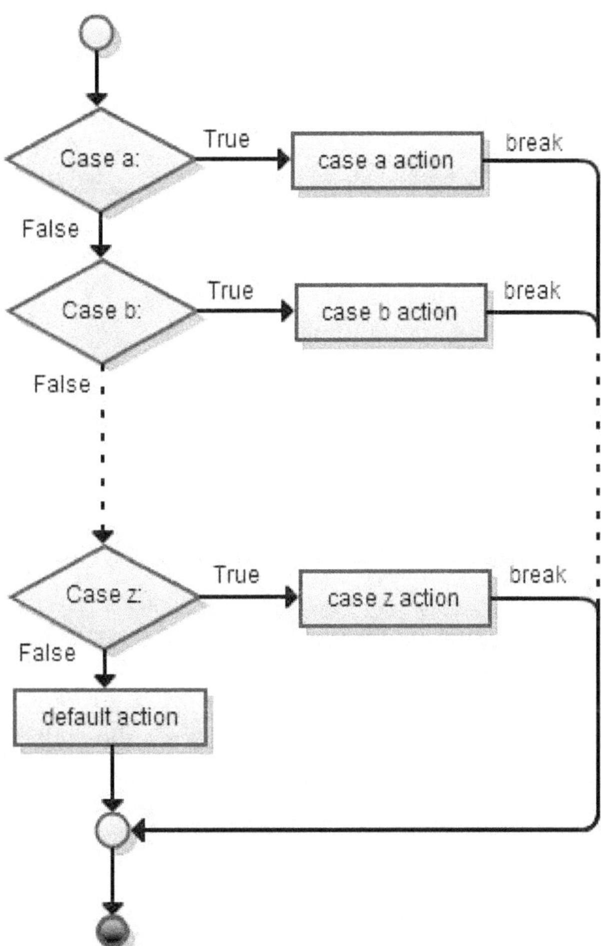

Switch-Case control flow

Example 5.3: Switch-Case condition

```
1.    /*Switch Case Example*/
2.    #include<stdio.h>
3.
4.    int main()
5.    {
6.         int x=2;
7.         printf("Please enter a number:");
8.         scanf("%d",&x);
9.         switch(x)
10.        {
11.        case 1:
12.             printf("x is 1");
13.             break;
14.        case 2:
15.             printf("x is 2");
16.             break;
17.        case 3:
18.             printf("x is 3");
19.             break;
20.        default:
21.             printf("value of x is unknown");
22.        }
23.        return 0;
24.    }
```

Output:
```
Please enter a number:2
x is 2
```

Analysis:
- Line 8:We have given value 2 to the variable x.

- Line 9:The variable x is passed to the switch statement. The value of x is 2 so the "case 2" block of code will be executed.

- Line 15:x is 2 is printed to the screen.

- Line 16:The break statement is reached which terminates the switch statement and the flow of control of the program will come to the line next to the switch that is line 23.

- Line 23:Program ends by returning value 0.

Note: break statement terminates the loop or switch statement and transfers execution to the statement immediately following the loop or switch.

If the variable passed in the switch is equal to some cash value, then the statements of the switch are executed until a break is found.

Example 5.4: Switch case fall through

```
1.     /*Switch Case fall-through Example*/
2.     #include<stdio.h>
3.
4.     int main()
5.     {
6.         int x=3;
7.         printf("Please enter a number:");
8.         scanf("%d",&x);
9.         switch(x)
10.        {
11.        case 1:
12.        case 2:
13.        case 3:
14.            printf("x is 1, 2 or 3");
15.            break;
16.        default:
17.            printf("value of x is unknown");
18.        }
19.        return 0;
20.    }
```

Output:

```
1.     Please enter a number:3
2.     x is 1, 2 or 3
```

Analysis: Line 11-13: Since there is no break statement in between so if case 1 is matched, case 2 is matched or case 3 is matched we will get the value "x is 1,2 or 3" printed to the screen.

Solved Examples

Problem 1: Find the largest value among the three given numbers

Example 5.5:

```
1.     int main()
2.     {
3.         int a, b, c, max;
4.         printf("Enter three variables: ");
5.         scanf("%d%d%d", &a, &b, &c);
6.         max = a;
7.         if(b > max)
8.             max = b;
9.         if(c > max)
10.            max = c;
11.
12.        printf("The largest value is %d\n", max);
13.        return 0;
14.    }
```

Output:

```
1.    Enter three variables: 21 12 30
2.    The largest value is 30
```

Analysis: Value of 'a' is stored in variable max. Value of max is compared with 'b' **if the value** stored in 'b' is larger than max **then the value** of max is updated to value of 'b'. Again value of max is compared with value of 'c' if value of 'c' is greater than max then max value is updated and value of 'c' is stored into it. Finally max contains the largest among the three input values.

Problem 2: Write a program to find if a given year is a leap year.
Conditions of leap year.
- Every 4th year we add an extra day
- Every 100th years we don't have a leap year
- Another rule says that every 400th years is a leap year again.

Hint: year % 4 == 0 && (year % 100 != 0 || year % 400 == 0)

Example 5.6:

```
1.    int main()
2.    {
3.        int year;
4.        printf("Enter year:: ");
5.        scanf("%d", &year);
6.        if (year % 4 == 0 &&  (year % 100 != 0 || year % 400 == 0))
7.        {
8.            printf("Given year is a leap year");
9.        }
10.    else
11.    {
12.        printf("Given year is not a leap year");
13.    }
14. }
```

Output:

```
1.    Enter year:: 2000
2.    Given year is a leap year
```

Analysis: To find if a given year is leap or not is tested using given calculation (year % 4 == 0 && (year % 100 != 0 || year % 400 == 0)).

Problem 3: Write a program to calculate the value of the basic expression with two operands and allowed operations are +,-,* and /.

Example 5.7:

```
1.    int main()
2.    {
3.        int a, b;
```

```c
4.          char op;
5.          printf("Please enter space separated expression:: ");
6.          scanf("%d %c %d", &a, &op, &b);
7.          switch(op)
8.          {
9.          case '+':
10.             printf("Result is %d", a+b);
11.             break;
12.         case '-':
13.             printf("Result is %d", a-b);
14.             break;
15.         case '*':
16.             printf("Result is %d", a*b);
17.             break;
18.         case '/':
19.             printf("Result is %d", a/b);
20.             break;
21.         default:
22.             printf("Unknown expression");
23.         }
24.         return 0;
25.     }
```

Output:
```
1.    Please enter space separated expression:: 2 + 5
2.    Result is 7
```

Analysis: Depending upon the operation symbol value of the expression is calculated and displayed.

Problem 4: WAP that finds whether a given number is even or odd.

Example 5.8:
```c
int main()
{
    int n;
    printf("Enter the number:: ");
    scanf("%d", &n);
    if(n%2 == 0)
        printf("Entered number is even.");
    else
        printf("Entered number is odd.");

    return 0;
}
```

Output:
```
Enter the number:: 22
Entered number is even.
```

Problem 5: WAP that accepts marks of five subjects and finds percentage and
prints grades according to the following criteria:
Between 90-100%--------------Print 'A'
80-90%---------------------------Print 'B'
60-80%-------------------------Print 'C'
Below 60%----------------------Print 'D'

Example 5.9:

```c
int main()
{
    int a, b, c, d, e;
    float sum, percentage;

    printf("Enter the marks of first subject:: ");
    scanf("%d", &a);
    printf("Enter the marks of second subject:: ");
    scanf("%d", &b);
    printf("Enter the marks of third subject:: ");
    scanf("%d", &c);
    printf("Enter the marks of fourth subject:: ");
    scanf("%d", &d);
    printf("Enter the marks of fifth subject:: ");
    scanf("%d", &e);

    sum = a+b+c+d+e;
    percentage = (sum /500)*100;

    printf("Sum is %f and Percentage is %.2f \n", sum, percentage);

    if(percentage > 90)
    {
        printf("Grade is A");
    }
    else if(percentage > 80)
    {
        printf("Grade is B");
    }
    else if (percentage > 60)
    {
        printf("Grade is C");
    }
    else
    {
        printf("Grade is D");
    }
}
```

Output:
```
Enter the marks of first subject:: 78
Enter the marks of second subject:: 77
```

```
Enter the marks of third subject:: 65
Enter the marks of fourth subject:: 80
Enter the marks of fifth subject:: 90
Sum is 390.000000 and Percentage is 78.00
Grade is C
```

Summary

1. Conditions "if" and "else" are used to execute a piece of code only when some condition is met.
2. Conditions are implemented using if statements. Which contains an expression enclosed within parentheses.
3. Boolean algebra is commonly used by three operators (and, or and not) to calculate the value of an expression as true or false.
4. The switch statement is used when we have some fixed set of values (not some range) and want to take some action, depending upon those values.

Questions & Answers

Question 1: when should I use if-else and when should I use a switch.
Answer: When we have some codes that need to be executed if some condition is met. E.g. some variable value less than, greater than or equal to something. We should use if-else.

The switch statement is used when we have some fixed set of values (not some range) and want to take some action depending upon those values.

Question 2: What is the difference between if(1 == i) and if(i == 1)?

Answer: There is no difference as such. However, it is a good practice to use the first one. In the second one by mistake, you can write it as if(i = 1), this is assigned the value 1 to variable I and it is always true if condition.

However, if by mistake, even if you write if(1 = i), the compiler will find this error for you.

Question 3: Which one is more efficient: a switch or if-else conditions?

Answer: Both statements are equally efficient, internally compilers implement both using the same instructions. We should use them depending upon our need. We should use if-else when we have some blocks of code which have to be executed depending upon Boolean value of some condition.

We should use switches when we have code that needs to be conditionally executed depending upon a list of values.

1. Write a program that takes input integers from the user to find if the input number is divisible by 3 or not.

2. Write a program that takes an integer input. Output if the entered number is positive, negative, or zero.

3. Write the output of the following code:

```c
int main()
{
    int x = 1;
    if (x > 4)
    {
        if(x ==1)
            printf("A");
    }
    else
    {
        if(x > 1)
            printf("B");
    }
    return 0;
}
```

4. Write a function to take the percentage of students and give output as pass or fail depending upon if the percentage is greater than 33%. Also display grades if the student has passed.
Between 80-100%-------------Grade 'A'
Between 70-80%-------------- Grade 'B'
Between 50-70%---------------Grade 'C'
Between 33-60%---------------Grade 'D'
Below 33%----------------------Grade 'F'

5. Draw flowchart of the above grade problem.

6. Write a program to tell a person whether he is fit, overweight or obese based on Body mass index of the person

7. What is the difference between a=0 and a==0 ?

8. What will be the output of this program

```c
#include<stdio.h>
int main()
{
    int a=-1;
    if( !(a++ && a++ && a++))
        printf("%d", a);
    else
        printf("nothing");
```

```c
        return 0;
}
```

Ans. It will print 1.

9. What will be the output of this program?
```c
#include<stdio.h>
int main()
{
    int a=-1;
    if( (a++||   a++ || a++))
        printf("%d", a);
    else
        printf("nothing");
    return 0;
}
```

Ans. It will print 0.

10. What will be the output of this program?
```c
#include<stdio.h>
int main()
{
    int a=-2;
    if( (++a &&   ++a && ++a))
        printf("%d", a);
    else
        printf("nothing");
    return 0;
}
```

CHAPTER 6: ITERATIONS AND LOOPS

Introduction

There are situations when we want to execute the same block of code multiple times. C programming language provides various control statements called loops, which are used to execute the same block of code multiple times. The various types of the loop we will see are "while-loop", "for-loop", "do.. while-loop" and "goto".

for-loop

There are situations in which we want to execute the same block of code multiple times. For this purpose, the C language has provided loops. Let us look into for-loops and analyze how loops work.

Syntax of for-loop:
```
for(initialization; condition; increment)
{
    statements;
}
```

There are three parts of for-loop: the first is the initialization which is executed only once when we enter the for-loop. The second is the condition that is checked at every iteration of the loop. If the condition is true, then the body of the loop is executed and if the condition is false, then we will come out of the for-loop. The third is the increment, which is used to increment/decrement the variables that are used in the condition. The below for-loop flow diagram will help you in understanding the for-loop properly.

Flow Diagram:

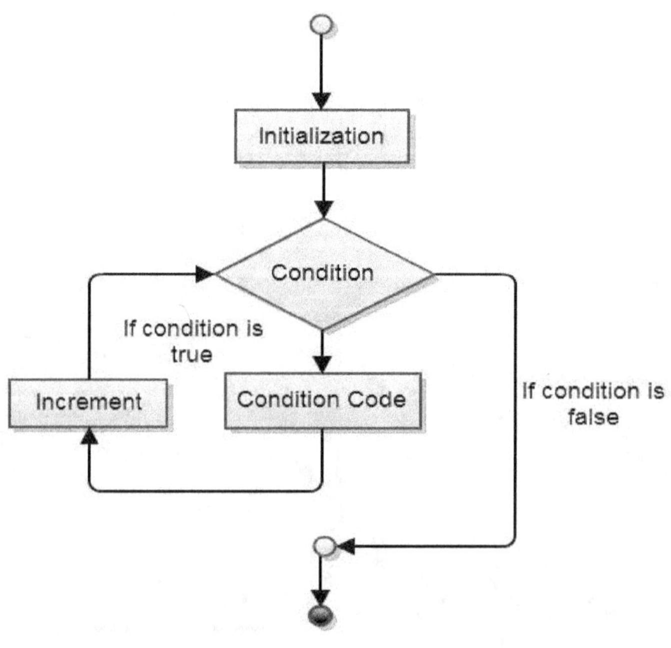

Example 6.1: for loop

```
1.    /* Using the "for" loop */
2.    #include<stdio.h>
3.
4.    int main()
5.    {
6.        int n;
7.        printf("Program will print 1 to 10\n");
8.        for(n=1; n<=10; n++)
9.        {
10.           printf("%d ",n);
11.       }
12.       return 0;
13.   }
```

Output:
```
Program will print 1 to 10
1 2 3 4 5 6 7 8 9 10
```

Analysis:
Line 8-11:

- ◆ In this line, we have initialized value 1 to a variable at the beginning of the for-loop. Note that initialization happens only once in for-loop.
- ◆ Then we are comparing n<=10, the for-loop will execute until this condition is true.
- ◆ Then we will print then number n.
- ◆ Then the increment step will take place in which we are increasing the value of n by one in each iteration.
- ◆ These steps are repeated many times until the condition is false. In our case when n is greater than 10 the for-loop will break and we will come out of the for loop to the next line.

Line 12 and 13: Once for loops end control flow, will come to line 12 and the program ends by calling return.

while-loop

A while-loop is used to execute the same block of code multiple times as long as a given condition is true.

Syntax of while-loop:
```
while(condition)
{
     statements;
}
```

Flow Diagram:

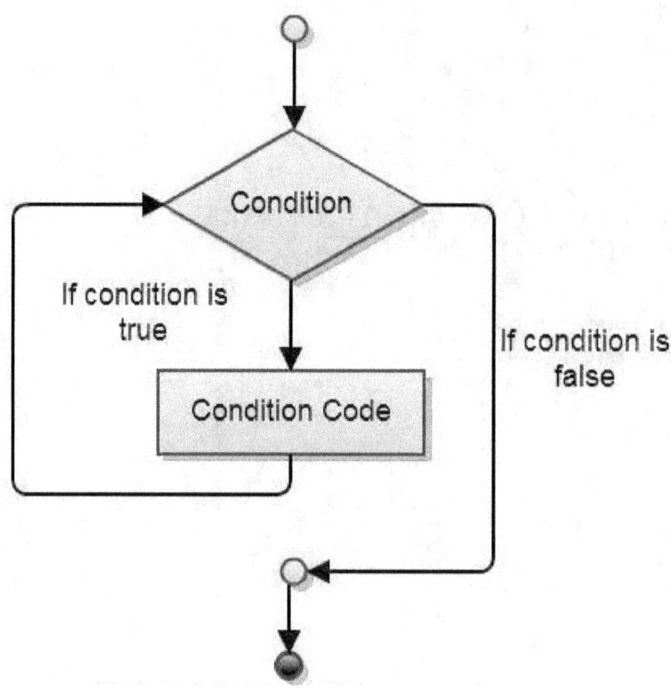

Example 6.2: while loop.
```
1.     /*Using the "while" loop*/
2.     #include<stdio.h>
3.
4.     int main()
5.     {
6.         int num=5;
7.         printf("Program will print decreasing counting\n");
8.         printf("Enter the starting number:: ");
9.         scanf("%d",&num);
10.
11.        while(num>0)
12.        {
13.            printf("%d ",num);
14.            num--;
15.        }
16.        return 0;
17.    }
```

Output:
```
Program will print decreasing counting
Enter the starting number:: 10
10 9 8 7 6 5 4 3 2 1
```

Analysis:
   ◆   Line 9: In this line, a value is assigned to num. In our example, we have assigned the value 5.

- Line 11-15: We have a while-loop condition of "num>0". As long as the value of num is greater than 0 then the loop will execute.
- Line 13: The value of num is printed to the screen.
- Line 14: In this line, we are decreasing the value of num by one.
- Line 16: When the value of num is 0, the while-loop ends and the program ends by calling return.

do..while-loop

A do..while-loop is similar to while-loop, but the only difference is that the conditional code is executed before the test condition. do..while-loop is used where you want to execute some conditional code at least once.

Flow Diagram:

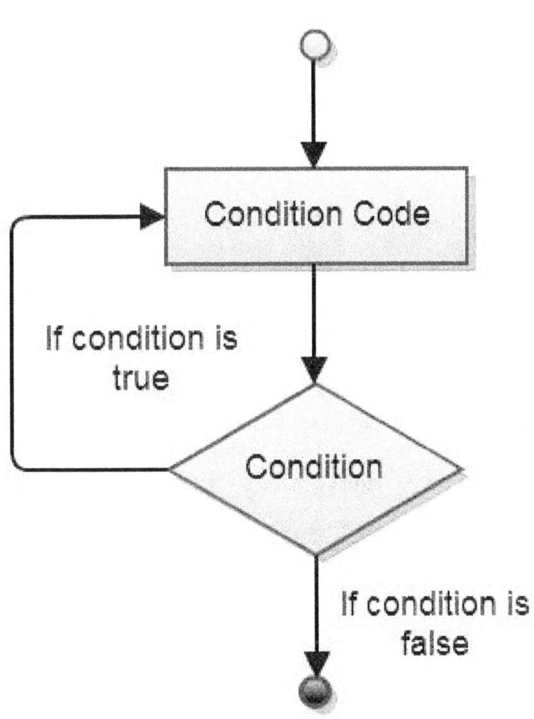

Example 6.3: do..while loop

```
1.    /* Using the "do..while" loop*/
2.    #include<stdio.h>
3.
4.    int main()
5.    {
6.        int num=5;
7.        printf("Program will print decreasing counting\n");
8.        printf("Enter the starting number:: ");
9.        scanf("%d",&num);
10.
11.       do
12.       {
13.           printf("%d ",num);
```

```
14.              num--;
15.          }
16.          while(num>0);
17.          return 0;
18.      }
```

Output:

```
Program will print decreasing counting
Enter the starting number:: 10
10 9 8 7 6 5 4 3 2 1
```

Analysis: Line 11-14: In this code, first the conditional statement is executed, then the value of num is manipulated (decreased) and at the end, the condition "num > 0" is checked. Whether the condition is false at the beginning or not the print statement on line 13 will execute at least once.

Loop with a break statement

When a break statement is executed inside a loop, then the loop is terminated. Similarly, if it is inside a block, then that block is skipped.

Example 6.4: break statement

```
1.      /* Using break inside loop */
2.      #include<stdio.h>
3.
4.      int main()
5.      {
6.          int num;
7.          for(num=10; num>0; num--)
8.          {
9.              if(num==3)
10.             {
11.                 break;
12.             }
13.             printf("%d ",num);
14.         }
15.         return 0;
16.     }
```

Output:

```
10 9 8 7 6 5 4
```

Analysis:
- Line 9: There is an "if" statement for condition "num==3" When num is equal to 3 Line 10-12 will be executed.
- Line 12: In this line, the break statement is used to break for-loop.
- Line 16: When a break statement is executed, the program control will come to the return statement.

Loop with a continue statement

When a continue statement is executed inside a loop, then all the statements in the loop which below continue are skipped and the next iteration of the loop proceeds.

Example 6.5: continue statement

```c
1.    /* Continue inside loop */
2.    #include<stdio.h>
3.
4.    int main()
5.    {
6.        int num;
7.        for(num=10; num>0; num--)
8.        {
9.            if(num==3)
10.           {
11.               continue;
12.           }
13.           printf("%d ",num);
14.       }
15.       return 0;
16.   }
```

Output:
10 9 8 7 6 5 4 2 1

Analysis: Line 9:When the num is equal to 3 the continue statement is executed. In the output, we can see that the value equal to 3 is not printed.

goto statement

A goto statement is used to jump from the goto to the labelled statement.

Example 6.6: Goto statement

```c
/*goto loop example*/
#include<stdio.h>

int main()
{
    int num=10;
loop:
    printf("%d ",num);
    num--;
    if(num>0)
        goto loop;

    return 0;
}
```

Output:
```
10 9 8 7 6 5 4 3 2 1
```

Analysis: Line 11:When this line is executed, then the flow of control is jumped to the label loop in line 7.

Note: You should not create a loop like this. It is bad practice to use goto.

Solved Examples

Problem 1: Given a number find the sum of all the digits of the number.

Hint: Modular number is used to find the least significant digit. Then divide can be used to get rid of the least significant digit.

Example 6.7:
```c
int main()
{
    int num, sum=0;
    printf("Enter a number:: ");
    scanf("%d", &num);
    while(num > 0)
    {
        sum += num%10;
        num /= 10;
    }
    printf("Sum of digits are:: %d", sum);
}
```

Output:
```
Enter a number:: 124
Sum of digits are:: 7
```

Problem 2: Given a number, create a number whose digits are reverse of the original number.

Example 6.8:
```c
int main()
{
    int num, num2=0;
    printf("Enter a number:: ");
    scanf("%d", &num);
    while(num > 0)
    {
        num2 = num2*10 + num%10;
        num /= 10;
    }
    printf("Reverse number is:: %d", num2);
}
```

Output:
```
Enter a number:: 124
The reverse number is:: 421
```

Problem 3: Given a number, find if it is a palindrome.

Hint: Reverse of a number is the same as the original number then it is a palindrome.

Example 6.9:
```c
int main()
{
    int num, num2=0, temp;
    printf("Enter a number:: ");
    scanf("%d", &num);
    temp = num;
    while(temp > 0)
    {
        num2 = num2*10 + temp%10;
        temp /= 10;
    }
    if(num == num2)
        printf("Given number %d is a palindrome", num);
    else
        printf("Given number %d is not a palindrome", num);
}
```

Output:
```
Enter a number:: 121
Given number 121 is a palindrome
```

Problem 4: Write a function to check if the given number is an Armstrong number.
Let us suppose the total number of digits is x. So calculate the sum of each digit of the number power by x. Then if the sum is equal to the number given then it is an Armstrong number else not. Let's suppose the given number is 153 so the total number of digits are 3. find sum $1^3 + 5^3 + 3^3 = 153$. The sum is equal to the given number so it is an Armstrong number.

Hint: Try to find the total number of digits. Then when we know the total number of digits then find the sum of desired power.

Example 6.10:
```c
#include<stdio.h>
#include<math.h>

int main()
{
    int num, sum=0, temp, digCount=0;
    printf("Enter a number:: ");
    scanf("%d", &num);
```

```c
    temp = num;
    while(temp > 0)
    {
        digCount += 1;
        temp /= 10;
    }
    temp = num;
    while(temp > 0)
    {
        sum += pow(temp%10, digCount);
        temp /= 10;
    }
    if(num == sum)
        printf("Given number %d is a armstrong", num);
    else
        printf("Given number %d is not a armstrong", num);
}
```

Output:

```
Enter a number:: 153
Given number 153 is a armstrong
```

Problem 5: Write a program to find if a given number is a prime number or not.
A prime number is greater than 1 and it should be divisible by 1 and itself only. It should not be divisible by any other number except 1 and itself.

Example 6.11:

```c
int main()
{
    int n, answer;
    printf("Enter any number:: ");
    scanf("%d", &n);

    if(n <= 1)
    {
        printf("Given number is not a prime.");
        return 0;
    }

    for(int i=2; i<n; i++)
    {
        if(n % i == 0)
        {
            printf("Given number is not a prime.");
            return 0;
        }
    }
    printf("Given number is a prime number.");
    return 0;
}
```

Further optimization on the number of comparisons.

Example 6.12:

```c
int main()
{
    int n, answer;
    printf("Enter any number:: ");
    scanf("%d", &n);

    if(n <= 1)
    {
        printf("Given number is not a prime.");
        return 0;
    }

    for(int i=2; i*i <= n; i++)
    {
        if(n % i == 0)
        {
            printf("Given number is not a prime.");
            return 0;
        }
    }

    printf("Given number is a prime number.");
    return 0;
}
```

Problem 6: Write a program to print Fibonacci series.

Example 6.13:

```c
int main()
{
    int n, answer;
    int sum, first=0, second=1;

    printf("Enter length of series:: ");
    scanf("%d", &n);

    if(n >= 0)
        printf("0 ");
    if(n >= 1)
        printf("1 ");

    while(n>2)    /* n - 2 > 0 , two values are already printed. */
    {
        sum = first + second;
        printf("%d ", sum);
```

```c
        first = second;
        second = sum;

        n -= 1;
    }
}
```

Output:
```
Enter length of series:: 4
0 1 1 2
```

Problem 7: Write a program to print prime numbers between 1 to N.

Example 6.14:
```c
int main()
{
    int n, answer, isPrime;

    printf("Enter upper limit number:: ");
    scanf("%d", &n);

    for(int i=2; i <= n; i++)
    {
        isPrime = 1;
        for(int j=2; j < i; j++)
        {
            if(i % j == 0)
            {
                isPrime = 0;
                break;
            }
        }
        if(isPrime == 1)
            printf("%d ", i);
    }
    return 0;
}
```

Output:
```
Enter upper limit number:: 10
2 3 5 7
```

Problem 8: Write a program to find the sum of Fibonacci series.

Example 6.15:
```c
int main()
{
    int num, sum=0, curr=1;
```

```c
        printf("Enter the number of elements:: ");
        scanf("%d", &num);

        for(int i=1; i <= num; i++)
        {
            /* From nth element to get (n+1)th element
             we need to multiply it by (n+1) */
            curr = curr*i;
            printf("%d ", curr);
            sum += curr;
        }
        printf("\nSum of all the elements:: %d", sum);
        return 0;
}
```

Output:
```
Enter the number of elements:: 6
1 2 6 24 120 720
Sum of all the elements:: 873
```

Problem 9: Write a program to find the sum of all the elements of series $x^n/n!$, given x and num of elements.

Example 6.16:
```c
int main()
{
    int num, x, sum=0, curr=1;

    printf("Enter the value of X:: ");
    scanf("%d", &x);

    printf("Enter the number of elements:: ");
    scanf("%d", &num);

    for(int i=1; i <= num; i++)
    {
        /* From nth element to get (n+1)th element
         we need to multiply it by x/(n+1) */
        curr = curr*x/i;
        sum += curr;
    }
    printf("Sum of all the elements:: %d", sum);
    return 0;
}
```

Output:
```
Enter the value of X:: 3
Enter the number of elements:: 3
Sum of all the elements:: 11
```

Problem 10: Write a program to print patterns given 'n' number of lines.

For n = 3

```
*
* *
* * *
```

Example 6.17:

```c
int main()
{
    int n;
    printf("Enter number of lines:: ");
    scanf("%d", &n);
    for(int i=1; i<= n; i++)
    {
        for(int j=1; j<=i; j++)
            printf("* ");
        printf("\n");
    }
}
```

Output:

```
Enter number of lines:: 5
*
* *
* * *
* * * *
* * * * *
```

Problem 11: Write a program to print the below pattern given the number of lines.

For n = 3

```
    *
  * *
* * *
```

Example 6.18:

```c
int main()
{
    int n;

    printf("Enter number of lines:: ");
    scanf("%d", &n);

    for(int i=1; i<= n; i++)
    {
        for(int j=i; j<=n; j++)
            printf("  ");

        for(int j=1; j<=i; j++)
            printf("* ");
```

```c
        printf("\n");
    }
}
```

Output:
```
Enter number of lines:: 5
          *
        * *
      * * *
    * * * *
  * * * * *
```

Problem 12: Write a program to print the below pattern given number of lines.
```
Number of lines:: 3
  1
 121
12321
```

Example 6.19:
```c
int main()
{
    int n;
    printf("Enter number of lines:: ");
    scanf("%d", &n);
    for(int i=1; i<= n; i++)
    {
        for(int j=i; j<n; j++)
            printf(" ");

        for(int j=1; j<=i; j++)
            printf("%d", j);

        for(int j=i-1; j>0; j--)
            printf("%d", j);

        printf("\n");
    }
}
```

Output:
```
Enter number of lines:: 4
   1
  121
 12321
1234321
```

Problem 13: Write a program to generate the following numbers structure:

12345
1234
123
12
1

Example 6.20:
```c
int main()
{
    int n;

    printf("Enter number of lines:: ");
    scanf("%d", &n);

    for(int i=n; i>= 1; i--)
    {
        for(int j=1; j<=i; j++)
            printf("%d", j);
        printf("\n");
    }
}
```

Problem 14: Write a program to find GCD of two numbers.

Example 6.21:
```c
int main()
{
    int a, b, divisor, dividend, rem;
    printf("Enter two numbers:: ");
    scanf("%d %d", &a, &b);

    if (a > b)
    {
        dividend = a;
        divisor = b;
    }
    else
    {
        dividend = b;
        divisor = a;
    }

    while(divisor != 0)
    {
        rem = dividend % divisor;
        dividend = divisor;
        divisor = rem;
    }
```

```c
        printf("GCD is %d", dividend);
        return 0;
}
```

Output:
```
Enter two numbers:: 20 5
GCD is 5
```

Problem 15: Write a function that will return the number of bits set in an integer.

Solution: use >> bitwise operator until the integer becomes zero. In the loop take a counter and increment the counter when bitwise & of integer and 1 gives 1 as result.

Example 6.22:
```c
int count(unsigned int num)
{
        int ctr = 0;
        while (num)
        {
                if (num & 1)
                {
                        ctr++;
                }
                num >>= 1;
        }
        return ctr;
}
```

Problem 16: Write a reverseBit function that will reverse the bits in an integer.

Example 6.23:
```c
int reverse(unsigned int num)
{
        unsigned int reverse=0;
        unsigned int bitsInInt = sizeof(int) * 8;

        for (int i = 0; i < bitsInInt; i++)
        {
                reverse = reverse | (num &1 );
                reverse <<= 1;
                num >>= 1;
        }
        return reverse;
}
```

Problem 17: WAP to print sum of even and odd numbers from 1 to N numbers.

Example 6.24:

```c
int main()
{
    int n, osum = 0, esum = 0;

    printf("Enter the number:: ");
    scanf("%d", &n);

    for(int i = 1;i<= n;i++)
    {
        if(i%2 == 0)
            esum += i;
        else
            osum += i;

    }
    printf("Odd Sum is %d \n", osum);
    printf("Even Sum is %d \n", esum);
    return 0;
}
```

Output:

```
Enter the number:: 10
Odd Sum is 25
Even Sum is 30
```

Problem 18: WAP to print the sum of all numbers up to a given number.

Example 6.25:

```c
int main()
{
    int n, sum =0;

    printf("Enter the number:: ");
    scanf("%d", &n);

    for(int i = 1;i<= n;i++)
        sum += i;

    printf("Sum is %d", sum);
    return 0;
}
```

Output:

```
Enter the number:: 10
Sum is 55
```

Summary

1. Loops are used if we want to execute some piece of code multiple times until some conditions are true.
2. ++ and -- operators are generally used with loops when we want to increment or decrement the value of a variable by 1.
3. A loop beginning and ending braces is not required when we have only one statement in the loop body. However, it is recommended to use braces even when the loop body contains only one statement.
4. An infinite loop is created using while(1) or similar loop statements. The program will execute indefinitely in the loop until some break statement is called.
5. While the condition is checked, then the loop body is executed.
6. do..while loop, once the body of the loop is executed, then the condition is checked.
7. For loop initial value of a variable, loop break condition, and increment/decrement. We do not expect a change in the value of the loop variable in the loop body.
8. The break statement terminates a loop and returns program control to the next statement following the end of the loop.
9. The continue statement passes over the remaining statement of the loop and continues with the next iteration of the loop.

Questions & Answers

Question 1: Will it be OK to use only one type of loop only in all places?
Answer: Yes, you can use it, but it is not advised.
Generally, when we want to execute some piece of code till some condition is true then we use a while loop.
do ..while is used when you want to execute some code at least once.
For loop is generally used when you have a fixed number of iterations.

Question 2: Why do we use a do-while loop in C? And tell its properties?
Answer: We use do-while loop when we want to execute a body of loop at least once. For example, while writing a menu-driven program, where the menu is to be shown at least once.

The properties of a do-while loop are:
1. The do-while loop condition is tested after the body is executed.
2. The body of the do-while loop is executed at least once.

Question 3: Explain the meaning of break and continue keyword in C?
Answer: Break: Break statement is used to terminate the loop or switch-case. When the break keyword is encountered within a loop or switch-case, the execution stops there, and control returns to the first statement after the loop or switch.
Syntax:
```
break;
```

Continue: When a continue statement is executed inside a loop, then all the statements in the loop which below continue are skipped and the next iteration of the loop proceeds.

Syntax:
```
continue;
```


1. Generate the below pattern
    ```
    $
    $$
    $$$
    $$$$
    ```

2. Generate the below pattern
    ```
    A
    BC
    DEF
    GHIJ
    ```

3. Generate the below pattern
    ```
    A
    BB
    CCC
    DDDD
    ```

4. Build an Odd-Even game that takes input from the user. Then it will validate if it is a number by using isdigit() function. (isdigit() is used to verify if the user has entered a digit or a non-digit letter).
    Using the remainder operator, find, if the number is divisible by 2. Then, depending upon whether it is even or odd, print "even"/ "odd" to the screen.

5. In the above program. Perform the same operation an infinite number of times (under a while loop). Until the user enters a number, it goes on printing, "even"/"odd" when the user enters some non-digit number and exits the loop (using break statement.)
    Hint to solve the problem using while(1), if-else (or switch) and isdigit().

6. Find if 10th bits of an integer is set or not.
    Solution: use and operator with power of 2.

7. Write a program to print the tables of all numbers from 1 to 20.

8. Write a program to determine if a given number is complete square or not?

9. What is the difference between while and do { }while(); ?

10. Comment when we have use for loop and when we should use while(){}.

CHAPTER 7: FUNCTIONS

Introduction

Functions are used to divide a large program into smaller subtasks. A function is a group of statements that together perform the subtask of the program. Sometimes the user of the function does not need to know the implementation of the function if its functionality and interface are well defined.

The basic prototype of function looks like this:
```
ReturnType FunctionName( ArgumentList )
{
      FunctionBody
}
```

The function has four parts: FunctionName, ReturnType, ArgumentList and FunctionBody
1. **FunctionName**: This is the actual name of the function. Whenever you want to call a function, you will use this same name to call it.
2. **ReturnType**: A function can return a value. The data type of the value may be int, double, char, etc. There is an option that the function will not return anything, in this case, Return Type will be void.
3. **ArgumentList**: An argument List will be used to pass a value to the function. The argument list is optional, so the function can take no arguments.
4. **FunctionBody**: The function body contains a collection of declarations and statements that defines the basic functionality of the function.

We have already looked into the main() function which is a function which is called by the system. main() is the starting point of the program.

Let us take an example of the sum() function which will add two numbers and return their sum.

Example 7.1:
```
/* function returning the sum of two numbers */
int sum(int num1, int num2)
{
    int result; /* local variable declaration */
    result=num1+num2;
    return result;
}
```

Function Declaration and Definition

The function declaration tells the compiler how the function looks. The actual implementation is not required in the function declaration.

Function declaration contains three parts:
1. Function named
2. Arguments to the function.
3. Return type of the function.

Syntax of function declaration:
```
return_type function_name(arguments);
```

For the above sum function, the function declaration will be:
```
int sum(int num1,int num2);
```

Or

```
int sum(int, int);
```

The function definition is the complete code of the function.
Function definition contains four parts:
1. Function named
2. Arguments to the function.
3. The return type of the function.
4. Body of the function.

Syntax:
```
return_type function_name(arguments)
{
    body of the function
}
```

Example 7.2:
```
int sum(int num1, int num2)
{
   return num1+num2;
}
```

Generally, the function declarations are kept in a separate file called header files with .h extension and the function definition resides in .c extension files, also called source files.

Calling Function

When you call a function the program control is passed to the called function, the code block inside the function starts executing. Moreover, when the called function returns or reaches the end of a function at the closing brace the program control is passed back to the calling function. Before calling a function, you need to provide the declaration of the function. To call a function, you need to provide the required arguments to the function name. If the function returns some value, you can store it in some variable.

Example 7.3: Demonstrating Function Calls
```
1.    #include <stdio.h>
```

```c
2.
3.    int sum(int num1, int num2); /* function declaration */
4.
5.    int main()
6.    {
7.
8.        int x = 10, y = 20, result;  /* local variable definition */
9.
10.       result = sum(x, y);  /* calling a function to find sum */
11.       printf("Sum is: %d\n", result);
12.       return 0;
13.   }
14.
15.   /* function returning the sum of two numbers */
16.   int sum(int num1, int num2)
17.   {
18.       int result;      /* local variable declaration */
19.       result= num1+num2;
20.       return result;
21.   }
```

Output:
```
The sum is: 30
```

Analysis:
- Line 3: function declaration of sum() function
- Line 10: Sum function is called from this main bypassing variable x and y with values 10 and 20, at this point control flow will go to line 16.
- Line 16: Variables passed to the sum function are copied into num1 and num2 local variables.
- Line 19 & 20: The sum is calculated and saved in a variable result. Then the variable result is returned. Control flow comes back to line number 10.
- Line 10-11: Return value of the sum function is saved in a local variable result. Then the value is printed to the screen.

Scope of variables

The scope of a variable is the region where that variable can be accessed or modified. Variables in C have two types of scope depending upon where they are declared. Their two types of scope are: Block Scope and Global Scope. Local variables have Block Scope and Global variables have Global Scope.

Global Variables

They are declared outside any function. These variables can be used throughout the program.

Example 7.4:
```c
1.    #include <stdio.h>
2.
3.    int var = 10;
```

```c
4.    int main()
5.    {
6.          printf("the value of a is %d\n", var);
7.          var = 2;
8.          printf("the value of a is %d\n", var);
9.          return 0;
10.   }
```

Analysis: The variable var is declared outside any function so it is a global variable.

Variables declared within a block are called local variables. These variables can be used only within the block (or function) in which they are declared. A block starts with an opening curly brace "{" and ends in a closing curly brace "}". A local variable is created upon entry into the block and destroyed before the exit of that block. If you create a variable in the main() function, then it can be used only within the main() function. That variable cannot be accessed by any other function that you may have created.

Arguments that are passed to the function are also local variables. They are created when you enter a function and are destroyed when you exit from the function.

Example 7.5:
```c
1.    #include <stdio.h>
2.
3.    int main()
4.    {
5.        int a;
6.        a = 2;
7.        printf("the value of a is %d\n",a);
8.        return 0;
9.    }
```

Analysis: The variable "a" is declared inside the main() function so it is a local variable.

Blocks inherit all variables from the global scope. When we declare variables with the same name as the global variable it hides (but not replace) the global variables if blocks are nested, variables declared in an inner block may hide variables, declared in an outer block variable, declared inside a block have a different scope of global variables, and may even be of a different type:

Example 7.6:
```c
1.    #include <stdio.h>
2.
3.    int var = 10;
4.    int main()
5.    {
6.        int var;
7.        var = 2;
8.        printf("the value of a is %d\n", var);
```

```
9.      {
10.         int var;
11.         var = 5;
12.         printf("the value of a is %d\n", var);
13.      }
14.      return 0;
15.  }
```

Analysis: Variable var is declared globally outside any function. But var is again declared inside the main() function so inside main it hides the global variable var.

Note: Use of Global variables is not recommended as they take more memory because the compiler has to keep them always in memory. Use of Global variables is not recommended as they can be changed from any part of the program and this kind of logical error is hard to find and fix.

Note: It is not recommended to use the same name for local and global variables, it can create confusions and programming errors.

Storage Classes

Storage classes are qualifiers which are used to define the scope (or visibility), lifetime, default value and storage location of a variable.

The four storage classes are:
1. auto (automatic)
2. static
3. extern
4. register

	Scope	Lifetime	Default Value	Storage Location
auto	Local	Life time of function	Garbage	RAM
static	Local	Life time of program	Default value, for example 0 for integer	RAM
register	Local	Life time of function	Garbage	Preferably Register otherwise RAM
extern	Global	Life time of program	Default value, for example 0 for integer	RAM

auto (automatic)

auto is the default storage class for local variables. Whenever you declare a variable in a function, it is by default "auto". You need not explicitly specify this qualifier.

Automatic variables have the following properties:
1. Their scope is local to the block/function in which they are declared.
2. The lifetime of an auto variable is the lifetime of the function in which they are declared. They are created when we enter the function and are destroyed when the function exits.

3. auto variable if not initialized they have garbage value inside them.
4. auto variables are stored in RAM.

Example 7.7:

```c
int display()
{
    auto int num = 0;   // auto keyword is optional.
    num += 10;
    printf("Num is %d \n", num);
}

int main()
{
    for(int i=0;  i<4;  i++)
        display();
}
```

Output:

```
Num is 10
Num is 10
Num is 10
Num is 10
```

Analysis: Function display() is called 4 times each time the variable num is created when control enters the function and is destroyed when control exits from the function. So we are getting the same output "Num is 10"

Static Storage: static

If static keyword is used inside a block or function, the compiler will create space for the variable that lasts for the life of the program

Static variables have the following properties:
1. Their scope is local to the block/function in which they are declared.
2. The lifetime of a static variable is the lifetime of the program.
3. Static variable if not initialized they have a default value for example for integer case they have value 0.
4. Static variables are stored in RAM.

Example 7.8:

```c
int display()
{
    static int num = 0;
    num += 10;
    printf("Num is %d \n", num);
}
```

```c
int main()
{
    for(int i=0; i<4; i++)
    {
        display();
    }
}
```

Output:
```
Num is 10
Num is 20
Num is 30
Num is 40
```

Analysis: Static variables have the lifetime of the program so it is initialized only once. So in each subsequent call of display() function, the static variable num is incremented by 10.

Private Variables: static

Another use for the static keyword is to ensure that code outside a file cannot modify variables that are globally declared in this file if declare.c has declared a variable farvar as "static int farvar;" then the extern int farvar statement in use.c would cause an error.

Optimization Hint: register

The register provides a hint to the compiler that the programmer thinks a variable will be frequently used, so store it in hardware registers instead of RAM. The register should only be used for variables that require quick access – such as counters. Registers are closer to the CPU and have much fast read and write compared with the RAM.

Note: Compiler is free to ignore register hints. If ignored, the variable is equivalent to an auto variable with the exception that you may not take the address of a register.
Note: In C programming, you should not try to find the address of a register variable. Register variables are rarely used since any modern compiler will do a better job of optimization than most programmers.

Register variables have the following properties:
1. Their scope is local to the block/function in which they are declared.
2. The lifetime of the Register variable is the lifetime of the function in which they are declared. They are created when we enter the function and are destroyed when the function exits.
3. Register variables if not initialized they have garbage value.
4. Register variables are preferably stored in Register but in case registers are not allotted to them then they stay in RAM.

Syntax:
```
Register datatype  variableName;
```

Example 7.9:

```c
int display()
{
    register int num = 0;
    num += 10;
    printf("Num is %d \n", num);
}

int main()
{
    for(int i=0; i<4; i++)
    {
        display();
    }
}
```

Output:

```
Num is 10
Num is 10
Num is 10
Num is 10
```

Analysis: Register variables behave just as auto behaviour. They are created when the control reaches at the start of the function display() and they are destroyed when the control flow reaches the end of the function. They are optimization hints to the compiler to store these variables in a fast register location.

Note: Do not expect that specifying all your variables as register type will speed up the program. Since there is a limited number of registers in a computer.

If a variable is declared (with global scope) in one file, but referenced in another, the extern keyword is used to inform the compiler of the variable's existence.

Note: that the extern keyword is for declarations, not definitions. An extern declaration does not create any storage; that must be done with a global definition, extern defines a global variable that is visible to ALL object modules. When you use 'extern', the variable cannot be initialized as all it does is point the variable name at a storage location that has been previously defined.

Example 7.10:

In declare.c:

```c
int var;
```

In use.c:

```c
int main()
{
    extern int var;
    int a;
```

```c
        a = var*2;
}
```

Analysis: variable var is declared in declare.c file and is used in use.c file. When the compiler compiles the use.c file at that time it will not give an error that the variable var is not declared. The extern keyword informs the compiler that an external global variable var exists.

Example 7.11:
File 1
```c
int count=5;
```

File 2
```c
extern int count;
int main()
{
        printf("count is %d\n",count);
}
```

Analysis: Count in 'File 1' will have a value of 5. If File 1 changes the value of count – File 2 will see the new value.

Arguments passed by value

Call by Value: When variables are passed to the function as arguments, the function creates local variables and the value passed as the argument is copied to the newly created variables. These variables are created upon entry into the function and are destroyed at the time the function exits. Since these are just a copy of the original arguments so if we make some change in them then the original variables are not changed.

Let us take an example of void increment (int value); the function which will increment the value of the passed argument variable.

Example 7.12: Passing arguments by Value
```c
1.      #include<stdio.h>
2.
3.      void increment(int value);
4.
5.      int main()
6.      {
7.          int i=10;
8.          increment(i);
9.          printf("The value of i is %d\n", i);
10.         return 0;
11.     }
12.
13.     void increment(int value)
14.     {
15.         value++;
```

```
16.        printf("The value of variable inside function is %d\n", value);
17.    }
```

Output:
```
1.    The value of variable inside function is 11
2.    The value of i is 10
```

Analysis:
- Line 8: When we pass a variable i into the function increment() as an argument, the value of variable i is copied into another variable value.
- Line 15:Then the value of the variable value is increased by one. Remember, it is not the variable i. It just contained the value stored in i.
- Line 16: We are printing the value in variable value which is 11. Then we exit from the function.
- Line 9: Finally, we printed the value of the variable i which is 10. This value is not incremented as it is not actually passed to the function; its value is copied to another variable value that is a local variable of the function and is destroyed when the function exits.

Pointers

What is a Pointer? The answer to this question is "A pointer is a type of variable which can store a memory address". To revisit the concept of pointer lets go to the concept of a variable once again.

A **variable** in a program is a memory location with a name that can store a value that can vary. The compiler assigns a block of memory within the ram to hold the value of that variable. The size of that block depends on the data type of the variable. For example, on a 32 bit PC the size of an integer variable is 4 bytes. This document assumes the use of a 32-bit system with 4-byte integers.

When we declare a variable, we inform the compiler of two things, the name of the variable and the data type of the variable.

For example, we declare a variable of type integer with the name var by writing:
```
int var;
```

When the compiler looks into the "int" part of the statement, then it reserves a memory of 4 bytes for this variable. Along with it, keep the name "var" of a variable in its symbol table. On the table, it keeps the relative address of this variable. So, in the program wherever it finds this symbol "var" it will look into its symbol table and know what is the value of "var" or where it needs to store some value on "var". So, if we write "var=10;" the compiler looks into the symbol table of "var", finds its memory location, and stores value 10 into it. Until this point, the compiler has compiled the program. A binary file is created which has all the addresses as a relative address. The relative address is an address calculated by considering the start of the program as address zero. When the program runs or when it is executed the absolute address is calculated by adding an offset of the executable to the relative address.

Absolute address = Offset of the exe + Relative address.

```
int a, b;
```

```
a=10;
b=a;
```

In the above code, there are two memory locations reserved with the name "a" and "b". Then a value of 10 is stored in the memory location of a. Then what value stored in "a" is read and stored in memory location "b".

If you want to store an address of a variable and use it in the program, then you need pointers. A **pointer** is a special type of variable that can store an address of a system. To declare a pointer, we use "*" after a datatype.

Example 7.13: Demonstrating pointers
```
1.      #include<stdio.h>
2.
3.      int main()
4.      {
5.          int a;
6.          int *ptrA = NULL;
7.          a = 10;
8.          ptrA = &a;
9.          printf("The memory location %p of ptrA contains:: %d \n", ptrA,
        *ptrA);
10.         return 0;
11.     }
```

Output:
```
The memory location 0x7ffc47035c7c of ptrA contains:: 10
```

Analysis:
- Line 5: A variable is declared and the compiler will allocate a memory location for this variable.

- Line 6: A pointer type variable ptrA is declared and the compiler will allocate how many bytes of memory are required to store an address in memory. We have used "int" to tell the compiler that we are going to store an address of an integer variable in this pointer ptrA. Therefore, we will call it as "ptrA" is a "pointer to an int". We have initialized a value NULL to the pointer. NULL is a macro. (We will learn about macros in coming chapters). For now NULL, it is some special value. We can test the value of ptrA as if (ptrA == NULL). So make a rule to initialize a pointer when declaring with some variable location or NULL if no such location is decided.

- Line 7: We have stored value 10 inside A.

- Line 8: ptrA is now pointing to the memory location of the variable "a". Operator "&" is used to get the address of a variable. Now, "ptrA" is pointing to "a". As ptrA stores the address of variable "a".

- ◆ Line 9: "*" " Dereference Operator is also used to access the value stored in the location pointed with a pointer. So, in our code *ptrA will return the value 10 because it is stored in the variable "a" this is pointed by ptrA.

Arguments passed by Reference / Pointer

What, if you want to modify the value of the variable (passed as argument) inside the function? For this pass-by-pointer or pass-by-reference is used.

Pass-by-pointer or Pass-by-reference: What we pass the pointer to the variable inside the calling function to the called function it is called pass-by-pointers. Since we know the address of the variable inside the called function, we can modify its value.

This method of passing variables is more efficient as new copies of variables are not created when passed by a pointer.

Example 7.14: Passing Arguments by Pointer

```
1.     #include<stdio.h>
2.
3.     void increment(int *value);
4.
5.     int main()
6.     {
7.         int i = 10;
8.         int *ptrInt = &i;
9.         increment(ptrInt);
10.        printf("The value of i is %d", i);
11.    }
12.
13.    void increment(int *ptrVar)
14.    {
15.        (*ptrVar)++;
16.        printf("The value of variable pointed by ptrVar is %d \n",
       *ptrVar);
17.    }
```

Output:
```
The value of variable pointed by ptrValue is 11
The value of i is 11
```

Analysis:
- ◆ Line 8: We have created, a pointer variable ptrInt and stored the address of variable i inside it.
- ◆ Line 9: We have passed the address stored inside ptrInt to the increment function this address is copied into the pointer variable ptrVar of the increment function.
- ◆ Line 15: We increased the value pointed by the pointer variable ptrVar, which is the variable i of the calling function. Therefore, the value of i is increased and will become 11.
- ◆ Line 16: We printed the value pointed by the ptrVar pointer. That is 11

◆ Line 10: We printed the value of the variable i which is also 11. The value of i was incremented inside increment() function.

Recursive Function

A recursive function is a function which calls itself, directly or indirectly (a function is part of a cycle in the sequence of function calls again.). A recursive function consists of two parts: Termination Condition and Body (which include recursive expansion).

Termination Condition / Base Case: A recursive function always contains one or more terminating conditions. A condition, in which recursive function processes a simple case and does not call itself.

Without a termination condition, the recursive function may run forever and will finally consume all the stack memory.

Body (including recursive expansion): The main logic of the recursive function is contained in the body of the function. It also contains the recursion expansion statement that in turn calls the function itself.

Example 7.15: Demonstrating the recursive function call.
```
1.    int factorial(int n)
2.    {
3.        /* Termination Condition */
4.        if(n<=1)
5.           return 1;
6.        /* Body, Recursive Expansion */
7.        return n * factorial(n-1);
8.    }
```

Analysis: In this above example, the factorial function is calling itself on line 7.
Following diagram represents factorial() function recursion calls:

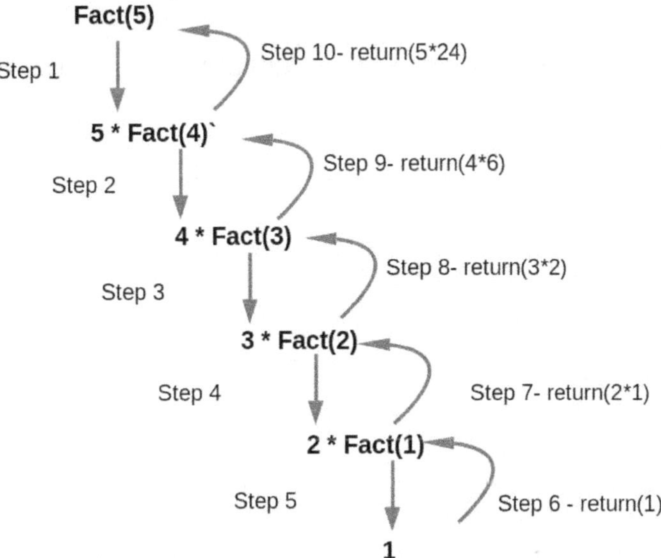

Note: The speed of a recursive program is slower because of stack overheads. If the same task can be done using loops and recursion, then we should prefer loops in place of recursion to avoid stack overhead.

Variable number of Arguments

It is sometimes required to have a function that can take a variable number of arguments. These functions are called a variadic function.

We have already seen scanf() and printf() functions that take a variable number of arguments. The declaration of scanf() and printf() function looks like:

```
int scanf (const char * format,...);
int printf (const char * format,...);
```

This "..." is called an ellipsis. It tells the compiler that there are more arguments to come. There are some macros in the C Standard Library, which help us in creating a variable argument function. The ellipsis can only be used if at least one named argument is there. All named arguments must precede the ellipsis.

There is no built-in way to determine the data type of arguments passed. Also, there is no built-in way to find the number of an argument passed. So, the solution is to pass a formatted string to find the type of argument and number of arguments. Alternatively, pass a count of arguments (like mean() function in the next example) and the user should know what kind of datatype it supports (in mean() function case it is an int).

The preprocessor macros are:
- va_list: Is a data-type to point to a variable list of arguments.
- va_start: Initialize variable list variable for num number of arguments
- va_arg: It is used to retrieve each element of an argument list.
- va_end: It is used to clean memory reserved for the variable list.

Let us make a verdict function mean() which takes a number of arguments and will return their mean value.

Example 7.16: Passing variable number of arguments to function.
```
1.    #include<stdio.h>
2.    #include<stdarg.h>
3.
4.    double mean(int num,...)
5.    {
6.        va_list varList;
7.        double sum=0.0;
8.        int i;
9.        /* initialize varList for number of arguments */
10.       va_start(varList,num);
11.       /* access all the arguments assigned to varList */
```

```c
12.        for(i=0; i<num; i++)
13.        {
14.            sum+=va_arg(varList,int);
15.        }
16.        /* clean memory reserved for varList */
17.        va_end(varList);
18.        return sum/num;
19.    }
20.
21.    int main()
22.    {
23.        printf("Mean of 2, 3, 4 & 5 = %f \n", mean(4, 2, 3, 4, 5));
24.    }
```

Output:

```
Mean of 2, 3, 4 & 5 = 3.500000
```

Analysis:

- Line 2: #include <stdarg.h>
  The header file stdarg.h needs to be included, it declares one type (va_list) and three macros (va_start, va_arg, and va_end).

- Line 4: double mean(int num,...)
  Ellipses i.e. three periods(...) tells the C compiler that there are more arguments that may come. An ellipsis is always the last argument of the function.
  The first argument generally represents the number of arguments to come as our example.

- Line 6: va_list varList;
  This array holds information needed by va_arg and va_end. When a called function takes a variable argument list, it declares an array of type va_list. In our case varList.

- Line 10: va_start(varList, num);
  This macro sets variable varList to point to the first of the variable arguments being passed to the function. va_start must be used before the first call to va_arg or va_end.
  The first argument is va_list type array varList and the second argument is the last fixed variable (lastfix) passed as an argument to the function that is "num" in our example.

- Line 14: sum += va_arg(varList, int);
  The first time macro va_arg is used, it returns the first argument in the list. Each successive time va_arg is used, it returns the next argument in the list. The first argument is the va_list type varList and the second argument is the type of variable that is an int. All the values returned by va_arg () are stored in a sum variable.

- Line 17: va_end(varList);
  The macro va_end is used to clean up the memory assigned to a va_list variable.

- Line 18:Finally, the sum is divided by the number of elements passed to the function and the mean is returned by the function.

◆ Line 23:The value of mean returned from the mean function is printed out as output.

Command-line Arguments

It is sometimes required to pass arguments to the program when it is run as a command. Command-line arguments are given to the name of the executable in the command line.
To understand the command line we need to understand the complete declaration of the main function:

```
int main (int argc, char *argv[] )
```

In the main function, there are two arguments argc and argv[] passed to it, argc stores the number of t command line arguments provided and argv contains the complete list of command-line arguments. argv is an array of character pointers that points to the list of all the arguments. argv[0] is the name of the program. After that, each consecutive element of the array contains the next command line argument provided to the program. argv[argc] is a null pointer.

Example 7.17: Demonstrating command line arguments
```
1.      #include<stdio.h>
2.
3.      int main(int argc,char *argv[])
4.      {
5.          if(argc==1)
6.          {
7.              printf("No command line argument provided.\n");
8.          }
9.          else if(argc==2)
10.         {
11.             printf("One command line argument provided.\n");
12.             printf("The command line argument is: %s\n", argv[1]);
13.         }
14.         else
15.         {
16.             printf("More than one command line argument provided.\n");
17.         }
18.     }
```

Execution:
```
./a.out test
```

Output:
```
One command-line argument provided
The command-line argument is: test
```

Analysis: In the above example, we have provided only one argument to the function so it will go into argc == 2 block. Then we have printed the argument provided to the program in the command line.

Library Functions

Functions which are already implemented in C programming language are called library functions. For example math.h file contains the declaration of various mathematical functions and stdio.h file contains the declaration of various i/o functions.

Difference between User-defined functions and Library Functions.

User-Defined Functions	Library Functions
These functions are implemented by the User.	These functions are predefined and are provided along with the compiler of C language.
These functions are created by the user as per their own requirements.	These functions are generic and are designed for use by the user community.
These functions are not required to be kept inside any file. They may be present in the files which are in the same location where they are used.	These functions are defined inside special library files. The user needs to include these files to use these functions.
For example, some sum() function is defined by the user.	For example stdio.h file functions like printf() and scanf().

The **math.h** header defines various mathematical functions in C language. All the mathematical functions used in C language are given below:

Function	Description
floor ( )	Returns the nearest integer which is less than or equal to the argument passed to this function.
round ( )	Returns the nearest integer value of the float/double/long double argument passed to this function.
ceil ( )	Returns nearest integer value which is greater than or equal to the argument passed to this function.
sin ( )	Calculate sine value of the argument.
cos ( )	Calculate cosine of the argument.
tan ( )	Calculate tangent of the argument.
sinh ( )	Calculate hyperbolic sine of the argument.
cosh ( )	Calculate hyperbolic cosine of the argument.
tanh ( )	Calculate hyperbolic tangent of the argument.
exp ( )	Calculate the exponential "e" raised to the argument.
log ( )	Calculates natural logarithm of the argument.
log10 ( )	Calculates base 10 logarithm of the argument.
sqrt ( )	Calculate the square root of the argument passed to this function.
pow ( )	Calculate the power of the given number
trunc()	Truncates the decimal value from floating point value and returns integer valu

The **stdio.h** header defines various input, output and file handling functions in C language. All the functions defined inside stdio.h are given below:

Function	Description
printf()	Formatted write onto the output screen.
scanf()	Formatted read data from keyboard.
getc()	Read character from file.
gets()	Read line from keyboard.
getchar()	Read characters from the keyboard.
puts()	Write line onto the output screen.
putchar()	Write a character to the output screen.
clearerr()	Clear the error indicators.
fopen()	Open file for reading.
fclose()	Closes an opened file.
getw()	Reads an integer from file.
putw()	Writes an integer to file.
fgetc()	Read a character from a file.
putc()	Write a character to file.
fputc()	Write a character to file.
fgets()	Read string from a file, one line at a time.
fputs()	Write string to a file.
feof()	Find end of file.
fgetchar()	Read a character from the keyboard.
fgetc()	Read a character from a file.
fprintf()	Write formatted data to a file
fscanf()	Read formatted data from a file.
fgetchar()	Read a character from the keyboard.
fputchar()	Write a character from the keyboard.
fseek()	Move file pointer position to given location
ftell()	Give current position of file pointer.
rewind()	Move file pointer position to the beginning of the file.
sprint()	Write formatted output to string.

sscanf()	Read formatted input from a string.
remove()	Delete a file.
fflush()	Flushes a file.

Solved Examples

Problem 1: Write a function isPrime() to check if a given number is prime or not.

Example 7.18:
```c
int isPrime(int n)
{
    if(n <= 1)
    {
        printf("Given number is not a prime.");
        return 0;
    }

    for(int i=2; i<n; i++)
    {
        if(n % i == 0)
        {
            printf("Given number is not a prime.");
            return 0;
        }
    }

    printf("Given number is a prime number.");
    return 1;
}

int main()
{
    int n, result;
    printf("Enter a number:: ");
    scanf("%d", &n);
    result = isPrime(n);
    printf("Entered value is prime:: %d", result);
}
```

Problem 2: Write a function sumDigit() to give the sum of all the digits of the input number.

Example 7.19:
```c
int sumDigits(int num)
{
    int sum=0;
```

```c
    while(num > 0)
    {
        sum += num%10;
        num /= 10;
    }
    return sum;
}

int main()
{
    int num, sum=0;
    printf("Enter a number:: ");
    scanf("%d", &num);
    printf("Sum of digits are:: %d", sumDigits(num));
}
```

Problem 3: Write a C program to calculate factorial of a given number using recursion.
Hint: f(N) = N * f(N-1)

Example 7.20:
```c
int factorial(int n)
{
    /*Termination Condition*/
    if(n<=1)
        return 1;
    /*Body,Recursive Expansion*/
    return n * factorial(n-1);
}
```

Problem 4: Write a C program to calculate factorial of a given number using a loop.
Hint: f(N) = N * f(N-1)

Example 7.21:
```c
int factorial(int n)
{
    int fact = 1;
    while (n > 1)
    {
        fact=fact*n;
        n--;
    }
    return fact;
}
```

Problem 5: Write a function to print numbers in the range start to end.

Example 7.22:
```c
void printNum(int start, int end)
{
```

```c
    while(start <= end)
    {
        printf("%d ", start);
        start++;
    }
}
```
or
```c
void printNum(int start, int end)
{
    while(start <= end)
        printf("%d ", start++);
}
```

Problem 6: Write a function to print numbers in the range start to end without using a loop.

Example 7.23:
```c
void printNum(int start, int end)
{
    if (start > end)
        return;
    printf("%d ", start++);
    printNum(start, end);
}
```

Problem 7: Write a program to convert decimal to any base (binary, hex etc...)

Example 7.24:
```c
void decimalToBaseX (int n, int base)
{
    if (n == 0)
        return;

    int remender;
    remender = n % base;
    decimalToBaseX (n / base, base);
    printf("%c", "0123456789abcdefghijklmnopqrstuvwxyz"[remender]);
}
```

Problem 8: Write a function to swap two variables without using a third variable.

Example 7.25:
```c
void swap1(int *a, int *b)
{
    *a = *a + *b;   // *a is A+B
    *b = *a - *b;   // *b is A+B-B i.e. A
    *a = *a - *b;   // *a is A+B-A i.e. B
}
```

```c
int main()
{
    int a = 1, b = 2;
    swap1(&a, &b);
    printf("value of a is %d & value of b is %d", a, b);
}
```

Output:
```
value of a is 2 & value of b is 1
```

Problem 9: Write a function to find if a given number is a palindrome or not.

Example 7.26:
```c
int isPalindrome(int num)
{
    int num2=0, temp;
    temp = num;

    while(temp > 0) // loop to find reverse of number
    {
        num2 = num2*10 + temp%10;
        temp /= 10;
    }

    if(num == num2)
        return 1;
    else
        return 0;
}

int main()
{
    int num;
    printf("Enter a number:: ");
    scanf("%d", &num);

    if(isPalindrome(num))
    {
        printf("Given number %d is a palindrome", num);
    }
    else
    {
        printf("Given number %d is not a palindrome", num);
    }
    return 0;
}
```

Output:
```
Enter a number:: 121
Given number 121 is a palindrome
```

Problem 10: Write a program to print Fibonacci series using recursion.

Example 7.27:
```c
int fibonacci(int n)
{
    if (n <= 1)
        return n;
    return fibonacci(n - 1) + fibonacci(n - 2);
}

int main()
{
    int count, i;
    printf("How many element you want to print: ");
    scanf("%d", &count);
    for(i=0; i<count; i++)
        printf("%d ", fibonacci(i));
}
```

Output:
```
How many element you want to print: 5
0 1 1 2 3
```

Problem 11: Write a program to print Fibonacci series without using recursion.

Example 7.28:
```c
void fibonacciSeries(int n)
{
    int sum, first=0, second=1;

    if(n >= 0)
        printf("0 ");
    if(n >= 1)
        printf("1 ");

    while(n>2)    /* n - 2 > 0 , two values are already printed. */
    {
        sum = first + second;
        printf("%d ", sum);

        first = second;
        second = sum;

        n -= 1;
    }
}

int main()
{
    int n;
```

```c
    printf("Enter length of series:: ");
    scanf("%d", &n);
    fibonacciSeries(n);
}
```

Output:
```
Enter length of series:: 5
0 1 1 2 3
```

Problem 12: Why Fibonacci series programs using recursion is inefficient.

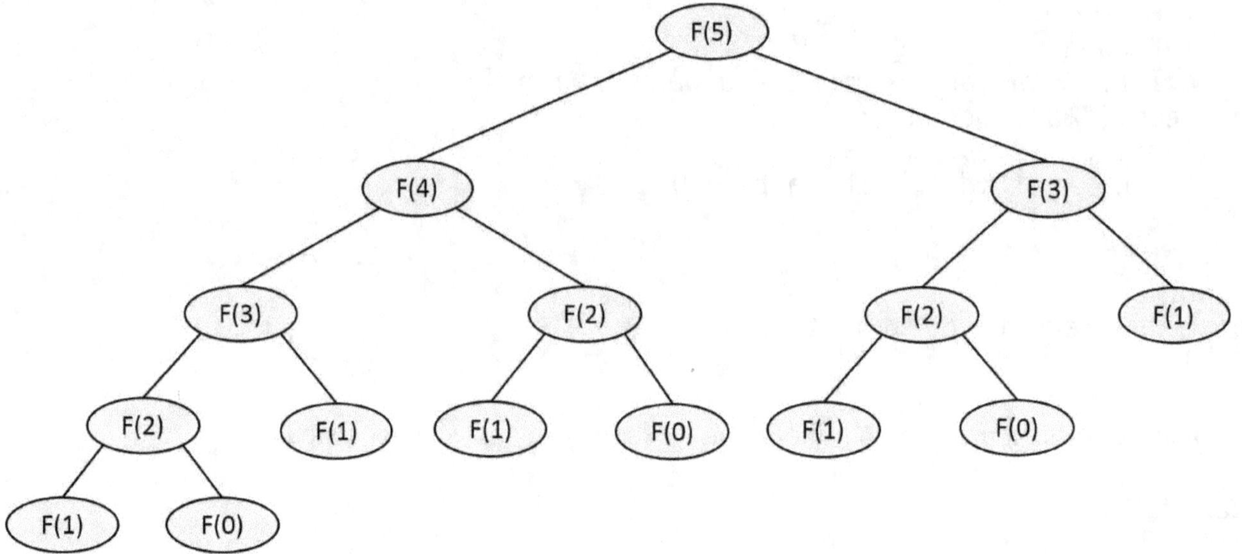

The same sub-problem is solved again and again, which reduces the performance of the algorithm. This algorithm has an exponential Time Complexity and linear Space Complexity.

Problem 13: Write a program to find the Armstrong number from 1 to 100.

Example 7.29:
```c
int isArmstrong(int num)
{
    int sum=0, temp, digCount=0;
    temp = num;
    while(temp > 0)
    {
        digCount += 1;
        temp /= 10;
    }
    temp = num;
    while(temp > 0)
    {
        sum += pow(temp%10, digCount);
        temp /= 10;
    }
}
```

```c
    if(num == sum)
        return 1;
    else
        return 0;
}

int main()
{
    int num, i;
    for(i=1; i<=100; i++)
    {
        if(isArmstrong(i))
            printf("%d is a armstrong number.\n", i);

    }
}
```

Output:
```
1 is an Armstrong number.
2 is an Armstrong number.
3 is an Armstrong number.
4 is an Armstrong number.
5 is an Armstrong number.
6 is an Armstrong number.
7 is an Armstrong number.
8 is an Armstrong number.
9 is an Armstrong number.
```

Summary

1. Function declaration: tells the compiler how the function looks the actual implementation
2. Function definition: contains the complete code of the function.
3. By default, arguments are passed by value in C, which involves making a local copy of the argument passed to the function.
4. Pointers can be used to pass arguments by a pointer.
5. A recursive function is a function that calls itself.
6. The recursive function consists of two parts: Termination Condition and Body (which include recursive expansion).
7. A global variable is declared outside any function. These variables can be used throughout the program.
8. Variables declared within a block are called local variables. These variables can be used only within the block (or function)
9. auto is the default storage class for local variables.
10. If a variable is declared (with global scope) in one file, but referenced in another, the extern keyword is used to inform the compiler of the variable's existence.
11. Static: If used inside a block or function, the compiler will create space for the variable which lasts for the life of the program

12. Another use for the static keyword is to ensure that code outside this file cannot modify variables that are globally declared inside this file.
13. The register provides a hint to the compiler that the programmer thinks a variable will be frequently used, so store it in hardware registers instead of RAM.
14. The macros definitions of variable arguments are defined in <stdarg.h> header file.
15. An ellipsis (...) in a function prototype indicates a variable number of arguments.
16. va_list : Is a data-type to point to a variable list of arguments.
17. va_start : Initialize variable list variable for num number of arguments
18. va_arg : It is used to retrieve each element of the argument list.
19. va_end : It is used to clean memory reserved for variable lists.
20. Command line arguments are passed to main function by including arguments int argc and char *argv[] in the arguments list of main.
21. Parameter argc receives the number of command-line arguments.
22. Parameter argv is an array of strings in which the actual command-line arguments are stored.
23. Function pointers are like other pointer variables, except that in place of the address of some variable it stores the address of a function.

Questions & Answers

Question 1: when should I use pass-by-value and pass-by-pointer?
Answer: Pass by value is used when we do not want to modify the argument variables inside the called function. On the other hand, a pass by the pointer is used when we want to modify the value of the argument variable passed to the called function. Pass by value is expensive if there is a huge data-structure passed as an argument and pass by value involves many copies. Pass-by-pointer will not involve copying. It just passes an address to the function, so it will be more efficient. Generally, we should prefer pass-by-value to pass-by-pointer. Pass-by-pointer is used only when we are strictly in need of it.

Question 2: Explain the difference between a function definition and function declaration.
Answer: Please refer to section function declaration and definition.

Question 3: What are the different uses of static?
Answer: 1) Static storage, a static variable inside a block retains its value throughout the life of the program.
2) Global static variables inside a file are global for the file, but cannot be accessed from outside the file.

Question 4: What are the Functions? What is the advantage of using multiple functions in a program?
Answer: A Function is a group of statements that together perform the subtask of the program. Functions are used to divide a large program into smaller subtasks.

Advantage of using multiple functions in a program
1. Easy to Develop: Dividing a large program to smaller subtasks makes the development process simple. Developers need to focus on the development and debugging of smaller pieces of code.
2. Re-Usability: It allows developers to reuse the function code by just knowing the interface of the function without writing the whole code.

3. Easy to Maintain: Small pieces of code need to be modified or updated. The interface is well defined for the function so it does not affect the user code.

Question 5: What is a re-declaration of a function error?
Answer: Like multiple declarations of variables, the same function is declared multiple times.

Question 6: What will happen if I provide more arguments to the function?
Answer: Compiler will complain about "too many arguments".

Question 7: What will happen if I provide a fewer number of arguments to the function?
Answer: Compiler will complain about "too few arguments".

Question 8: What are inline functions?
Answer: Making a function inline will make a request/ suggestion to the compiler to copy the code of the function to all the places where the function is called. The benefit of the inlining is that the function call overhead will be prevented.
Inline is used for only short functions. Most advanced compilers will do such optimizations themselves without instructions from developers.

Syntax of inline.
```
inline int fun()
{
….
}
```

We should make a function inline only if:
1) They are small.
2) They are called many times.
3) They are in the time-critical path.

Question 9: How can a function return multiple values?
Answer: There are various ways to achieve the same:
1. You can pass a memory location to a function and the function can populate inside it.
2. You can get a structure returned from a function.
3. You can populate some global variables.

Question 10: What is the difference between Global and Extern variables.
Answer: A global variable can be accessed from any part of the program. They are declared outside all the functions or blocks.
An external storage class tells that a global variable is declared somewhere else. The purpose of extern keyword is to facilitate the use of the same global variable among different files of the same program.

1. Write a function declaration / prototype for isOdd function. The function takes an integer as an argument and returns 1 if it is an odd number or 0 if it is an even number.

2. Write function definition / implementation of the above isOdd function.

3. Write a function declaration / prototype for "biggerNumber" function. The function takes two integers as an argument and returns the bigger of the two numbers.

4. Write function definition / implementation of the above biggerNumber function.

5. Write a function int isPrime(int num) to check if a given number is prime or not.
   Hint: Prime number program is explained in the loop section.

6. Explain Recursion and write a program to solve the factorial of a number using recursion.

7. Write a C program to calculate factorial of a given number.
   Hint: You can write a "for" loop to do your job.

8. Write a program, which will demonstrate the use of extern.

9. Write a program, which will demonstrate the use of static inside a block that retains its value.

10. Write a program that will demonstrate a global static variable that is global inside a file but cannot be accessed from outside.

11. Difference between Pass-by-value and Pass-by-pointer/ reference.

12. Write a program to display sum of digits?

13. Write a C program to reverse the digits of a given number.

14. Write a c program to count the number of digits in increasing order in a given number.

CHAPTER 8: ARRAYS

Introduction

If you want to store more than one variable of the same datatype. As a group of integers, then Array is used. An array is a group of variables under the same array name and each variable is accessed using an index number.

Note: An Array always has a fixed size, once it is declared then it cannot shrink or expand.

Syntax of Arrays declaration
```
datatype arrayName[arraysize];
```

Let us suppose you want to store the height of 10 students. Therefore, you need 10 integer variables. Alternatively, an array that contains 10 integer variables.

E.g.
```
int height[10];
```

The index in an array starts from 0. In the above case the individual variables or array are height[0], height[1], height[2]........., height[9]. The first element of the array is height[0], second height[1], and so on. The last element is height [9] this is the tenth element.

We can store the value inside array elements and read from array elements.
```
Height[0] = 165;
firstHeight = height[0];
```

An array can be initialized or assigned values at the deceleration time as
```
int weight[] = {55, 65, 75, 85};
```

If you are initializing the array at the deceleration time, then the compiler knows the size of the array and you are not required to provide its size. The above statement is the same as.
```
int weight[4] = {55, 65, 75, 85};
```

An array can be initialized at runtime also.
```
int weight[4];
for(int i = 0; i < 4; i++)
    scanf("%d", &weight[i]);
```

Example 8.1: Demonstrating Compile time initialization of Array
```
1.      #include<stdio.h>
2.
3.      int main()
4.      {
5.          int weight[] = {55,65,75,85};
6.          int length = sizeof(weight)/sizeof(int);
```

```c
7.          int index;
8.          for(index = 0; index<length; index++)
9.          {
10.             printf("Weight of student no %d is %d\n", index+1,
       weight[index]);
11.         }
12.         return 0;
13.  }
```

Output:

```
Weight of student no 1 is 55
Weight of student no 2 is 65
Weight of student no 3 is 75
Weight of student no 4 is 85
```

Analysis:

- Line 5: We have declared an array weight and assigned values to it. The compiler will know the size of the array by looking into the number of assigned values.

- Line 6: Sizeof(weight) will give the number of bytes there in the array weight including all its internal variables. Sizeof (int) will give the size of each variable. sizeof(weight)/sizeof(int) will give the number of the variable in the array.

- Line 8-11: For loop is used to print all the variables in the array. Each element is accessed using indexing, This is done by line weight[index].

Example 8.2: Demonstrating runtime initialization of an array.

```c
3.    #include<stdio.h>
4.
5.    int main()
6.    {
7.          int weight[4];
8.          int index;
9.          printf("Enter weight of 4 students: ");
10.         for(index = 0; index<4; index++)
11.         {
12.             scanf("%d", &weight[index]);
13.         }
14.
15.         for(index = 0; index<4; index++)
16.         {
17.             printf("Weight of student no %d is %d\n", index+1,
       weight[index]);
18.         }
19.         return 0;
20.  }
```

Output:
```
Enter weight of 4 students: 45 50 55 60
Weight of student no 1 is 45
Weight of student no 2 is 50
Weight of student no 3 is 55
Weight of student no 4 is 60
```

Analysis: Array is declared with length 4. Then values of individual elements are entered by the user. Finally entered values are printed to the screen.

Single Dimensional Array

The array we were using in the previous chapter is a single dimensional array. A one-dimensional array is a sequence of values.
Below is an example of a one-dimensional array named "arr":

```
int arr[2];
```

You can initialize the value of these two elements as:
```
arr[0]=1;
arr[1]=2;
```

Alternatively, we can initialize them at the time of declaring:
```
int arr[2]={1,2};
```


Two-dimensional Array

The two-dimensional array has rows and columns. Below is an example of a two-dimensional array:
int arr[2][2];

You can initialize the value of various fields of two-dimensional array as:
```
arr[0][0]=1;
arr[0][1]=2;
arr[1][0]=3;
arr[1][1]=4;
```

The array will look like:
```
1 2
3 4
```

Note: a[0][0] contains the value 1. a[0][1] contains the value 2. a[1][0] contains the value 3. a[1][1] contains the value 4.

A nested loop is used to traverse a two-dimensional array.

The below example will demonstrate a two-dimensional array. We will initialize the value to the array and then prints each element:

Example 8.3: Two-dimensional array.

```
1.    int main()
2.    {
3.        int a[4][2] = {{1, 2}, {3, 4}, {5, 6}, {7, 8}};
4.        int i, j;
5.        for(i=0; i<4; i++)
6.        {
7.            for(j=0; j<2; j++)
8.            {
9.                printf("a[%d][%d]=%d\n", i, j, a[i][j]);
10.           }
11.       }
12.       return 0;
13.   }
```

Output:
```
arr[0][0]=1;
arr[0][1]=2;
arr[1][0]=3;
arr[1][1]=4;
arr[2][0]=5;
arr[2][1]=6;
arr[3][0]=7;
arr[3][1]=8;
```

Analysis:
- Line 3: We have declared and initialized an array of 2 rows and 4 columns. You can initialize the value at some separate place.
- Line 9: The various elements of the array from arr[0][0] ...arr,[3][1] are printed to the screen.

Multi-dimensional arrays

Like one-dimensional and two-dimensional, an array can be of n-dimensional. The general syntax of an array is.

```
data type Name[size1][size2]...[sizeN];
```

Note: Accessing the value of the array without initializing will lead to an array bound error. Which might give a garbage value or may lead to a segmentation fault.

Common errors while using arrays

Array Bound Read (ABR)

It is a logical error in which users try to access an array beyond its length. In case of array bound read issue garbage value will be returned. The compiler will not be able to catch such errors.

Example 8.4: Array bound read problem

```
1.      #include<stdio.h>
2.
3.      int main()
4.      {
5.          int weight[] = {55,65,75,85};
6.          printf("The weight of 6th boy is %d\n", weight[5]);
7.          return 0;
8.      }
```

Output:
```
The weight of 6th boy is 32765
```

Analysis: Line 6:You try to access a value weight [5] that is the 6th element of the array, but the array has only 4 elements so this is an error called array bound to read. This is a logical error and the c compiler will not be able to catch it.

Array Bound Write (ABW)

This is a logical error in which users try to write something into an array beyond its length. The compiler will not be able to catch such errors.

Example 8.5: Array bound write problem

```
1.#include<stdio.h>
2.int main()
3.{
4.      intweight[]={55,65,75,85};
5.      weight[5]=70;
6.      return 0;
7.}
```

Analysis: Line 5: You try to write some value into the weight[5] that is the 6th element of the array, but the array has only 4 elements so this is an error, called array bound to write. This is a logical error and the c compiler will not be able to catch it.

Uninitialized Memory Read (UMR)

It is a logical error in which the user accesses array elements without its initialization. Such memory access will return garbage values. Users should always initialize a variable before accessing its value. In the same way you should first initialize an array before using it. So, in the Example below, we have accessed an array before actually initializing the value to it, so this is an error.

Example 8.6: Uninitialized memory read problem

```
1.      #include<stdio.h>
2.
3.      int main()
4.      {
5.              int weight[4];
```

```c
6.          int length = sizeof(weight)/sizeof(int);
7.          int index;
8.          for(index = 0; index<length; index++)
9.          {
10.             printf("Weight of student no %d is %d\n",index+1,
    weight[index]);
11.          }
12.          return 0;
13.    }
```

Output:
```
Weight of student no 1 is 566755856
Weight of student no 2 is 21965
Weight of student no 3 is 566749056
Weight of student no 4 is 21965
```

Analysis:

- Line 10: We are doing the Uninitialized Memory Read (UMR) error. We are accessing array variables before initializing the value to it, so garbage value is printed to the screen. The actual result will depend on your system condition. We should avoid this error.

- This is a logical error and the c compiler will not be able to catch it. Therefore, you should be careful not to use a variable before initializing them.

Arrays as Parameters

Arrays are passed to a function using pointers. Along with the pointer array, size is also passed as an argument. The below example demonstrates passing array and its size to a function

Example 8.7: Passing array as argument
```c
1.     void print(int *arr,int size);
2.
3.     int main()
4.     {
5.         int a[5]= {1, 2, 3, 4, 5};
6.         print(a, 5);
7.         return 0;
8.     }
9.
10.    void print(int *arr, int size)
11.    {
12.        int i;
13.        for(i=0; i<size; i++)
14.        {
15.            printf("%d ",arr[i]);
16.        }
17.        printf("\n");
18.    }
```

Output:
```
1 2 3 4 5
```

Analysis:
- Line 6: The array is passed to the function. The array tag name is a constant pointer to the first element of the array. Along with it, the size of the array is also passed.

- Line 10-18: In this function, array passed is used as if it is declared inside this function. The size of an array is passed as an argument.

Passing arrays as functions arguments

Sometimes, there is a requirement to send an array as an argument of the function. Passing an array to the function is the same as passing a pointer as the name of an array is a constant pointer. However, as we are passing a pointer, which is pointing to the first element of the array, then we also require passing the count of the number of elements in the array.

A function that is going to take an array, as an argument, has to declare the argument type as an array, by a pair of braces [].

```c
void PrintArray(int arr[], int count);
```

This is the same as declaring the argument of type pointer to int. Therefore, the above declaration is the same as using "pointer to int" as the first argument of the PrintArray function.

Example 8.8: Passing array as function argument
```c
1.    void PrintArray(int arr[], int count);
2.
3.    int main()
4.    {
5.        int arr[] = {2, 4, 6, 8};
6.        int count = 4;
7.        PrintArray(arr,count);
8.        return 0;
9.    }
10.
11.   void PrintArray(int arr[], int count)
12.   {
13.       int i=0;
14.       for(i=0; i<count; i++)
15.       {
16.           printf("%d ",arr[i]);
17.       }
18.       printf("\n");
19.   }
```

Output:
```
2 4  6  8
```

Analysis:

- ◆ Line 11: The first argument is "int arr[]", which is a pointer to a variable of type int. The second argument is the count of the number of elements in the array.

- ◆ Line 11 to 19: We are printing the elements of the array.

- ◆ Line 7: We have passed an array name, which is a pointer to the first element of the array. This will be same as PrintArray(&arr[0], count);

Return array from functions

You can only return pointers to dynamically allocated memory located outside the function.
You should not return a pointer to a local array since its memory location is not valid once you return from a function.

Example 8.9: Correct Way to return an array from a function
```c
int *ReturnArray(int count)
{
    int *arr=(int*)malloc(count*sizeof(int));
    /* Other operations on the array. */
    return arr;
}
```

You have created a memory location, which can contain a count number of integers and finally return the pointer to that memory location.

Example 8.10: Wrong-Way to return an array from a function
```c
int *ReturnArray(int count)
{
    int arr[count];
    return arr;
}
```

In this code, an array is created inside the function and then its pointer to the first element is returned. However, there is an error that the array will be destroyed when we return from this function, so the returned pointer is pointing to some invalid memory location which is an error.

Solved Examples

Problem 1: WAP that simply takes elements of the array from the user and finds the sum of these elements.

Example 8.11:
```c
int main()
{
    int n, sum =0, arr[100];
    printf("Enter the number of elements:: ");
    scanf("%d", &n);
    printf("Enter elements ::");
    for(int i = 0;i< n;i++)
        scanf("%d", &arr[i]);

    for(int i = 0;i< n;i++)
        sum += arr[i];

    printf("Sum is %d", sum);
    return 0;
}
```

Output:
```
Enter the number of elements:: 5
Enter elements ::1 2 3 4 5
Sum is 15
```

Problem 2: Write a program to find the largest and second-largest in the given array.

Example 8.12:
```c
int main()
{
    int arr[100], count;
    int first, second, i;
    printf("Enter the number of elements ( greater than 2) : ");
    scanf("%d", &count);
    printf("Enter the array: ");
    for(i=0; i<count ; i++)
        scanf("%d", &arr[i]);

    if(arr[0] > arr[1])
    {
        first = arr[0];
        second = arr[1];
    }
    else
    {
        first = arr[1];
        second = arr[0];
    }

    for(i = 2; i< count; i++)
    {
        if(arr[i] > first)
        {
```

```c
            second = first;
            first = arr[i];
        }
        else if(arr[i] > second)
        {
            second = arr[i];
        }
    }
    printf("The largest and second largest are %d & %d", first, second);
}
```

Output:

```
Enter the number of elements ( greater than 2) : 9
Enter the array: 9 1 2 5 4 8 7 3 6
The largest and second-largest are 9 & 8
```

Analysis:
- First, the largest and smallest among the first two elements are assigned to first and second.
- Then all the rest of the elements of the array are traversed.
- All the elements are compared if they are greater than first then they are greater then second too. In this case, both the first and second are modified.
- If the element is greater then second and less than first then only second will be modified.

Problem 3: Write a program to find the product of two matrices.

Example 8.13:

```c
int main()
{

    int a[20][20], b[20][20];
    int r1, c1, r2, c2;
    int i, j, k, p;
    printf("Enter dimensions of first matrix: ");
    scanf("%d%d", &r1, &c1);

    printf("Enter dimensions of second matrix: ");
    scanf("%d%d", &r2, &c2);

    if(c1 != r2) /* Number of columns of the first matrix should be the
same as the number of rows of the second. */
    {
        printf("Matrix multiplication not possible.");
        return 0;
    }
    printf("Enter first matrix:\n");
    for(i=0; i<r1; i++)
        for(j=0; j<c1; j++)
            scanf("%d", &a[i][j]);
```

```c
    printf("Enter second matrix:\n");
    for(i=0; i<r2; i++)
        for(j=0; j<c2; j++)
            scanf("%d", &b[i][j]);

    printf("Matrix multiplication is:: \n");
    for(i=0; i<r1; i++)
    {
        for(j=0; j<c2; j++)
        {
            p = 0;  /* Resetting the product */
            for(k=0; k<c1; k++)  /* Calculating product */
                p += a[i][k] * b[k][j];
            printf("%d ", p); /* Printing the product */
        }
        printf("\n");
    }
    return 0;
}
```

Output:

```
Enter dimensions of first matrix: 2 3
Enter dimensions of second matrix: 3 2
Enter first matrix:
1 2 3
4 5 6
Enter second matrix:
7 8
9 10
11 12
Matrix multiplication is::
58 64
139 154
```

Problem 4: Write a program to add two matrices.

Example 8.14:

```c
int main()
{

    int a[20][20], b[20][20], c[20][20];
    int r1, c1, r2, c2;
    int i, j, k, p;
    printf("Enter dimensions of first matrix: ");
    scanf("%d%d", &r1, &c1);

    printf("Enter dimensions of second matrix: ");
    scanf("%d%d", &r2, &c2);
```

```c
    if(c1 != c2 || r1 != r2) /* Number of columns and rows of the first
matrix should be the same as the second.*/
    {
        printf("Matrix addition not possible.");
        return 0;
    }
    printf("Enter first matrix:\n");
    for(i=0; i<r1; i++)
        for(j=0; j<c1; j++)
            scanf("%d", &a[i][j]);

    printf("Enter second matrix:\n");
    for(i=0; i<r2; i++)
        for(j=0; j<c2; j++)
            scanf("%d", &b[i][j]);

    printf("Matrix addition is :: \n");
    for(i=0; i<r1; i++)
    {
        for(j=0; j<c1; j++)
        {
            c[i][j] = a[i][j] + b[i][j];
            printf("%d ", c[i][j]); /* Printing the sum */
        }
        printf("\n");
    }
    return 0;
}
```

Output:

```
Enter dimensions of first matrix: 2 3
Enter dimensions of second matrix: 2 3
Enter first matrix:
1 2 3
4 5 6
Enter second matrix:
7 8 9
1 2 3
Matrix addition is ::
8 10 12
5 7 9
```

Problem 5: Write a program to find the transpose of a matrix.

Example 8.15:

```c
int main()
{
    int a[20][20], b[20][20];
    int r1, c1, r2, c2;
    int i, j, k, p;
```

```c
    printf("Enter dimensions of the matrix: ");
    scanf("%d%d", &r1, &c1);

    r2 = c1;
    c2 = r1;

    printf("Enter the matrix:\n");
    for(i=0; i<r1; i++)
        for(j=0; j<c1; j++)
            scanf("%d", &a[i][j]);

    printf("Transpose matrix is :: \n");
    for(i=0; i<r1; i++)
        for(j=0; j<c1; j++)
            b[j][i] = a[i][j];

    for(i=0; i<r2; i++)
    {
        for(j=0; j<c2; j++)
            printf("%d ", b[i][j]);
        printf("\n");
    }

    return 0;
}
```

Output:

```
Enter dimensions of the matrix: 2 3
Enter the matrix:
1 2 3
4 5 6
Transpose matrix is ::
1 4
2 5
3 6
```

Problem 6: Given an Array, you need to rotate its elements K number of times. For example, an Array [10,20,30,40,50,60] rotate by 2 positions to [30,40,50,60,10,20]

Hint: To right rotate an int array A of N elements by K position.
- First, write a general array reversal function. void reverse(int A[], int startposition, int length)
- Second, apply reverse array function to first K elements. Then apply the same function to next N- K elements.
- Finally, apply the reverse function to the whole array.

Example 8.16:

```c
void rotateArray(int *a,int n,int k)
{
    reverseArray(a,k);
```

```c
    reverseArray(&a[k],n-k);
    reverseArray(a,n);
}

void reverseArray(int *a,int n)
{
    int temp, i, j;

    for(i=0,j=n-1; i<j; i++,j--)
    {
        temp = a[i];
        a[i] = a[j];
        a[j] = temp;
    }
}
```

Analysis:
- The rotating list is done in two parts tricks. In the first part, we first reverse elements of the list first half and then the second half.

  1,2,3,4,5,6,7,8,9,10   =>   5,6,7,8,9,10,1,2,3,4
  1,2,3,4,5,6,7,8,9,10   =>   4,3,2,1,10,9,8,7,6,5   =>   5,6,7,8,9,10,1,2,3,4

- Then we reverse the whole list thereby completing the whole rotation.

Problem 7: Write a program to copy the contents of one array into another in the reverse order.

Example 8.17:
```c
int main()
{
    int a[100]={1,2,3,4,5,6,7,8,9};
    int n = 9;
    int b[100];

    for(int i=0;i<n;i++)
    {
        b[i] = a[n-i-1];
    }

    for(int i=0;i<n;i++)
    {
        printf("%d ", b[i]);
    }
}
```

Problem 8: Write a program in C to find the largest number of elements in 4*4 matrix.

Example 8.18:
```c
#include <stdio.h>
```

```c
int max(int arr[4][4], int n)
{
    int max = arr[0][0];
    int i, j;

    for (i = 0; i < n; i++) {
        for (j = 0; j <= n; j++) {
            if (arr[i][j] > max) {
                max = arr[i][j];
            }
        }
    }
    return max;
}

int main()
{
    int arr[4][4] = { { 1, 9, 11, 2 },
                      { 4, 5, 7, 14 },
                      { 9, 8, 6, 4 },
                      { 10, 12, 13, 3 } };
    printf("Largest number:: %d", max(arr, 4));
    return 0;
}
```

Output:
Largest number:: 14

Problem 9: WAP that finds the sum of diagonal elements of a mxn matrix.

Example 8.19:
```c
int main()
{

    int arr[20][20];
    int row, col, sum = 0;
    int i, j, k, p;
    printf("Enter dimensions of first matrix: ");
    scanf("%d%d", &row, &col);
    printf("Enter the matrix:\n");
    for(i=0; i<row; i++)
        for(j=0; j<col; j++)
            scanf("%d", &arr[i][j]);

    for(i=0; i<row && i <col; i++)
        sum += arr[i][i];

    printf("Sum of diagonal elements is %d ", sum);
    return 0;
}
```

Output:
```
Enter dimensions of first matrix: 3 3
Enter the matrix:
1 2 3
4 5 6
7 8 9
Sum of diagonal elements is 15
```

Problem 10: WAP that inputs two arrays and saves the sum of corresponding elements of these arrays in a third array and prints them.

Example 8.20:
```c
int main()
{
    int n, sum =0, a[100], b[100], c[100];

    printf("Enter the number of elements:: ");
    scanf("%d", &n);

    printf("Enter elements of first array ::");
    for(int i = 0;i< n;i++)
        scanf("%d", &a[i]);

    printf("Enter elements of second array ::");
    for(int i = 0;i< n;i++)
        scanf("%d", &b[i]);

    for(int i = 0;i< n;i++)
        c[i] = a[i] + b[i];

    printf("Sum Array is:: ");
    for(int i = 0;i< n;i++)
        printf("%d ",c[i]);

    return 0;
}
```

Output:
```
Enter the number of elements:: 5
Enter elements of first array ::1 2 3 4 5
Enter elements of second array ::6 7 8 9 0
Sum Array is:: 7 9 11 13 5
```

Summary

1. A Variable in a program is a memory location that can store a value.
2. An Array is a group of similar types of variables, which have contiguous memory segments.

3. Individual variables in an array are called elements. Elements in an array are accessed by an index number.
4. Loops are used to iterate through each element of an array.
5. The Size of an Array will return the total number of bytes allocated to the array variable.
6. Nested loops are used to iterate through a two-dimensional array.
7. A pointer to an array can be created to point to the first element of an array.
8. Arrays are passed to the function using pointers. Along with pointer, array-size is also passed as an argument.

Questions & Answers

Question 1: What is special about the name of an array?
Answer: It is a pointer, which stores the address of the first element of an array. It is a const pointer that means it cannot point to some other location. You can directly store its value to another pointer of the same type.

Question 2: If a[] is an array, is a++ valid?
Answer: No, "a" is a const pointer, which means it cannot point to some other location.

Question 3: How to find the number of elements in an array arr[]?
Answer: Use sizeof(arr)/sizeof(arr[0]);

Exercises

1. A program that uses a single dimension array and stores 10 numbers into it. Find the sum of all the numbers by looping through the array. Print the total sum into the screen. Find the average value entered. Print the average to the screen.

2. Write a program to add two matrices of dimension 3*3 and store the result in another matrix.

3. Write a program to display transpose of a given matrix.

4. Consider a 2-d array of doubles arr[4][5] with base address 3000 and computer the address of arr[2][3].

5. Write a c program to count numbers in an array of integers which are in increasing order.

6. Write a c program to count unique numbers in an array of integers.

7. What is the difference between row major order and column major order of representation of 2-D array?

8. Write a C program to print the largest and smallest numbers in an array.

9. Write a C program to print prime numbers in a given array of positive integers.

CHAPTER 9: STRINGS

Introduction

In C language, Strings are represented by arrays of characters. The end of a string is marked with a special character called the null character ('\0'), which simply characterizes the ASCII value 0. (Note this null character has no relation with a NULL pointer.)

Declaring Strings

We have two ways of declaring strings, one as an array of characters and second a char pointer pointing to a string literal.

1) char a[] = "Hello World!"
In this, the "Hello World!" which is a string literal is copied into the char array a. When you define an array "a" and put a string of characters inside the double inverted comma, like "Hello World!" the C compiler creates an array of characters and terminates it with null char. We do not require providing the size of an array as C compiler will look for the null character and then make the proper size of an array. So finally, array "a" will look like.

H	e	l	l	o		W	o	r	l	d	!	\0

Since it is an array, you can change the content of an array. However, the "a" is the start of the array so you cannot point it to anything else.

2) char* a= "Hello World!"
In this second example, the char pointer "a" is pointing to "Hello World!" which is a string literal. String literals are constants and you cannot change the content of a string literal. However, in this case, "a" is just a pointer to char so you can make it point to any other char.

a ----------> H e l l o   W o r l d ! \0

In our entire example, we will use the first type of declaring a string.
char a[] = "Hello World!";

Example 9.1: String as an array of char.
```c
#include<stdio.h>
int main()
{
	char a[]="Hello, World!";
	int i;
	for(i=0; a[i] != '\0'; i++)
		printf("%c", a[i]);
}
```

Output:
```
Hello, World!
```

Analysis:
- You can loop through the various characters of the string.
- This will print all the characters of the string one by one and when it reaches the end of the string, the loop will break.

Reading and Writing String

Two ways to take user input are using scanf() and gets() functions. Scanf is used to take a formatted string and it considers blank space, tab and newline as end of input. Puts consider only the newline as the end of string.

```c
char a[50];
printf("Please enter your name:: ");
scanf("%s", a);
```

As we had already used printf, which is used to print a string to screen and scanf can be used to take a string as input from the user into a char array. These input-output functions are defined in library stdio.h.

We have created an array of 50 characters and taken the input from the user into this array. You should allocate enough space in an array a[] so that the user input will not cause array bound write error. The input will be stored in the array and at the end null '\0' char is stored.

```c
char a[50];
printf("Please enter your name:: ");
gets(a);
```

puts() function works similar to scanf() but we can input strings with spaces.

The character will be stored to delimit the string.

Example 9.2: Taking string input in char array using scanf
```c
1.     int main()
2.     {
3.         char a[50];
4.         printf("Please enter your name:: ");
5.         puts(a) /* scanf("%s", a); */
6.         printf("Hello %s", a);
7.         return 0;
8.     }
```

Output:
```
Please enter your name:: Kartik
Hello Kartik
```

Analysis:
- Line 4: Print a text to the screen.
- Line 5: Taking input from a user and storing it into an array a[] using the %s identifier.
- Line 6: Print string to screen and use the %s identifier to print the user name to the screen.

Error In string handling

Remember that strings are stored as arrays. Moreover, the only way to change the contents of an array in C is to make changes to each element in the array.

Therefore, we cannot do the following:

```c
char name[30];

name = "Hemant Jain"; //This is wrong-------Error
                      //name is constant pointer
                      //you can't dereference it again.

name = anotherName; //This is wrong too-----Error
                    //name is constant pointer
                    //you can't dereference it again.
```

String Manipulation (string.h library)

A C library string.h file has string manipulation functions implemented in it. The following are the most useful string functions that we will discuss.

strlen

```c
unsigned long strlen (const char *str);
```

This library function returns the length of a string. (Will not include null char)

Example 9.3:
```c
int main()
{
    char name[]="Kartik";
    int length=strlen(name);
    printf("Length is:: %d \n", length);
    return 0;
}
```

Output:
```
Length is:: 6
```

Strcpy

```
char *strcpy (char *dest, const char *src);
```
This library function is used to copy the source string to the destination string.

Example 9.4:
```
int main()
{
    char src[]="hello world.";
    char dest[20];
    strcpy(dest,src);
    printf("Source: %s \n Destination: %s \n", src, dest);
}
```

Output:
```
Source: hello world.
Destination: hello world.
```

Note: strcpy() will not perform any boundary checking. It assumes that the dest points to a buffer of enough length to hold the src string.

strcmp

```
short strcmp (const unsigned char *first, const unsigned char *second);
```

This library function is used to compare two strings. If the first string is greater than the second string, a number greater than 0 is returned. If the first string is equal to the second string, 0 is returned. If the first string is less than the second string, a number less than 0 is returned.

Example 9.5:
```
int main()
{
    char *first = "Hello";
    char *second = "Hello";
    char *third = "World";
    printf("Compare first & second %d \n", strcmp(first, second));
    printf("Compare first & third %d \n", strcmp(first, third));
}
```

Output:
```
Compare first & second 0
Compare first & third -15
```

strcat

```
char *strcat (char *dest, const char *src);
```

This library function is used for appending two strings. strcat will append the content of src to the end of dest. (Overwrite the null terminating char of dest). The length of the resulting string will be strlen(dest) +strlen(src). strcat will return a pointer of the concatenated string that is dest.

Note: It assumes that the dest points to a buffer of enough length to hold the concatenated string.

Example 9.6:
```c
int main()
{
    char dest[30] = "Hello, ";
    char src[]="World!";
    strcat(dest, src);
    printf("%s \n", dest);
}
```

Output:
```
Hello, World!
```

Strstr

```c
char *strstr (const char *str, const char *substr);
```

This library function is used to search the first occurrence of the substring substr inside string str. strstr() function returns a pointer to the element in str where substr begins (points to substr in str). If substr does not occur in str, strstr() returns NULL.

Example 9.7:
```c
int main()
{
    char text[30] = "Hello how are you kartik. ";
    char token[]="how";
    char *temp = strstr(text, token);
    printf("%s \n", temp);
}
```

Output:
```
How are you kartik.
```

Other string functions:
1. The atof() function converts a string to a floating-point number.
2. The atoi() function converts a string to an integer.
3. tolower() and toupper() are used to convert a single character to lowercase and uppercase.

Problem 1: Write your own user-defined strlen() function.

Example 9.8:
```c
int strlen2(char str[])
{
    int count=0;
    while(str[count] != '\0')
        count++;

    return count;
}
```

Analysis: All the elements of the string array are traversed and counted.

Problem 2: Write a program to implement user defined strcpy() function.

Example 9.9:
```c
void strcpy2(char dst[], char src[])
{
    int i=0;
    while(src[i] != '\0')
    {
        dst[i] = src[i];
        i++;
    }
    dst[i]='\0';
}
```

Analysis: Content of src string is copied to dst string char by char.

Problem 3: Write a user defined strcmp() function.

Example 9.10:
```c
int strcmp2(char a[], char b[])
{
    int count=0;
    while (a[count] != '\0' && b[count] != '\0' && a[count] == b[count])
        count++;
    return (a[count] - b[count]);
}
```

Problem 4: Write your own strcat() function, to concatenate two given strings.

Example 9.11:
```c
void strcat2(char dst[], char src[])
{
```

```c
    int i = 0, j = 0;
    while(dst[i] != '\0')
        i++;

    while(src[j] != '\0')
    {
        dst[i] = src[j];
        i++;
        j++;
    }
    dst[i] = '\0';
}
```

Problem 5: Write a program in C to reverse a string.

Example 9.12:
```c
void reverseString(char a[])
{
    int lower = 0;
    int upper = strlen(a) - 1;
    char tempChar;
    while(lower<upper)
    {
        tempChar=a[lower];
        a[lower]=a[upper];
        a[upper]=tempChar;
        lower++;
        upper--;
    }
}
```

Problem 6: Write a program in C to reverse a string by using a pointer.

Example 9.13:
```c
void reverseString(char *a)
{
    char *lower = a;
    char *upper = a + strlen(a) - 1;
    char tempChar;
    while(lower < upper)
    {
        tempChar=*lower;
        *lower=*upper;
        *upper=tempChar;
        lower++;
        upper--;
    }
}
```

```c
int main()
{
    char hello[] ="hello, world!";
    reverseString1(hello);
    printf("reverse: %s \n", hello);
}
```

Problem 7: Write a user defined function to compare two strings where they are identical or not.

Example 9.14:
```c
int isIdentical(char a[], char b[])
{
    int count=0;
    while (a[count] != '\0' && b[count] != '\0' && a[count] == b[count])
        count++;

    if(a[count] == '\0' && b[count] == '\0')
        return 1;
    else
        return 0;
}

int main()
{
    char *first ="hello, world!";
    char *second ="hello, world!";
    printf("isIdentical: %d", isIdentical(first, second));
}
```

Problem 8: Write a program to sort a set of names stored in an array in alphabetical order

Example 9.15:
```c
#include <stdio.h>
#include <stdlib.h>
#include <string.h>

int compare(const void *first, const void *second){
    // first and second are pointer to the elements
    // of array which is an array of pointer
    // so first and second are pointers to pointers.
    // so they are casted to pointer to pointer of char.
    return strcmp(*(const char**)first, *(const char**)second);
}

// Function to sort the array
void sort(const char* arr[], int n) {
    qsort(arr, n, sizeof(const char*), compare);
}
```

```c
int main()
{
    const char* arr[] = { "Cat", "Apple", "Dog", "Bat"};
    int n = sizeof(arr) / sizeof(char*);
    int i;
    sort(arr, n);
    // Print the sorted array
    printf("\nSorted array of names:\n");
    for (i = 0; i < n; i++)
        printf("%d: %s \n", i, arr[i]);
    return 0;
}
```

Output:
```
Sorted array of names:
0: Apple
1: Bat
2: Cat
3: Dog
```

Problem 9: Write a reverse string function that will reverse char by char. The last char will become first and first char will become last and so on.

Input: "Hello, world!"

Output: "!dlrow ,olleH"

Example 9.16:
```c
void reverseString(char a[],int lower,int upper)
{
    char tempChar;
    while(lower<upper)
    {
        tempChar=a[lower];
        a[lower]=a[upper];
        a[upper]=tempChar;
        lower++;
        upper--;
    }
}
```

Problem 10: Write a reverse word function that will reverse words. Last word will become first and first word will become last and so on.

Input: "Hello, world!"

Output: "world! Hello,"

Example 9.17:
```c
void reverseWords(char a[])
{
    int length = strlen(a);
    int lower, upper = -1;
```

```c
        lower = 0;
        for (int i = 0; i <= length; i++)
        {
            if (a[i] == ' ' || a[i] == '\0')
            {
                reverseString(a, lower, upper);
                lower = i + 1;
                upper = i;
            }
            else
            {
                upper++;
            }
        }
    reverseString(a, 0, length-1); //-1 because we do not want to reverse
'\0'
}

int main()
{
    char st[100] = "One Two Three";
    reverseWords(st);
    printf("%s\n", st);
    return 0;
}
```

Output:
```
Three Two One
```

Problem 11: Write a C program to check if given string is a palindrome?
E.g. "abccba", "aba", "abcba" are palindrome.

Example 9.18:
```c
int isPalindrome(char str[])
{
    int i = 0, j = strlen(str) - 1;
    while (i < j && str[i] == str[j])
    {
        i++;
        j--;
    }
    if (i < j)
    {
        printf("%s is not a Palindrome.\n", str);
        return 0;
    }
    else
    {
        printf("%s is a Palindrome.\n", str);
        return 1;
```

```c
        }
}

int main()
{
    char *st = "HELLOLLEH";
    isPalindrome(st);

    st = "HELLOOLLEH";
    isPalindrome(st);

    st = "HELLOOLLEHA";
    isPalindrome(st);
    return 0;
}
```

Output:
```
HELLOLLEH is a Palindrome.
HELLOOLLEH is a Palindrome.
HELLOOLLEHA is not a Palindrome.
```

Problem 12: Given two strings A and B, how would you find out if the characters in B are a subset of the characters in A?

Example 9.19:
```c
int isSubset(char a[], char b[])
{
    int counter[256];
    int i;

    for(i=0; i<256; i++)
        counter[i]=0;

    for(i=0; a[i]!='\0'; i++)
        counter[a[i]]++;

    for(i=0; b[i]!='\0'; i++)
    {
        if(!counter[b[i]])
        {
        printf("b is not a subset of a");
        return(0);
        }
        else
            counter[b[i]]--;
    }
    printf("b is subset of a");
    return(1);
}
```

Problem 13: Write your own tolower() and toupper() functions.

Example 9.20:
```c
char ToUpper(char s)
{
    if (s >= 97 && s <= (97 + 25))
        s = s - 32;
    return s;
}

char ToLower(char s)
{
    if (s >= 65 && s <= (65 + 25))
        s = s + 32;
    return s;
}
```

Summary

1. The string is a grouping of characters. In C, characters are not just a-z and A-Z, they also include the digits 0-9 and other characters.
2. A string is created using a character array and a terminating NULL character.
3. Character array created by assigning a string literal will create a char array of the required number of elements with terminating NULL character.
4. Printf function with %s conversion specifier is used to print a string to the screen.
5. strcpy(str1, str2) Copies str2 into str1.
6. strcat(str1, str2) Concatenates str2 onto the end of str1.
7. strcmp(str1, str2) Returns 0 if str1 and str2 are the same; less than 0 if str1<str2; greater than 0 if str1>str2.
8. strlen(str1) Returns the length of str1. Returns the number of characters in the string up to the NULL character, but not including the NULL character.
9. strchr(str1, ch1) Returns a pointer to the first occurrence of ch1 in str1.
10. strstr(str1, str2) returns a pointer to the first occurrence of str2 in str1.

Exercises

1. Create a program that performs the following functions:
    - Uses character arrays to read a user's name from standard input.
    - Tells the user how many characters are there in his or her name. (Using strlen())
    - Displays the user's name in uppercase. (Using toupper())
    - Displays the user's name in lowercase. (Using tolower())

2. Create a program in which two strings are there, the first string will have a text "C is simple" and the second string will have the text "simple" stored inside it. Find the location of the second string inside the first string using srtstr() function. Create a third string which stores "sample" inside it and then search the occurrence of a third-string in the first string and observe the return value of strstr() function.

3. Create a program that has two strings, the first string contains text "Bilbo" inside it. The second string contains "Baggins' ' inside it. Concatenate both the string using srtcat() function and print the concatenated result to the standard output.

4. What is string? Also explain different string functions with examples.

5. Write a C program to display whether a given string is palindrome or not.

6. Implement strlen, strcat, strrev function without using string.h header file.

7. Write a C program to sort a given array of fruits in alphabetical order ["orange", "grapes", "apple", "mango", "banana", "guava", "cherry"].

8. Write a C program to count the occurrence of a word in a string.

9. Write a C program to index of last the occurrence of a word in a string.

CHAPTER 10: STRUCTURES

Introduction

As we have already seen that an array is a data structure, which can hold a collection of elements of the same data type. Similarly, **A Structure is a user-defined data-type. Structure creates a data-type to hold various elements inside it and the elements can be of a different data type.** The structure is defined by struct keyword.

The structure has the following syntax:
```
struct StructureName{
    DataType1 element1;
    DataType2 element2;
};
```

Let us take some examples of structures.
Let us consider that you want to make an entry of students with their enrolment number and name.
```
struct Students{
    int enrolNo;
    char name[50];
    char gender[10];
};
```

In this above example, we have a structure type Students, and each student has his or her enrolment number "enrolNo" and his or her corresponding name and gender.

Declaring Structure Variable: A structure variable can either be declared with structure declaration or as a separate declaration like basic types.

```
struct Students{
    int enrolNo;
    char name[50];
    char gender[10];
}st;
```

Here "st" is a "structure Student" type variable.

Similarly, we can declare structure variables like basic types.

```
struct Student st;
```

Similarly, if you want to store coordinates of any point, then you will declare a chord structure and it will have element x and y for x-axis and y-axis coordinates.

Example 9.1: Demonstrating Structure

```
1.    struct coord
2.    {
3.         int  x;
4.         int y;
5.    };
6.
7.    int main()
8.    {
9.         struct coord point;
10.        point.x=10;
11.        point.y=10;
12.        printf("X axis coord value is %d\n",point.x);
13.        printf("Y axis coord value is %d\n",point.y);
14.        printf("Size of structure is %d bytes\n",sizeof(point));
15.        return 0;
16.   }
```

Output:
```
X axis coord value is 10
Y axis coord value is 10
Size of structure is 8 bytes
```

Analysis:

- Line 1-5: We have declared the structure "coord", which contains two elements inside it. The two elements x and y correspond to the x-axis and y-axis coordinates.

- Line 9: We have declared a variable "point" of type "struct coord".

- Line 10-11: We have assigned coordinate (10, 10), to x and y element of the "point". Various elements of a structure are assessed using the dot(.) operator.

- Line 12-13: We are printing the value stored in the x and y elements of the point that is of type struct coord.

- Line 14: We are printing the size of struct point. Since structure consists of more than one element, then the size of a structure is the sum of all the elements inside it.

Difference between Structure and Array

Array	Structure
Array refers to a collection consisting of elements of the homogeneous data type.	Structure refers to a collection consisting of elements of a heterogeneous data type.
Array elements are accessed using subscript operator or "[ ]" (square bracket).	Structure elements are accessed using Dot operator or "."
An array is pointer as it points to the first element of the collection.	The structure is not a pointer

Array declaration is done simply using "[ ]".	Structure declaration is done using the "struct" keyword.

data_type array_name[size];	struct sruct_name{
	data_type1 ele1;
	data_type2 ele2;
	};

typedef (User-defined data type)

The keyword "typedef" helps to create an alias for a data type and use this aliased name instead of the actual data type name. To declare a typedef you have to use the typedef keyword, followed by the data type name and the alias name:

The syntax of the typedef is:
```
typedef dataTypeName alisaName;
```

The typedef does not define new data types, they are just aliases or alternate names for already existing data types. In the above example, we have "struct coord" data structure and in order to declare a variable of type coord we have written "struct coord variableName;". We can declare an alias using typedef.

```
typedef struct coord coord_t;
```

Alternatively, at the time of structure declaration like:
```
typedef struct coord2
{
    int x;
    int y;
} coord_t;
```

Now we can declare a point variable of coord type by simply writing

```
coord_t point;
```

Example 9.2: Using typedef keyword
```
1.    typedef struct coord2
2.    {
3.         int x;
4.         int y;
5.    } coord_t;
6.
7.    int main()
8.    {
9.         coord_t point;
10.        point.x=10;
11.        point.y=10;
12.        printf("X axis coord value is %d\n", point.x);
13.        printf("Y axis coord value is %d\n", point.y);
```

```
14.        printf("Size of structure is %d bytes\n", sizeof(point));
15.        return 0;
16.    }
```

Analysis:

- Line 1-5:We have declared a struct coord which contains two elements x and y of type int. Moreover, we have declared an alias name of "struct coord" as "coord_t". Now in the code we can directly use coord_t in place of "struct coord".

- Line 9:We have declared a point variable of type "struct coord" but coord_t type is an alias of "struct coord"

Note: Same typedef can be used in many places where you want to simplify some complex data type by giving it an alternate name.

Union

The union is like structures and contains elements of a different data type. However, all the elements of the union share the same storage space in the computer memory. Since they are sharing the same memory location, so at a time only one can be used.

The syntax of the union is:
```
union unionName{
    datatype1 element1;
    datadype2 element2;
};
```

Elements of a union are accessed using the dot operator (.).

Take an example of a union.
```
union data
{
    char c;
    int i;
    double d;
};
```

Declaring a union
```
union data myData;
```

Accessing the members of the union using "." operator.

Example 9.3:
```
int main()
{
    myData.c = 'a';
    printf("%c \n", myData.c);
    myData.i=10;
```

```c
    printf("%d \n", myData.i);
    myData.d=10000;
    printf("%f \n", myData.d);
    printf("Size of union is: %d", sizeof(myData));
}
```

Output:
```
a
10
10000.000000
Size of union is: 8
```

The storage allocated for a union is the storage required for the largest member of the union, plus any padding required for the union to end at a natural boundary. If we call sizeof on myData, it will return 8 considering the size of the double is 8 bytes.

A typedef can be used by the union

```c
typedef union data2
{
    char c;
    int i;
    double d;
} data_u;
```

```c
data_u myData;
```

Difference between Structure and Union.

Structure	Union
"struct" keyword is used to define a structure.	"union" keyword is used to define a union.
Every member element of the structure has its unique memory address.	All the member elements share the same memory location.
Changing the value of one member element does not change the value of the other member elements.	Changing the value of one member element changes the value of all the other member elements.
It enables initializing several member elements at once.	Only one member can be initialized and used at a time.
Total size of the structure is the sum of the size of every member element.	The size of the union is the size of the largest member element.
It is used for storing various data types at once.	It is used for storing one of many data types.
We can initialize and use various data types using struct.	We can use only one of the member elements of the available members.

Structure within a Structure

Structures can also contain structures inside it. Let us take an example of a structure circle, which contains another structure centre inside it.

Example 9.4: Demonstrating structure within structure

```
1.    typedef struct coord
2.    {
3.          int x;
4.          int y;
5.    } coord_t;
6.
7.    typedef struct circle
8.    {
9.          coord_t centre;
10.         int radius;
11.   } circle_t;
12.
13.   int main()
14.   {
15.        circle_t myCircle;
16.        myCircle.centre.x=50;
17.        myCircle.centre.y=50;
18.        myCircle.radius=10;
19.        printf("X:%d, Y:%d & Radius:%d \n", myCircle.centre.x,
      myCircle.centre.y, myCircle.radius);
20.        return 0;
21.   }
```

Output:
```
X:50, Y:50 & Radius:10
```

Analysis:
- Line 1-5:We have defined a structure radius which contains two integers x and y.

- Line 7-11:We have declared a structure circle, which contains another structure centre and an integer radius inside it.

- Line 15:We have declared a variable myCircle of the type struct circle.

- Line 16-19:We have assigned the x and y coordinates to the radius of myCircle. Moreover, assign a value to the variable radius. We have accessed the radius of myCircle using the dot operator (.) and then accessed x and y coordinates using another dot operator (.).

Bitfield

Bitfield is a kind of optimization in the space required by some variables inside the structure. If you know how much space an element can hold the Bit Field can be useful. Let us consider that we want to store age and sex inside some variable person. So we know that the age of a person can be between 0-120 (I never heard anyone older than 120) and sex can be male or female so just two values.

```c
struct person1
{
    unsigned int age;
    unsigned int sex;
};
```

This is a big waste of memory as we are giving a large space to age and sex. Moreover, we already know the max limit, which is a small number 0-120 and 0-11

```c
struct person2
{
    unsigned int age:7;
    unsigned int sex:1;
};
```

Example 9.5: Demonstrating Bitfields
```c
int main()
{
    struct person1 p1;
    struct person2 p2;
    printf("size of struct person1 without bitfield: %d\n", sizeof(p1));
    printf("size of struct person2 with bitfield: %d\n", sizeof(p2));
    return 0;
}
```

Output:
```
size of struct person1 without bitfield: 8
size of struct person2 with bitfield: 4
```

Analysis: In this example, we can see that the sizeof the structure variable decreases as we have defined the bitfield and told the compiler that we are going to use only 7 bits for the age and only one bit for the sex variable.

Enum / Enumeration type

An enumeration consists of a set of named integer constants. An enumeration type declaration gives the name of the enumeration and defines the set of named integer constants called "enumeration set" or members. A variable with enumeration type stores one of the values of the enumeration set defined by that type.

Syntax of enum:
```c
enum EnumName { enumeration set };
```

Let us take an example of BOOLEAN, which can have only two values true or false.

Example 9.6: Demonstrating Enums
```c
1.    enum BOOLEAN
2.    {
```

```
3.          false,
4.          true
5.      };
6.
7.      int main()
8.      {
9.          enum BOOLEAN flag;
10.         flag=true;
11.         if(flag==true)
12.         {
13.             printf("flag is true");
14.         }
15.         else
16.         {
17.             printf("flag is false");
18.         }
19.     }
```

Output:
```
flag is true
```

Analysis:
- Line 1-5: We have declared an enum data type name BOOLEAN. With two values true and false in the enumeration list. Enumeration list members are integer constants so compilers assign them with values false = 0 and true = 1.

- Line 9: We have declared enum BOOLEAN type variable flags that can store two values true or false.

- Line 10: We have assigned the value true to the flag. The actual integer value stored in a flag is 0.

- Line 11: We are comparing the value of flag with true in the "if statement". In the above example, we have declared an enum variable, assigned value to it, and then compare it with enum integral constant. By default, enum starts numbering its integral constant members from 0 (zero). However, we can define values yourself or tell the compiler to start numbering from some other integer value.

```
1.enum BOOLEAN
2.{
3.    false=1,
4.    true
5.};
```

Since we have told the compiler to give the constant value 1 to false and enum values are incremental so true will be equal to 2

```
1.enum BOOLEAN
2.{
3.    false=1,
4.    true=4
5.};
```

In this example, we have assigned value 1 to false and value 4 to true.

Example 9.7: Demo on starting Enum of days in a week from Sunday to Saturday.
```
1.     enum Days {Sunday=1,Monday, Tuesday, Wednesday, Thursday, Friday,
       Saturday};
2.
3.     int main()
4.     {
5.         enum Days TheDay;
6.         int j=0;
7.         printf("Please enter the day of the week (1to7)\n");
8.         scanf("%d",&j);
9.         TheDay=(enum Days)j;
10.        if(TheDay==Sunday||TheDay==Saturday)
11.            printf("Enjoy this weekend\n");
12.        else
13.            printf("Have to work\n");
14.        return 0;
15.    }
```

Output:
```
Please enter the day of the week (1to7)
5
Have to work
```

Analysis:
- Line 1:In this line, we have declared data structure Days of type enum. Enumerations set for Days enum are {Sunday =1, Monday, Tuesday, Wednesday, Thursday, Friday, Saturday}. The integral value which the compiler assigns to Sunday=1, Monday =2 and so on until Saturday =7. By default integral value of Enumeration, the set starts with 0, but we have initialized value 1 to Sunday so it will start from 1.

- Line 5: We have declared TheDay variable of type enum Days.

- Line 7-8: In these lines, we have taken input from the user.

- Line 9: In this line, we have converted user input into enum Days and stored in TheDay variable.

- Line 10-13:In this line, we have checked that the value of The Day is Sunday or Saturday. In a case when users input Saturday or Sunday, "Enjoy this weekend" will be printed to the screen. Otherwise, "Have to work" will be printed to the screen.

Note: Enumerations provide an alternative to the #define a preprocessor directive with the advantages that the values can be generated for you and obey normal scoping rules.

Array of structure

In the previous chapters, we have read about structures used to store a record of many data-types. In C, you can declare an array of structures to store a list of such records.

```
struct student
{
    int id;
    char name[20];
    char gender[10];
};

struct student studentList[40];
```

In this example, we have a structure student that contains roll-No of the student and first and last name. Then we are declared a list of student studentList that can store data of 40 students.

Example 9.8: Array of structure.
```
1.      struct student
2.      {
3.          int id;
4.          char name[20];
5.          char gender[10];
6.      };
7.
8.      int main()
9.      {
10.         int i=0, num, id=0;
11.         struct student studentList[100];
12.         printf("Enter the number of students::");
13.         scanf("%d", &num);
14.         for(i =0; i<num; i++)
15.         {
16.             studentList[i].id= id++;
17.             printf("Enter student name: ");
18.             scanf("%s", studentList[i].name);
19.             printf("Enter student gender: ");
20.             scanf("%s", studentList[i].gender);
21.         }
22.
23.         for(i=0; i<num; i++)
24.         {
25.             printf("RollNo: %d, Name: %s, Gender: %s \
        n",studentList[i].id,
26.                     studentList[i].name,studentList[i].gender);
```

```
27.          }
28.          return 0;
29.    }
```

Output:
```
Enter the number of students::2
Enter student name: Mohan
Enter student gender: Male
Enter student name: Radha
Enter student gender: Female
RollNo: 0, Name: Mohan, Gender: Male
RollNo: 1, Name: Radha, Gender: Female
```

Analysis:

- ◆ Line 11: We have declared an array studentList, which is of type struct student, this can contain maximum 100 student data.

- ◆ Line 12-21: We had taken the total number of student count and the student information from the user.

- ◆ Line 23-27: The data input is displayed to the screen.

Pass Structure to a Function

We can pass a structure to a function and can take structure as a return type of a function. However, in both the cases, you are making a copy of the structure, all the elements of a structure are copied so this operation can be quite memory intensive.

Example 9.9: Pass Structure to a Function
```
1.    void printCoord(struct coord point)
2.    {
3.          printf("X coordinate is %d\n",point.x);
4.          printf("Y coordinate is %d\n",point.y);
5.    }
6.
7.    int main()
8.    {
9.          struct coord point;
10.         point.x=10;
11.         point.y=20;
12.         printCoord(point);
13.         return 0;
14.    }
```

Output:
```
X coordinate is 10
Y coordinate is 20
```

Analysis:
- Line 9-11: We have declared a struct coord type variable name point. We had initialized values 10 and 20 to x and y-axis.

- Line 3-6: The variable point is passed by value to the printCoord() function which will print the coordinates.

Note: Argument is passed by value so all the elements of the structure will be copied.

Pass Pointer to Structure to a Function

In the above example, we have passed structure as an argument to the function and return structure from the function. Since all the elements of the structure are copied so this operation can be quite memory intensive. The solution to this problem

Example 9.10: Pass Pointer to Structure to a Function

```
1.    struct coord* GetCoord(int x,int y)
2.    {
3.        struct coord* ptrPoint=(struct coord*)malloc(sizeof(struct
      coord));
4.        ptrPoint->x=x;
5.        ptrPoint->y=y;
6.        return ptrPoint;
7.    }
8.
9.    void printCoord(struct coord* ptrPoint)
10.   {
11.       printf("X coordinate is %d\n", ptrPoint->x);
12.       printf("Y coordinate is %d\n", ptrPoint->y);
13.   }
14.
15.   int main()
16.   {
17.       struct coord* ptrPoint;
18.       ptrPoint=GetCoord(10,20);
19.       printCoord(ptrPoint);
20.       return 0;
21.   }
```

Output:
```
X coordinate is 10
Y coordinate is 20
```

Analysis:
- Line 1: We have declared a function GetCoord which takes x and y-axis value. This function will return a pointer to the structure coord.

- Line 3: We have declared a pointer "ptrPoint" of type struct coord and then allocated memory using malloc function.

- Line 4-6: We have assigned value x and y to the structure pointed by ptrPoint. Finally, we have returned a pointer to structure ptrPoint. The return is by pointer/reference so the elements of the structure will not be copied.

- Line 9: We have declared function printCoord. This takes a pointer to structure coord as an argument.

  Note: Argument is passed by the pointer so the structure will not be copied.

- Line 11-12: We are printing the x and y coordinates of the struct variable pointed by ptrPoint.

- Line 18: We are calling GetCoord function by passing its value 10 and 20 for x and y coordinates. It returns a pointer to a structure. The return is by the pointer so there will be no copy.

  Note: Memory is allocated from heap so it will not be destroyed once we come out of the scope of GetCoord function.

- Line 19: We are calling a printCoord function to print the value of the point. In this, structure is passed by the pointer so again there will be no copy.

Problems on Structure

Problem 1: Write a program in C to create a database of fifty students to store personal details such as roll no, name and marks. Print all the details of the student whose name is entered by the user.

Program 9.11:
```c
#include<stdio.h>
struct student
{
    int rollNo;
    char name[20];
    int marks;
};

int main()
{
    int i=0, num, id=0;
    struct student studentList[100];
    printf("Enter the number of students::");
    scanf("%d", &num);
    for(i =0; i<num; i++)
    {
        printf("Enter student Roll number: ");
```

```c
        scanf("%d", &(studentList[i].rollNo));
        printf("Enter student name: ");
        scanf("%s", studentList[i].name);
        printf("Enter student marks: ");
        scanf("%d", &(studentList[i].marks));
    }

    for(i=0; i<num; i++)
    {
        printf("RollNo: %d, Name: %s, Marks: %d \n",studentList[i].rollNo,
                studentList[i].name,studentList[i].marks);
    }
    return 0;
}
```

Problem 2: Write a program in C to create a database of fifty students to store personal details such as roll no, name and marks.. Display the content of the student whose name is given as input.

Example 9.12:

```c
int main()
{
    int i=0, num, id=0;
    char name[100];
    struct student studentList[100];
    printf("Enter the number of students::");
    scanf("%d", &num);
    for(i =0; i<num; i++)
    {
        printf("Enter student Roll number: ");
        scanf("%d", &(studentList[i].rollNo));
        printf("Enter student name: ");
        scanf("%s", studentList[i].name);
        printf("Enter student marks: ");
        scanf("%d", &(studentList[i].marks));
    }

    printf("\nEnter the name of the student whose details you need: ");
    scanf("%s", name);
    for(i=0; i<num; i++)
    {
        if(strcmp(studentList[i].name , name) == 0)
        {
            printf("RollNo: %d, Name: %s, Marks: %d \
n",studentList[i].rollNo, studentList[i].name,studentList[i].marks);
        }
    }
    return 0;
}
```

Problem 3: Write a program to compare two dates. To store date use structure say date that contains three members namely date, month, and year. If the dates are equal then display the message as "Equal" otherwise "Unequal".

Example 9.13:

```c
struct date
{
    int date;
    int month;
    int year;
};

int main()
{
    struct date d1, d2;

    printf("\n Enter date 1 day:: ");
    scanf("%d", &d1.date);
    printf("\n Enter date 1 month:: ");
    scanf("%d", &d1.month);
    printf("\n Enter date 1 year:: ");
    scanf("%d", &d1.year);
    printf("\n Enter date 2 day:: ");
    scanf("%d", &d2.date);
    printf("\n Enter date 2 month:: ");
    scanf("%d", &d2.month);
    printf("\n Enter date 2 year:: ");
    scanf("%d", &d2.year);

    if(d1.date == d2.date && d1.month == d2.month && d1.year == d2.year)
        printf("Both dates are equal.");
    else
        printf("Both dates are unequal");
}
```

Summary

1. The structure is a data-structure, which can hold a collection of variables of different data-type.
2. The structure is defined using the struct keyword followed by curly braces to enclose various members of the structure. At the time of definition, memory is not allocated to the structure.
3. When we create an instance of a structure, then memory is allocated to various objects of it.
4. typedef helps to create an alias for a data-type and use this aliased name instead of the actual data type name.
5. Unions provide a more economical way to build objects with attributes by reserving a single memory space for its largest member.
6. Bitfield is a kind of optimization in the space required by some variable inside the structure.
7. Enum defines a group of constants of type int

8. We can pass a structure to a function and can take structure as a return type of a function. However, in both the cases you are making a copy of the structure.
9. A pointer to a structure can be passed to a function in this case, copy is not made.
10. In C, you can declare an array of structure to store a list of some records.

Questions & Answers

Question 1: What will happen if a structure is passed as an argument and its member contains a pointer?

Answer: Passing structure to function by value does shallow copy. A shallow copy means if the argument value passed contains some pointer, then the copy also contains a pointer, which will point to the same location, and no new pointer location will be created. If you free that memory location inside the function then the structure variable, that is passed, contains a dangling pointer, which will give an error / even crash when accessed.

Question 2: Can we compare two structures using the equality operator (==)?

Answer: No, we need to compare each individual element if we want to compare two structures.

Question 3: What is the difference between enumeration variables and the pre-processor #define?

Answer:

Functionality	Enumerations	#defines
Numeric values are assigned automatically.	YES	NO
Can the debugger display the symbolic values?	YES	NO
Obey block scope?	YES	NO

Question 4: How to create a structure?

Answer: 'struct' keyword is used to create structure.
```
struct Point {
    int x;
    int y;
};
```

Question 5: How to declare structure variables?

Answer: A structure variable can either be declared with structure declaration or as a separate declaration like basic types variables.
```
// A variable declaration with structure declaration.
struct Point {
    int x;
    int y;
} pt1; // The variable pt1 is declared with 'Point' structure
```

```c
// A variable declaration like basic data types
struct Point {
    int x;
    int y;
};

int main()
{
    struct Point pt1; // Variable pt1 is declared like a basic data type.
}
```

Exercises

1. Write down the difference between array and structure.

2. Create a structure called Student with the following members.
   First Name
   Last Name
   Stream
   Address.
   Create an instance of type Student, assign it with some student information and output the same student information to the standard output.

3. Create an array of structure called Students which have 30 instances of structure Student with the following members
   First Name
   Last Name
   Stream
   Address.
   In a "for" loop, take input of all the students and then output to the standard output the list of students stored in the students array.
   After every student details entered, the user should have the option to print the whole list or enter another student until all the 30 student details are entered after which the program should print the student details and exit.

4. Create an enum IsIndian with two values Yes and No. Add this field to the student structure above. Then Create an instance of type Student, assign it with some student information and output the same student information to the standard output.

5. Create a struct variable point with x-coor and y-coord. Write c Program to calculate the distance between two points using this struct.

6. Create a struct variable for a complex number and write a C program to display addition, subtraction and multiplication of two complex numbers.

Pointers

What is a Pointer? The answer to this question is "A pointer is a type of variable which can store a memory address". To revisit the concept of pointer lets go to the concept of a variable once again.

Variables

A variable in a program is a memory location with a name that can store a value that can vary. The compiler assigns a block of memory within the computer to hold the value of that variable. The size of that block depends on the data type of the variable. For example, on a 32 bit PC the size of an integer variable is 4 bytes. This document assumes the use of a 32-bit system with 4-byte integers.

When we declare a variable, we inform the compiler of two things, the name of the variable and the data type of the variable.

For example, we declare a variable of type integer with the name a by writing:
```
int a;
```

When the compiler looks into the "int" part of the statement, then it reserves a memory of 4 bytes for this variable. Along with it, keep the name "a" of a variable in its symbol table. On the table, it keeps the relative address of this variable. So, in the program wherever it finds this symbol "a" it will look into its symbol table and know what is the value of "a" or where I need to store some value on "a". So, if we write "a=10;" the compiler looks into the symbol table of "a" , finds its memory location, and stores value 10 into it. Until this point, the compiler has compiled the program. A binary file is created which has all the addresses as a relative address. The relative address is an address calculated by considering the start of the program as address zero. When the program runs or when it is executed the absolute address is calculated by adding an offset of the executable to the relative address.

Absolute address = Offset of the exe + Relative address.
```
int a, b;
a=10;
b=a;
```

Therefore, in the above code, there are two memory locations reserved with the name "a" and "b". Then a value of 10 is stored in the memory location a. Then what value stored in "a" is read and stored in memory location "b".

Pointers

If you want to store an address of a variable and use it in the program, then you need Pointers. **A pointer is a special type of variable that can store an address of a system. To declare a pointer, we use "*" after a datatype.**

Syntax:
```
datatype *variableName;
```

For example:
```
int *ptr;    /* ptr is pointer to address which holds int data type */
```

How to use a pointer?
- Define a pointer variable using a unary operator (*).
- Assign the address of a variable to a pointer using the unary operator (&), which returns the address of that variable.
- Accessing the value stored in the address using a unary operator (*), which returns the value of the variable stored in the location whose address is contained in the pointer.

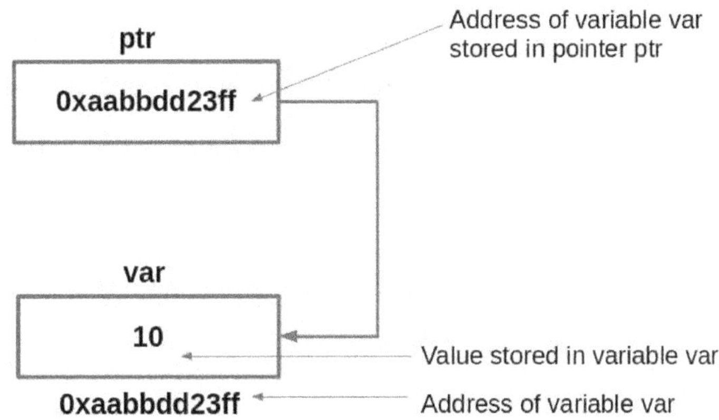

Example 10.1: Demonstrating pointers
```
1.      #include <stdio.h>
2.
3.      int main()
4.      {
5.          int a;
6.          int *ptrA = NULL;
7.          a = 10;
8.          ptrA = &a;
9.          printf("The memory location pointed by ptrA contains:: %d \n",
        *ptrA);
10.         return 0;
11.     }
```

Output:
```
The memory location pointed by ptrA contains:: 10
```

Analysis:
- Line 5: A variable is declared and the compiler will allocate a memory location for this variable.

- Line 6: A pointer type variable ptrA is declared and the compiler will allocate memory required to store an address of memory. We have used "int" to tell the compiler that we are going to store an address of an integer variable in this pointer ptrA. Therefore, we will call it as "ptrA" is a "pointer to an int" We have initialized a value NULL to the pointer. NULL is a macro. (We will learn about macros incoming chapters). For now NULL, it is some special value. We can test the value of ptrA as if (ptrA == NULL). (previously if pointers are used carelessly, then programs can write in operating system memory and corrupt the operating system). So make a rule to initialize a pointer when declaring with some variable location or NULL if no such location is decided.

- Line 7: We have stored value 10 inside A.

- Line 8: ptrA is now pointing to the memory location of the variable. Operator "&" is used to get the address of a variable. Now, "ptrA" is pointing to "a". As ptrA stores address of variable "a"

- Line 9: "*" " Dereference Operator is also used to access the value stored in the location pointed with a pointer. So, in our code *ptrA will return the value 10 because it is stored in the variable "a" this is pointed by ptrA.

Memory Allocation

Until this point, we have learned about local variables of various data type and function calls. Let us go in deep and know about their memory allocation. Broadly speaking when a program is loaded into memory three types of memory are used as Code Section, Stack Section, and Heap Section.

Code Section

Code Section is a memory location where the compiled code of the program remains. It includes the code that the programmer has written along with the required code of the library that is used in the program.

Stack Section

The stack Section is a location where the local variable inside a function and the function call resides. Memory is allocated when a local variable is created or a function is called and the same memory is returned to the system or deallocated when a local variable goes out of scope or a function returns. The stack is "last in, first out" which means the variables and a function, that is allocated last, will be deallocated first.

Example 10.2: Understanding system stack.

```
int main()
{
    int a;
    first();
}
```

```
void first()
{
    int b;
    second();
}

void second()
{
}
```

When second function is called at that point stack will look like:

second()
int b;
first()
int a;
main()

First main() function is allocated memory, Then there is a variable int a; inside main which is allocated memory, followed by first() function call, Inside first() function, memory is allocated to int b; and then…finally second() function is called from first so memory is allocated to second. As it had already explained that stack is "last in, first out" so when the second() function returns, then the memory allocated to it is freed, then the int b; is freed before the first() function exits when the first function exits then the memory allocated to it is also free. At the end int a; memory is deallocated before the main() function exits and once main function exits the memory reserved for it is also returned to the system.

Example 10.3: Block Scope
```
1.      int main()
2.      {
3.          int a;
4.          {
5.              int b;
6.          }
7.      }
```

In this code the scope of variable "int a" is inside the main() function. Integer variable "a" is created at the beginning of the main() function and will exist until the end of the main() function. However, variable "int b" is created inside a block starting with a "{" and ends with a "}". Therefore, its scope is between line 4 and 6. At the start of the block, the int b is created and at the end of it, its memory is deallocated.

Heap Section

The heap section provides persistent storage of data. The memory allocated from the heap section remains in existence during the lifetime of the program. Therefore, the Global variable and Static variable are allocated memory from Heap Section.

Along with Static and Global variables, the heap section is used in the allocation of Dynamic Memory. The dynamic memory of the desired size is created by the programmer. The programmer specifies the amount of memory it wants from the heap section and it is the programmer's responsibility to return this memory to the system. The memory allocated by the heap area is initialized to zero at the program start until they are zero until the programmer changes them so there is no chance of containing garbage value (Uninitialized local variable contains garbage value.).

There are two types of memory allocation
1) Static memory allocation: In this type of allocation, the compiler knows the exact size of the memory used at the compile time. This type of memory comes from the stack section. All the local variables are allocated memory using static allocation.
2) Dynamic memory allocation: This type of memory is allocated during run-time. The compiler does not know about the exact sizes of memory that is required. This memory is allocated by the runtime system.

Dynamic Memory Allocation

Dynamic memory allocation refers to managing system memory at runtime. In C language, dynamic memory is allocated using the malloc(), calloc() and realloc() functions. The dynamic memory is required to be freed using the free() function. These four memory management functions are defined in "stdlib.h" header file.

Malloc function:

Definition of the malloc function is as below.

```
void *malloc(size_t size);
```

It allocates a memory block of length "size" bytes and returns a pointer to the block. It will return NULL if the system does not have enough memory.

The C standard defines void* is a generic pointer that is required to be casted to required type. Most C compilers need this casting. However, the latest ANSI C standard does not require it.

E.g.
```
int* p = (int *) malloc (100 * sizeof(int));
```

Since the size of int is 4 bytes, this statement will allocate 400 bytes of memory. And, the pointer p holds the address of the first byte in the allocated memory.

Calloc function:

Definition of calloc function is as below.

```c
void *calloc(size_t num, size_t size);
```

It allocates a memory block of length "num * size" bytes and return a pointer to the block. It will return NULL if the system does not have enough memory. One thing more it does, that is, it initializes every byte to zero.

E.g.
```c
int* p = (int *) calloc (100, sizeof(int));
```

This statement allocates contiguous space in memory for 100 elements each with the size of int.

Realloc function:

Definition of realloc function is as below.

```c
void *realloc(void *ptr, size_t newSize);
```

It is used to change the memory block size of a previously allocated block of memory pointed by ptr. It returns a memory block of the newSize. If the block size is increased then the content of the old memory block is copied to a newly allocated region. If the pointer returned by the function is different from the old pointer ptr. Then ptr will no longer point to a valid location. So, in general, you should not use ptr once it is passed to realloc() function. If ptr is NULL, realloc works the same as malloc().

Note: You need to cast the return value of malloc/calloc/realloc before using it.
e.g. int *i = (int *) malloc(size);

Free Function:

The memory that is allocated using malloc(), calloc() or realloc() needs to be freed using a free() function. The syntax of the free() function is as below.

```c
void free(void *pointer);
```

A pointer to previously allocated memory is passed to free() function. The free() function will put the allocated memory block back to the heap section.

Memory Errors

Memory Allocation and Pointers give great power to C language. However, "with power comes specific obligations". Therefore, many bugs can come because of misuse of memory and pointers. It is extremely important that you should understand these bugs, this will help you in writing robust code and help you in fixing these bugs with minimal effort.

Memory errors are broadly classified as Stack Section Errors and Heap Section Errors. Various errors under the Stack section and Heap section are as below.

- Uninitialized memory read
- Array bound read/write
- Beyond stack read/write

- Null pointer read/write
- Invalid pointer read/write
- Free memory read/write
- Memory leak
- Freeing non-heap memory
- Freeing unallocated memory

Mistake 1: Uninitialized memory read

This error occurs when we are using a memory location that is not initialized. A simple example is as mentioned below.

```
int i;
printf("value of i is %d\n", i);
```

The variable "i" is not initialized and its value is printed using printf so a garbage value will be printed to the screen.

Mistake 2: Array bound read / write

Reading or writing beyond the size of the array will cause array bound read/write error.

```
int weight[4];
weight[4]=10;
printf("value of weight of 5th candidate is %d\n", weight[4]);
```

Remember that the index of an array starts from zero. Therefore, we have declared an array of size 4. Therefore, the elements will be weight [0], weight [1], weight [2] and weight [3]. However, in the next line, we are writing into the fifth element of the array that is beyond the array boundary; this error is called array bound write. In the next line, we are printing or reading the value of the fifth element of the array that is again beyond the array boundary so this error is called array bound read.

Mistake 3: Beyond stack read / write

When a local variable goes out of scope, then its memory is destroyed and given back to the system. If somehow this memory is stored in some global variable or accessed in some way, then this leads to beyond stack read and writes error.

```c
char *strGen()
{
    char str[]="hello, world!";
    return str;
}

int main()
{
    char *temp;
    temp=strGen();
    printf("%s\n", temp);
}
```

This program demonstrates the Beyond stack read error. Variable str is freed when we exit from function strGen(). But it is accessed again. Similarly, there will be beyond stack write error if you try to write something into temp.

Mistake 4: Null pointer read / write

NULL is not a valid memory address. If you try to read from NULL or write into it, you will get this error. Null pointer reads / writes mostly leads to segmentation faults. In a case when malloc() is not able to return memory as the system does not have memory then malloc() return NULL. If it does not check for null value, then this will lead to Null pointer read / write error.

```c
int fun()
{
    int *ptr;
    ptr=(int*)malloc(sizeof(int));
    *ptr=4;
    return*ptr;
}
```

If the malloc is failed, then this leads to a NULL pointer write, followed by NULL pointer read. What we need is checks for NULL == ptr.

```c
ptr=(int*)malloc(sizeof(int));
if(NULL==ptr)
    return 0;
```

Mistake 5: Free memory read / write

When malloc() is used, the system allocates memory from the heap and when the pointer to that memory location is passed to free() then the memory is de-allocate and returned to the system. After this, the memory should not be accessed and the pointer should be set to NULL.

However, it is also possible that there is more than one pointer pointing to the same memory location. Then maybe if one pointer used a free() function to free this memory location, then the other pointer will become dangling pointers. For this, memory can be reallocated by the system, so, if this memory is accessed using these dangling pointers then the system behavior is undefined.

The basic code below has a free memory read and free memory write error.

```
ptr=(int*)malloc(sizeof(int));
free(ptr);
printf("value stored in ptr %d", *ptr);
*ptr=4;
```

Mistake 6: Freeing non-heap memory

The memory of an array is allocated from the stack section and if called free() over it, then Free Non-Heap Memory error will come. The below code demonstrates this.

```
int a[10];
free(a);
```

Mistake 7: Memory leak

When there is no pointer pointing to some memory location, then this is called memory leaks. Such memory location cannot be accessed by the program. Memory leaks generally lead to slow the system and finally lead to halting the program. It is one of the most common problems when there is a system of thousands of lines where you allocate some memory and then the pointer pointing to it is again used to point something else or set to NULL before calling free() over it.

Case 1
```
int *ptr = (int*)malloc(sizeof(int));
ptr = NULL;
```

Case 2
```
int *ptr = (int*)malloc(sizeof(int));
ptr = (int*)malloc(sizeof(int));
```

In both of these examples, the memory pointed by ptr that is allocated at the first line is lost as ptr is pointing to something else. Moreover, the previously allocated memory is not freed.

Mistake 8: Segmentation fault

Segmentation faults are caused when your program tries to access memory it does not own. This is an umbrella term for ABR / ABW when your program tries to access an array element that is out of bounds or tries to use a pointer that is not allocated.

Mistake 9: Arithmetic Error

Arithmetic errors are the result of illegal mathematical operations, such as dividing a number by zero.

Pointer to an Array

Pointers do not require a pointer to a single variable they can point to an array.
For example, we can write:

```
int *ptr;
int arr[10]={1, 2, 3, 4, 5, 6, 7, 8, 9, 10};
ptr = arr;
```

Array name "arr" is a constant pointer to the first element of the array. Pointer ptr is assigned to arr, this is the same as &arr[0]. In this example, ptr is pointing to the first element of the array. Since we have a pointer pointing to an array. We can do pointer arithmetic on it.

```
printf("second element is %d \n",*(ptr + 1));
```

It will print the second element of the array.

Example 10.4: Pointer to array

```
1.      #include<stdio.h>
2.
3.      int main()
4.      {
5.          int arr[10]= {1, 2, 3, 4, 5, 6, 7, 8, 9, 10};
6.          int j;
7.          for(j=0; j<10; j++)
8.          {
9.              printf("%d",*(arr+j));
10.         }
11. }
```

Analysis: Line 9: In this line, all the various elements of an array are printed. The various elements are accessed using the pointer arithmetic.

Array of Pointers

Just like an array of integers or characters, there can be an array of pointers too.

An array of pointers can be declared as:
```
type* name[elementsCount];
```

For example:
```
char* ptr[2];
```

The above line declares an array of two-character pointers.
Let us take a working example:

Example 10.5: Array of pointers
```
1.      #include<stdio.h>
2.
3.      int main()
4.      {
5.          char*p1="Hello,";
6.          char*p2="World!";
7.          char*arr[2];
8.          arr[0]=p1;
9.          arr[1]=p2;
10.         printf("\n%s %s\n", arr[0], arr[1]);
11.         return 0;
12.     }
```

Output:
```
Hello, World!
```

Analysis: In the above code, we have two pointers pointing to two strings. Then we declared an array that can contain two pointers. We have assigned the pointers "p1' and "p2' to the 0 and 1 index of the array.

Pointer to structure

Pointers can be used to access the various elements of a structure. The various elements of a structure are accessed by pointer using -> operator.

Example 10.6: Pointer to structure
```
1.      #include<stdio.h>
2.
3.      struct student
4.      {
5.          int rollNo;
6.          char *firstName;
7.          char *lastName;
8.      };
9.
10.     int main()
11.     {
```

```
12.          int i=0;
13.          struct student stud;
14.          struct student *ptrStud;
15.          ptrStud=&stud;
16.          ptrStud->rollNo=1;
17.          ptrStud->firstName="john";
18.          ptrStud->lastName="smith";
19.          printf("RollNo: %d Student Name: %s %s", ptrStud->rollNo,
        ptrStud->firstName, ptrStud->lastName);
20.
21.          return 0;
22.  }
```

Analysis:

- Line 3-8: We have declared a struct student that contains roll-no, first and last name of a student.

- Line 13: We have declared a pointer to struct students.

- Line 15-18: Pointer ptrStud is pointing to stud. We have used ptrStud to assign a value to struct stud. We have used -> operator to access the various elements of the structure pointed by ptrStud.

  Note: If we have used the stud to assign, we would have used "." operator. The same structure, when assessed using a pointer, we use the indirection operator "->".

- Line 19: We have finally printed all the various elements of structure variable stud.

  Note: In the same way you can use -> operator to access elements of the Union.

Function Pointer

In this section, you will read about a pointer that can store the address of a function. Function pointers are like other pointer variables, except that, in place of the address of some variable it stores the address of a function. Consider the following function:

```
int compare (int first, int second)
{
    return first > second;
}
```

Just as the array name is a constant pointer to the first element of an array, the Function name is also a constant pointer to a function. When a function pointer is dereferenced by an operator "()" the execution changes to the function code.

You can declare a non-constant pointer to a function. The syntax of doing so is as mentioned below. You have to add a pointer "*" to the function and then close them inside parentheses "(" and ")". The syntax of a function pointer.

Function declaration:
```
ReturnType FunctionName ( ParamTypes )
```

Function pointer declaration:
```
ReturnType (* FunctionPointerName )( ParamTypes )
```

Note: Function pointer declaration is same as function declaration just you have to add "(*" & ")" to a function name. For the above compare() function, the function pointer declaration will be:

```
int (*ptrCompare) (int first, int second);
```

Note: The parentheses around the function pointer name is important, otherwise it will be a declaration of a function that returns a pointer to int.

Using Function Pointers

Function pointers are used to assign a function to a function pointer and then call the function using function pointers. Let us take the above example of compare() function and function pointer.

Example 10.7: Demonstrating function pointer.
```
1.     #include<stdio.h>
2.
3.     int compare(int first,int second)
4.     {
5.         return first > second;
6.     }
7.
8.     int main()
9.     {
10.        int a = 20;
11.        int b = 10;
12.        int result = 0;
13.        int(*ptrCompare)(int first, int second);
14.        ptrCompare = compare;
15.        result = ptrCompare(a, b);
16.        return 0;
17.    }
```

Analysis:
- Line 13: We have declared a function pointer ptrCompare. ptrCompare is a pointer to a function which takes two int as arguments and which return an integer.

- Line 14: In this line, we have assigned compare function to ptrCompare. ptrCompare will contain the address of function compare.

◆ Line 15: In this line, the function compare is called using a ptrCompare function pointer. Two variables a & b are passed to it and the return value of the function is stored in the result variable. You can print this value of the result and see that the compare function is called.

Why are we using function pointers?

We can call compare function directly and assign it to some function pointer and then call the function. Well, the answer is that this is just an example and the actual implementation is very different. Function pointers are very important tools when we want to write generic code, which can handle changes. (Some of the important implementations of function pointer are callbacks and state-machines) Let us look into the bubble sort example and understand why we need a function pointer.

Example 10.8: Bubble sort algorithm
```
1.    void BubbleSort(int *list,int count)
2.    {
3.        int i,j,temp;
4.        for(i=0; i<(count-1); i++)
5.        {
6.            for(j=0; j<count-i-1; j++)
7.            {
8.                if(list[j]>list[j+1])
9.                {
10.                   /*Swapping*/
11.                   temp=list[j];
12.                   list[j]=list[j+1];
13.                   list[j+1]=temp;
14.               }
15.           }
16.       }
17.   }
```

In this BubbleSort function what we are going to do is if we compare and find list[j] > list[j+1] then we will swap them. So it is going to arrange the elements of the function in ascending order and if the input array contains {3, 5, 4, 6, 7, 8, 9, 1, 2} then after calling this BubbleSort function, it will contain {1, 2, 3, 4, 5, 6, 7, 8, 9}. What will happen if you want the descending order sort function which will give the output {9, 8, 7, 6, 5, 4, 3, 2, 1} for this you need to change the comparison to list[j] < list[j+1]. For this small change, you need to make a change in the complete BubbleSort function or need to define another function to make this change.

Note: Good programmer tries to reduce duplicate code. As the duplicate code is a waste of energy. It is error-prone as the bug is fixed in one copy but not in another. The solution to this problem is two different compare functions in for ascending and one for descending order and use a function pointer in the comparison.

Example 10.9: Using function pointers
```
1.    #include<stdio.h>
2.
3.    int ascCompare(int first, int second)
```

```c
4.    {
5.        return first > second;
6.    }
7.
8.    int desCompare(int first,int second)
9.    {
10.        return first < second;
11.    }
12.
13.    void BubbleSort2(int *list, int count, int(*ptrCompare)(int first,
    int second ))
14.    {
15.        int i, j, temp;
16.        for(i=0; i<(count-1); i++)
17.        {
18.            for(j=0; j<count-i-1; j++)
19.            {
20.                if(ptrCompare(list[j], list[j+1]))
21.                {
22.                    /*Swapping*/
23.                    temp=list[j];
24.                    list[j]=list[j+1];
25.                    list[j+1]=temp;
26.                }
27.            }
28.        }
29.    }
30.
31.    int main()
32.    {
33.        int a[] = {3, 5, 4, 6, 7, 8, 9, 1, 2};
34.        int b[] = {3, 5, 4, 6, 7, 8, 9, 1, 2};
35.        int i;
36.        int n = sizeof(a)/sizeof(int);
37.        BubbleSort2(a, n, ascCompare);
38.        for(i=0; i<n; i++)
39.        {
40.            printf("%d ", a[i]);
41.        }
42.        printf("\n");
43.        n=sizeof(b)/sizeof(int);
44.        BubbleSort2(b, n, desCompare);
45.        for(i=0; i<n; i++)
46.        {
47.            printf("%d ",b[i]);
48.        }
49.        return 0;
50.    }
```

Output:
```
1 2 3 4 5 6 7 8 9
9 8 7 6 5 4 3 2 1
```

Analysis:

- Line 3-6: ascCompare is an ascending order comparison function. What it will do is it will return 1 if the first argument is greater than the second argument.

- Line 8-11: desCompare is a descending order comparison function. What it will do is it will return 1 if the first argument is smaller than the second argument.

- Line 13: void BubbleSort(int* list, int count, int (* ptrCompare) (int first, int second))
  BubbleSort function that takes a list of integers and their count, and the third argument is a function pointer. The function pointer is a pointer that can store an address of a function that takes two integer arguments and return an integer.
  We can pass any function as an argument in the function pointer. The only restriction should be that it should take two integer arguments and return an integer.
  E.g. ascCompare and desCompare

- Line 20: ptrCompare (list[j], list[j+1])
  In this line, the actual comparison depends upon the type of the argument passed to the function pointer ptrCompare.
  If ptrCompare returns 1 then those values will be replaced.

- Line 37: In this line, the BubbleSort function is used by passing an ascCompare function as an argument to the ptrCompare. So the output will be ascending order as "1 2 3 4 5 6 7 8 9"

- Line 43:In this line, the BubbleSort function is used by passing a desCompare function as an argument to the ptrCompare. So the output will be descending order as "9 8 7 6 5 4 3 2 1"

Solved Examples

Problem 1: Write the function so that we get the two dimensional array and memory is assigned to it using malloc function.

Example 10.10:
```c
int** myArray(int m,int n)
{
    int ** a;
    a=(int **)malloc(sizeof(int )*m);
    for(int i=0;i<m;i++)
        a[i]=(int *)malloc (sizeof(int)*n);
    return a;
}
```

Problem 2: How to find the size of a structure without using sizeof () operator?

Solution: use a pointer to a structure and then increment it by 1 position and take the difference of the two addresses.

Example 10.11:
```c
struct SomeStruct
{
    int data1;
    int data2;
};

int main()
{
    struct SomeStruct *ptr=0;
    int size = ((char*)(ptr+1))-((char*)ptr);
    printf("\nSIZE : %d \n", size);
    return 0;
}
```

Problem 3: Out of the given functions, which function will be able to return string properly?
```c
char* function1()
{
    char arr[50];
    scanf("%d", arr);
    return arr;
}

char* function2()
{
    char arr[50]="Hello, World!";
    return arr;
}

char* function3()
{
    char arr[50] = { 'H', 'e', 'l', 'l', 'o', ' ', 'W', 'o', 'r', 'l',
'd', '!', '\0' };
    return arr;
}

char *function4()
{
    char *arr = "Hello, World!";
    return arr;
}

char* function5()
{
    char* arr = (char *) malloc (50 * sizeof(char));
    strcpy(arr, "Hello, World!");
    return arr;
```

```c
}

void function6(char** dptr)
{
    *dptr = (char *)malloc(50 * sizeof(char));
    strcpy(*dptr, "Hello, World!");
}
```

Solution:
Out of these, the first three functions will not work, they are returning a local variable, which is created inside a function that will be destroyed once we exit the function.
Function4() will work because the string literal location is passed.
Function5() this will also work as we are allocating a memory in a heap and then returning its address.
Function6() this will also work as data is saved in memory allocated in the heap.

Problem 4: Write C code to return a string from a function. This is one of the most popular interview questions. Which of these C programs will not work.

```c
char* function1()
{
    char arr[50];
    scanf("%d", arr);
    return arr;
}

char* function2()
{
    char arr[50]="Hello, World!";
    return arr;
}

char* function3()
{
    char arr[50] = { 'H', 'e', 'l', 'l', 'o', ' ', 'W', 'o', 'r', 'l', 'd',
'!', '\0' };
    return arr;
}

char *function4()
{
    char *arr = "Hello, World!";
    return arr;
}

char* function5()
{
    char* arr = (char *) malloc (50 * sizeof(char));
    strcpy(arr, "Hello, World!");
    return arr;
}
```

```c
void function6(char** dptr)
{
    *dptr = (char *)malloc(50 * sizeof(char));
    strcpy(*dptr, "Hello, World!");
}
```

In function1() function2() and function3(), the return pointer is a local variable that will be freed when the function returns. So the returned pointer should be to a static buffer (like static char buffer[20];), or to a buffer passed in by the caller function, or memory allocated using a malloc(), but not to a local array.

The function4() function5() and function6() will work as they are returning a static literal constant or memory allocated from the heap.

Problem 5: How to initialize a pointer inside a function?

Solution: When we call a function and pass a pointer to it. Then the memory stored in the passing pointer is copied into the new pointer variable (copy of the pointer). If you change the pointer inside the function, then the same result will not be shown in the original pointer, which is passed.

These functions will not work.
```c
void myfunction(int *ptr)
{
    int var = 100;
    ptr = &var;
}
```

There are two problems in this example. First, we try to pass the address of a local variable, which will be freed when this function exits.

The second problem is that we try to set some address inside the copy of the pointer so the result will not be reflected in the calling code.

```c
void myfunction(int *ptr)
{
    ptr = (int*)malloc(sizeof(int));
}
```

We try to set memory allocated from malloc into a ptr, which is a copy of the passed pointer so the result will not reflect in the calling code.

The two solutions of this problem is to use a double pointer or make the function return a pointer:
```c
void myfunction(int** dptr)
{
    *dptr = (int*) malloc(sizeof(int));
}
```

```
int* myfunction()
{
    int *ptr = (int*)malloc(sizeof(int));
    return ptr;
}
```

Problem 6: Write a program, which will dynamically allocate one and two-dimensional array..

Solution: dynamically allocation means we have to use the malloc() function.
One-dimensional array is simple, we have to create a contiguous memory location using malloc.

```
int* single (int size)
{
    int * arr = (int*) malloc(size * sizeof(int));
    return arr;
}
```

The calling code will access the array elements simply using arr[i].
For a two-dimensional array, it is a bit tricky. There are three methods to do so.

Method 1: in this method, we will create a single-dimensional contiguous memory location using malloc () of size "(number of columns) * (number of rows)" And will access the elements with a mapping. arr[i][j] = arr [i* number of column + j]

```
int* doubleArr(int rows, int cols)
{
    int * arr = (int*)malloc(cols * rows * sizeof(int));
    return arr;
}
```

Method 2: what if we want to access the various elements in the same fashion as arr[i][j], to do this we have to create an array of pointers, allocate memory to it and then finally return it.

```
int** doubleArr(int rows, int cols)
{
    int **arr = (int **)malloc(rows * sizeof(int *));
    for (int i = 0; i < rows; i++)
    {
        arr[i] = (int *) malloc(cols * sizeof(int));
    }
    return arr;
}
```

Method 3: In the above code, malloc is called for each row entry so can we optimize this function.

```
int** doubleArr(int rows, int cols)
{
    int **arr = (int **)malloc(rows * sizeof(int *));
    arr[0] = (int *) malloc(rows * cols * sizeof(int));
    for (int i = 0; i < rows; i++)
    {
```

```c
        arr[i] = myarray[0] + (i * cols);
    }
    return arr;
}
```

Summary.

1. A Pointer is a variable that can store a memory address.
2. A Pointer is variables that contain a memory address that point to another variable.
3. The indirection operator (*) in front of the variable name to declare a pointer.
4. The address of operator (&) is used to find the address of a variable.
5. Pointer variables should always be initialized with the address of another variable or with the NULL keyword.
6. The %p conversion specifier is used for the printing address of variable or pointer value.
7. Code Section is a memory location where the compiled code of the program will remain.
8. Stack Section where the local variable inside a function and the function call resides.
9. The heap section provides persistent storage of data. The memory allocated from the heap section remains in existence during the lifetime of the program.
10. Heap section memory is reserved by malloc(), calloc() and realloc() function.
11. The malloc() function tries to reserve a dedicated memory segment from the heap section. Malloc() function returns a pointer to the beginning of the memory reserved.
12. In case of failure when malloc() function is not able to allocate memory it will return a null pointer.
13. The free() function is used to free memory allocated using malloc(). The free() function takes a pointer to the memory and free the memory pointed by it.
14. Like malloc() function, calloc() function tries to reserve contiguous segments of memory from the heap.
15. Unlike malloc(). Calloc() helps to initialize each memory segment allocated.
16. The realloc() function provides a feature for expanding the continuous block of memory while retaining the original contents.
17. An array of the pointer is just a collection of some type of pointers.
18. Pointers can be used to access the various elements of a structure. The various elements of a structure are accessible by pointer using -> operator.

Questions & Answers

Question 1: how does free() find out how much memory need to be free?

Answer: Bookkeeping, Keep the length of the allocated memory in the header preceding the allocated memory. This is a standard approach and requires an extra word for every allocated block.

Question 2: how does malloc() find the allocated memory?

Answer: Implicit list finding a free block is done using various algorithms
- First fit: Search list from the beginning, chooses the first free block that fits
- Next fit: Like first-fit, but search list from the location of the end of the previous search
- Best fit: Search the list, choose the free block with the closest size that fits

Pros and Cons:
First and next Fit leaves the memory fragmented. Best fit leaves memoryless fragmented but it is slow as each time we have to traverse the whole list for this.

Question 3: What is the difference between the following?
1. char* p;
2. const char* p;
3. char* const p;
4. const char* const p;

Answer:

```
char* p;
```

p is mutable and the value pointed by p is also mutable.

```
const char* p;
```

p is mutable, it can point to some other location. However, the value pointed by p cannot be modified using pointer p.

```
char* const p;
```

p is a const pointer, but the value pointed by it can be modified.

```
const char* const p;
```

p is a const pointer it cannot point to some other location and the value pointed by can not be modified using p pointer.

Note: The trick for this is * and const position. If const is in the left of * then it is saying data is immutable. However, if const is on the right side of the * then the pointer is immutable.

Question 4: What is a NULL pointer?

Answer: Pointers that are assigned a NULL value are called NULL pointers.
When we define:

```
int* p = NULL;
```

We are telling the compiler that pointer p is pointing to NULL. Which, in other words, is a pointer that points to nothing.

In C NULL pointer is defined as:
```
#define NULL 0
```

Which means that the NULL pointer is pointing to the base address of the segment.

It is always a good practice to assign some value to a pointer when we create it or assign a NULL value to it.

Question 5: What do you mean by dynamic memory allocation? Explain the malloc() and calloc() function in detail.
Hint: Refer Dynamic Memory Allocation section.

Question 6: What is a Callback function?
Answer: A callback function is a function pointer that is passed as an argument in another method and which is invoked after some kind of event by that method.

A callback function is a function you provide to another piece of code, allowing it to be called by that code. A callback is called as the called function is passed a function pointer as an argument from calling the function. Besides, the called function uses the function pointer passed as an argument to call the code of the calling function.

Application code calls the API of a library and the response of the API call is sent back to the application as a callback function call.

The main motive of a callback function is to make a function call "Non-blocking" and "asynchronous". Which means the caller will not wait for the called function to complete its job. When the called function is done, it will use the function pointer to invoke the calling code.

Note: Callback is a bit tedious to understand by now. However, when you are done with reading this book you can come back and read this again.

Question 7: What is a void pointer?
Answer: It is a generic pointer, which can point to any kind of object (structure/variables etc.). It is used when a pointer is declared but its type is not known.

void pointer is returned by the malloc function that just knows how many bytes of memory need to be reserved but does not know what kind of object is stored in it.

Question 8: What is a dangling pointer?
Answer: A pointer that is pointing to some memory location that is already freed.

Question 9: What are the various valid arithmetic operators in Pointers?
Answer: Valid Arithmetic operator for the pointer

Incrementing Pointer	i++
Decrementing Pointer	i--
Addition of Pointer and Number	i+=5
Subtraction of Pointer and Number	i-=5
Differencing between two pointers	i- j
Comparing two Pointers	i < j i >= j i == j i != j i == Value , i == NULL.

Invalid Arithmetic operators are the rest of all. E.g. Addition /Multiplication or division of two pointers.

Question 10: What is casting in C? What are its uses?
Answer: Casting allows the programmer to forcibly convert one data type to another. They are generally used when we are dealing with void pointers. Their use should be ideally avoided. However, sometimes they are used to suppress compiler warnings.

Question 11: Let us suppose p is a pointer, which is pointing to some integer value.
Then what does *p++ do?
1. It increments p to the next pointer location
2. It will increase the value pointed by p

Answer: The increment operator "++" has higher precedence, then prefix dereference operator "*". Therefore, the pointer p will be incremented first and will point to the next pointer location. Then the value of p is dereferenced.

Question 12: What should I do if I want to increase the value pointed by p and then dereference the value stored at its location.

Answer: use parenthesis, (*p) ++.

Question 13: What is the difference between char *a and char a[]?

Answer:
```
char a[] = "hello, world!";
```
The declaration char a[] asks for space for 14 characters and that it is known by the name "a".
In the above case, it is legal to call
a[0] = 'H';//this statement is fine.

```
char *a = " hello, world!";
```
The declaration char *a, asks for a pointer that is known by the name "a". This pointer "a" can point anywhere. In this case,it is pointing to an anonymous array of 14 characters.

In the above case, it is illegal to call
a[0] = 'H'; // this statement will give error

Question 14: What is the difference between int (*x)[10] and int *x[10].
Answer:
int (*x)[10] a pointer to an array of 10 ints
int *x[10] array of 10 pointers to ints

1. Build a program in which there is a pointer to integer iPtr that points to an integer iNum=10. You can print the value of both variable and value pointed by iPtr using *iPtr, both the value printed should be 10.

   Then print iPtr value and &iNum both using a %p conversion specifier, both of these address values should be the same.

   Now modify the value of iNum to 20 and print value if variable pointed by iPtr (print *iPtr). It should be 20.

   Now do the other way modify the value of the variable pointed by iPtr to 30 and then print the value of iNum it should be 30.

2. Create a program to allocate a memory of 100 characters using malloc(). Ask the user to enter his name. Read the response with scanf() function and assign the user name to the allocated memory. Finally display the username to the screen.

3. In the above program this time allocated using the calloc() function. Take the user name input and store it into the memory allocated. Print the user name at the end and print the number of chars in the username.

4. Create an array of char pointers of capacity four and store four strings "Apple", "Banana", "Mango" and "Orange". Then traverse through a loop to print all the stored literals.

5. Compiler will shout, at which line no?
```
int p=5;
int q=10;
int *ptp= &p;
int *ptq=&q;
int *const * c=&ptp;
*c= &p;
```

   Hint: Double pointer c is a pointer to a constant pointer to int. So we cannot change the value of the address stored in *c.

CHAPTER 12: FILE HANDLING

Files in C

Until this point, we are keeping our data into memory that is lost once our program exits. There is a requirement of retaining information intact even when a computer shuts down. For retaining this information intact, we need to write the information into a file, which is stored in the secondary storage.

Opening a file

Before you can read or write information to a file we must open a file. For opening a file, fopen() function is used. Opening a file establishes a link between the program and the operating system.

```
FILE* fopen(char* filename, char* mode)
```

fopen() function return FILE pointer. The FILE is a data structure that is defined in the header file stdio.h contains information about the file being used, such as its current size, its location in memory, etc. The fopen() function takes two arguments, first filename and the second mode of opening the file.

Various modes of opening text file are:

Mode	Operation
r	Open a file for reading. The file must exist.
w	Create an empty file for writing. If a file with the same name already exists, its content is erased and the file is treated as a new empty file.
a	Append to a file. Writing operations append data at the end of the file. The file is created if it does not exist.
r+	File is opened at the beginning both for reading and writing.
w+	Same as "w" except both for reading and writing.
a+	Same as "a" except both for reading and writing.
rb	Open a binary file for reading.
wb	Open a binary file for writing.
ab	Open a binary file for appending.

In case of success fopen() function, return a pointer to a FILE structure. In case of failure, the fopen function will return NULL.

Closing a file

A file must be closed as soon as all operations on it have been completed. This would close the file associated with the file pointer.

Syntax to close the file
```
int fclose(FILE *fp)
```

Example 12.1 : Demonstrating fopen() and fclose() functions.
```
1.      #include <stdio.h>
2.
3.      int main()
4.      {
5.          FILE *fp;
6.          char name[100];
7.          printf("Enter file name:: ");
8.          gets(name);
9.          fp=fopen(name,"r");
10.
11.         if(fp!=NULL)
12.         {
13.             /*File handling code when file exist*/
14.         }
15.         fclose(fp);
16.         return 0;
17.     }
```

Analysis:
- Line 1: The FILE pointer structure is defined in stdio.h file, so this file is required to be included.

- Line 5: We have declared file pointer fp of type FILE.

- Line 8-9: To open the file we have called the function fopen( ). It would open a file entered file name in "read" mode. The first argument of fopen() is the file name and the second argument is the mode of opening. When a file exists, then file pointer is returned and if the file does not exist then null will be returned.

- Line 15: This line demonstrates the closing of the file at the end when its work is done.

Note: If you are opening a file for reading, writing or appending always check the return value.

Writing a character to a file

The syntax for fputc() function to write a character to a file.

```
int fputc(int c, FILE *fp);
```

This function will write a character to the file pointed by file pointer fp. It returns the written character in case of success and in case of failure, it will return EOF and sets the error indicator.

Example 12.2 : Demonstrating fputc() function.

```c
1.    #include<stdio.h>
2.
3.    int main()
4.    {
5.        FILE *fp;
6.        char *ch="Hello, World!";
7.        int i, size ;
8.        char name[100];
9.        printf("Enter file name:: ");
10.       gets(name);
11.       fp=fopen(name,"w");
12.
13.       if(fp!=NULL)
14.       {
15.           size = strlen(ch);
16.           for(i=0; i<size; i++)
17.           {
18.               fputc(ch[i],fp);
19.           }
20.           fclose(fp);
21.       }
22.   }
```

Analysis:

- Line 6:In this line, we have declared a character string ch, which contains the text "Hello, World!". Our aim is to put this text into the entered file.

- Line 16-19: In these lines, we are running a for-loop for the number of characters in the text "Hello World!"

- Line 18: In this line, we are putting one character at a time to the opened file pointer by fp. In case there are some errors in writing a character to file, then the function fputc will return EOF. In the case of error, some error actions need to be taken. We will read about this in the error section topic below.

Writing a string to a file

The syntax for fputs() function to write a null-terminated string to a file.

```c
int fputs( char * str, FILE * fp)
```

This function will write a null-terminated string to the file pointed by file pointer fp. In case of success, it will return a non-negative value. In case of failure, it will return EOF and set the error indicator.

Example 12.3 : Demonstrating fputs() function.

```
1.      #include<stdio.h>
2.
3.      int main()
4.      {
5.          FILE *fp;
6.          char ch[]="Hello, World!";
7.          char name[100];
8.          printf("Enter file name:: ");
9.          gets(name);
10.         fp=fopen(name,"w");
11.
12.         if(fp!=NULL)
13.         {
14.             fputs(ch, fp);
15.             fclose(fp);
16.         }
17.     }
```

Analysis:

- Line 6: In this line, we have declared a character string ch, which contains the text "Hello, World!". We aim to put this text into the entered file.

- Line 15: In this line, we are writing a null-terminated string to the opened file pointer by fp. In case there is an error in writing a string to file, fputs will return EOF. In the case of error, some error actions need to be taken. We will read about it in the error section topic below.

Writing a formatted string to a file

for fprintf() function to write a formatted string to a file.

```
int fprintf(FILE *fp, const char *format,...)
```

The syntax of fprintf is the same as printf with the only difference is that it is also taking file pointer as an argument and the output will be written to the file in place of a screen. In case of success, it will return the number of characters written to the file. In case of failure, it will return a negative value.

Example 12.4 : Demonstrating fprintf() function

```
1.      #include<stdio.h>
2.
3.      int main()
4.      {
5.          FILE *fp;
6.          int index=1;
7.          char *ch="Hello, World!";
8.          char name[100];
9.          printf("Enter file name:: ");
```

```
10.          gets(name);
11.          fp=fopen(name,"w");
12.
13.          if(fp!=NULL)
14.          {
15.              fprintf(fp,"%d %s\n", index, ch);
16.              fclose(fp);
17.          }
18.      }
```

Analysis:

- Line 7: In this line, we have declared a character string ch, which contains the text "Hello, World!". We aim to put this text into the destination file.

- Line 15: In this line, we are writing a formatted string using a fprintf() function, which takes a FILE pointer as its first argument that points to the destination file. In case of error in writing a string to file the function fprintf() will return a negative value. In the case of error, some error actions need to be taken. we will read about it in the error section topic below.

Note: fputc(), fputs() and fprintf() all return a negative value in case of error, so it is best to check against a –ve value in place of EOF or putc and puts. Error checks for fputc(), fputs(), and fprintf() can be:
1. if(fputc(ch[i],fp) < 0)
2. if(fputs(ch, fp) < 0)
3. if(fprintf(fp, "Input Line %d :: %s\n", index, ch) < 0)

Note: fprintf() is just like printf in syntax the only difference is that in fprintf we are writing into a file stream and in printf we are writing into standard output, which is the screen.

```
fprintf(stdout, formatted string,...)
```

Is same as
```
printf(formatted string,...)
```

Reading a character from a file

The syntax for fgetc() function to read a character to a file.
```
int fgetc(FILE *fp)
```

This function will read a character from the file pointed by file pointer fp. It returns the next character read in case of success and in case of failure, it would return EOF and sets the error indicator.

Example 12.5: Demonstrating fgetc() function
```
1.      #include<stdio.h>
2.
3.      int main()
4.      {
```

```
5.          FILE *fp;
6.          char ch;
7.          char name[100];
8.          printf("Enter file name:: ");
9.          gets(name);
10.         fp=fopen(name, "r");
11.
12.         if(fp!=NULL)
13.         {
14.             while((ch=fgetc(fp))!=EOF)
15.             {
16.                 printf("%c", ch);
17.             }
18.             fclose(fp);
19.         }
20.     }
```

Analysis: Line 16: we are reading a single character from file pointed by file pointer fp. At the end of the file, the fgetc() function will return the EOF character that will finally lead to the break of the loop.

Reading a string from a file

The syntax for fgets() function to read a string from a file.
```
char * fgets( char * str, int num, FILE * fp)
```

Reads at most (num-1) characters from the stream into str Null-terminates the string read (adds a '\0' to the end) Stops after a newline character is read Stops if the end of the file is encountered. This function will return a pointer to str in case of success and will return NULL case of failure.

Example 12.6: Demonstrating fgets() function.
```
1.      #include<stdio.h>
2.
3.      int main()
4.      {
5.          FILE *fp;
6.          char name[100], buff[100];
7.          printf("Enter file name:: ");
8.          gets(name);
9.          fp=fopen(name,"r");
10.
11.         if(fp!=NULL)
12.         {
13.             while(fgets(buff,100,fp)!=NULL)
14.                 printf("%s",buff);
15.             fclose(fp);
16.         }
17.     }
```

Analysis:

- ◆ Line 6: We have declared a buffer space buff.

- ◆ Line 9: We are reading a string of character from the file with file pointer fp. Each time fgets() is called buffer is read from the file into the buffer space buffer passed to fgets() function. Max buffer size is also passed to fgets() function that will tell that maximum how much the buffer can store. At the end of the file, fgets() function will return NULL character which will finally lead to the break of the loop.

Reading formatted data from a file

The syntax for fscanf () function to read a formatted string from a file.

```
int fscanf(FILE *stream, const char *format,...)
```

The syntax of fscanf() is the same as scanf() with the only difference being that it is also taking a file pointer as an argument and the input will be read from the file in place of standard input that is the keyboard. In case of success, it will return the number of characters read from the file. In case of failure, it will return EOF.

fscanf() take various format specifiers. Like:
%d for integer
%c for char
%s for string

Example 12.7: Demonstrating fscanf() function.
```
1.    #include<stdio.h>
2.
3.    int main()
4.    {
5.        FILE *fp;
6.        int index;
7.        char name[100], buff[100], num[20];
8.        printf("Enter file name:: ");
9.        gets(name);
10.       fp=fopen(name,"r");
11.       if(fp!=NULL)
12.       {
13.           fscanf(fp, "%s %s\n", num, buff);
14.           printf("%s %s\n", num, buff);
15.           fclose(fp);
16.       }
17.   }
```

Analysis: Line 13: we are reading a string of characters from the file that is pointed by file pointer fp. However, at this time we need to be a bit more careful in reading this data. The file should be in some specific format so that we can read an integer, then a string and so on. At the end of the file, the fscanf() function will return the EOF character that will finally lead to the break of the loop.

Note: There is a problem of Buffer overflow, here as the string that is read from the file may be longer than the size of the buffer. Hackers can exploit this feature to execute arbitrary code so it is recommended not to use scanf(), fscanf(), which does not limit the size of the input. The solution is to use fgets() like functions that have the max limit of the number of characters they can take input.

End of a file

feof() is a macro that is used to test if the file pointer is at the end of a file.

```c
int feof( FILE * stream );
```

If file pointer fp is at the end of file, then a non-zero value is returned, else 0 is returned.

Note: This function will check the end of the file indicator which is set by fgetc(), fgets() etc.

Example 12.8: Demonstrating feof() function

```c
1.      #include<stdio.h>
2.
3.      int main()
4.      {
5.          FILE*fp;
6.          char name[100], ch;
7.          printf("Enter file name:: ");
8.          gets(name);
9.          fp=fopen(name,"r");
10.
11.         if(fp!=NULL)
12.         {
13.             while(!feof(fp))
14.             {
15.                 ch=fgetc(fp);
16.                 putchar(ch);
17.             }
18.             fclose(fp);
19.         }
20.     }
```

Analysis:
- Line 13: In this line, we are using the feof() function which checks whether we have reached the end of the file. Function feof() will return false till we are not at the end of the file and once we are at the end of the file it will return true, which will break the loop.

- Line 15 & 16: In this line, we are reading one character at a time and printing it to the standard output.

Example 12.9: Demonstrating fgets() with feof() function.

```c
1.      #include<stdio.h>
2.      #define BUFFER_SIZE 70
3.
4.      int main()
5.      {
6.          FILE*fp;
7.          fp=fopen("DemoFile.txt","r");
8.          char buff[BUFFER_SIZE];
9.          if(fp!=NULL)
10.         {
11.             while(!feof(fp))
12.             {
13.                 fgets(buff,BUFFER_SIZE,fp);
14.                 printf("%s",buff);
15.             }
16.             fclose(fp);
17.         }
18.     }
```

Analysis:

- Line 11: In this line, we are using the feof() function which checks whether we have reached the end of the file. feof() function will return false till we are not at the end of the file and once we are at the end of the file it will return false, which will break the loop.

- Line 13 & 14: In this line, we are reading a buffer of characters and then printing it to the screen as reading a single character at a time is not a good idea for effective point of view. Then we are printing a buffer of character to the standard output.

Error Handling

Three functions are provided to handle the error. The functions are ferror(), perror() and clearerr().

```c
int ferror( FILE* fp);
```

This function is used to check if the error indicator associated with a file pointer is set. If the error indicator is set, this function returns a non-zero integer otherwise returns 0.

```c
void perror( const char* str);
```

This function is used to print the value of the global variable errno and the string passed as an argument to the stderr that is by default screen.

```c
void clearerr( FILE* fp);
```

This function is used to reset both the error indicators and the EOF indicators of the stream.

Example 12.10: Demonstrating ferror(), perror() and clearerr() function.

```c
1.      #include<stdio.h>
2.
3.      int main()
4.      {
5.              FILE*fp;
6.              fp=fopen("DemoFile.txt","r");
7.              char ch;
8.              if(fp!=NULL)
9.              {
10.                     while(!feof(fp))
11.                     {
12.                             ch=fgetc(fp);
13.                             if(ferror(fp))
14.                             {
15.                                     perror("Error in reading file");
16.                                     clearerr(fp);
17.                                     break;
18.                             }
19.                             putchar(ch);
20.                     }
21.                     fclose(fp);
22.             }
23.     }
```

Analysis: Line 15: This line will print the errno value along with the string passed to it "Error in reading file". To the standard output, which is generally a computer screen.

Moving to the beginning of the file

rewind() function is used to set a file pointer to the beginning of the file.
```c
void rewind( FILE * stream );
```

Function rewind() does the following function:
1) Moves file pointer to the beginning of file
2) Resets end-of-file indicator
3) Reset error indicator
4) Forgets any virtual characters from ungetc

Example 12.11 : Demonstrating frewind() function
```c
1.      #include<stdio.h>
2.
3.      int main()
4.      {
5.              FILE*fp;
6.              fp=fopen("DemoFile.txt","w");
7.              char ch[]="Hello, World!";
8.              if(fp!=NULL)
9.              {
```

```
10.              fputs(ch,fp);
11.              rewind(fp);
12.              fputs(ch,fp);
13.              fclose(fp);
14.          }
15.  }
```

Analysis:

- ◆ Line 10: This line will write "Hello, World!" to the DemoFile.txt file.
- ◆ Line 11: This line will rewind the file pointer fp and it will again point to the start of the file.
- ◆ Line 12: This line will again write "Hello, World!" to the DemoFile.txt file. However, since the file pointer is rewind the"Hello, World!" if rewritten by second and we will see only one "Hello, World!" in the DemoFile.txt when we open it.

Moving to a location in a file

fseek() function is used to set the file pointer to a new position defined by adding an offset to a reference position specified by origin.

```
int fseek ( FILE * fp, long int offset, int origin )
```

Three arguments of fseek function:
1. A pointer to a file(fp) which has been opened correctly.
2. The number of bytes(offset) to move the file pointer.
3. The place to start counting from:
    a. SEEK_SET = measure from the beginning of the file
    b. SEEK_CUR = measure from the current position
    c. SEEK_END = measured backward from the end of theFile

Example 12.12 : Demonstrating fseek() function.
```
1.   #include<stdio.h>
2.
3.   int main()
4.   {
5.       FILE*fp;
6.       fp=fopen("DemoFile.txt", "w");
7.       char ch[]="I love apples.";
8.       char ch2[]="bananas";
9.       if(fp!=NULL)
10.      {
11.          fputs(ch,fp);
12.          fseek(fp,-7,SEEK_CUR);
13.          fputs(ch2,fp);
14.          fclose(fp);
15.      }
16.  }
```

Analysis:

- Line 11: This line will write "I love apples." to the DemoFile.txt file.
- Line 12: This line will rewind the file pointer fp by 7 character negative from the current position. Therefore, the file pointer now will be pointing to the place where "a" of "apples"is written.
- Line 13: This line will write "bananas." to the DemoFile.txt file. Since the file pointer is pointing to "a" of "apples" this operation will overwrite "apples" by "bananas" When we open DemoFile.txt, We will see "I love bananas".

Other File Functions

Function getw( )

The getw() function is used to read an integer value from a file.

Syntax:
```
int getw(FILE *fp);
```

Function putw()

The putw() function is used to write an integer value from a file.

Syntax:
```
int putw(int number, FILE *fp);
```

Function fread()

The fread() function is used to read data from a file.

Syntax:
```
size_t fread (void* ptr, size_t size, size_t count, FILE* fp);
```

ptr: pointer to memory where the read data will be stored.
size: size of data elements (in byte) to be read.
count: number of data elements to be read.
stream: pointer to the file from which the data will be read.

Types of files

There are two kinds of files, text files and binary files. Many operating systems like Linux do not distinguish between text and binary files. However, there are operating systems like windows, which have two kinds of files called text and binary files. When you read a file normally in a text mode, some characters may be hidden from the program. These characters are still there in the file, but your program cannot read it. Therefore, this filter is applied when you open the file in text mode.

ANSI standard for C does not specify what filtering should be used while opening the file in text mode. For example, when you are using a windows environment, when a file is opened in text mode the line ending carriage-return is filtered out. That has the effect of CR/LF pair being changed to LF. This behavior is compiler dependent.

Therefore, if you want to access every byte in the file, you have to open the file in binary mode (If you are working in the Windows environment). Any file can be opened in binary mode, you just have to add "b" in the opening mode.

Mode	Description
"rb"	Open a binary file for reading. The file must exist.
"wb"	Create an empty binary file for writing. If a file with the same name already exists, its content is erased and the file is treated as a new empty file.
"ab"	Append to a binary file. Writing operations append data at the end of the file. The file is created if it does not exist.
"r+b"	Binary file is opened at the beginning for both reading and writing.
"w+b"	Same as "wb" except both for reading and writing
"a+b"	Same as "ab" except both for reading and writing.

You can open the file in binary mode for reading as below.
```
FILE *fp = fopen("myfile.bin", "rb");
```

Line termination character in Linux, Mac, and Windows.
1. Linux/Unix and Mac OsX (and later versions)use LF also called linefeed as the line ending character. LF is the same as Ctrl-J or ^J or hex 0A.
2. Mac(Older versions) uses CR also called a carriage return as the line ending character. CR is the same as Ctrl-M or ^M or hex 0D.
3. Windows uses CRLF as the line ending, which is two characters for line ending. When you edit a file in text mode in Windows and Mac or open in normal mode in Linux/Unix then every \n will be converted into the terminating character. Therefore, if you have a file written in windows and want to read it on Linux, you have to keep it in mind what is the terminating character of the source and the target machine.

Solved Examples

Problem 1: Write a program to read from file demo.txt and then find the following counts
   ◆ Number of characters
   ◆ Upper letters characters
   ◆ Lower letter character
   ◆ Number of words
   ◆ Number of digits

Example 12.13:
```c
int main()
{
    FILE *fp;
    char ch;
    int chCount=0, upCount=0, loCount=0, wCount=0,digCount=0;
    char name[100];
    printf("Enter file name:: ");
    gets(name);
    fp=fopen(name, "r");

    if(fp!=NULL)
    {
        while((ch=fgetc(fp))!=EOF)
        {
            chCount++;
            if(ch == ' ' || ch == '\n' )
                wCount++;
            if(ch >= 'a' && ch <= 'z')
                loCount++;
            if(ch >= 'A' && ch <= 'Z')
                upCount++;
            if(ch >= '0' && ch <= '9')
                digCount++;
        }
        printf("Character count %d \n", chCount);
        printf("Upper case character count %d \n", loCount);
        printf("Lower case character count %d \n", upCount);
        printf("Word count: %d \n", wCount);
        printf("Digit count %d \n", digCount);
        fclose(fp);
    }
}
```

DemoFile.txt file
1234567890
Live and let live.
Honesty is the best policy.
#define

Output:
```
Enter file name:: DemoFile.txt
Character count 66
Upper case character count 40
Lower case character count 2
Word count: 11
Digit count 10
```

Problem 2: Write a C program to copy contents of one file to another file.

Example 12.14:
```c
int main()
{
    FILE *fp1, *fp2;
    char src[100], dst[100], c;
    printf("Enter the input file name: ");
    scanf("%s", src);
    fp1 = fopen(src, "r");
    if(fp1 == NULL)
    {
        printf("Cannot open file %s", src);
        return 0;
    }
    printf("Enter the output file name: ");
    scanf("%s", dst);
    fp2 = fopen(dst, "w");
    if(fp2 == NULL)
    {
        printf("Cannot open file %s", dst);
        return 0;
    }

    c = fgetc(fp1);
    while(c != EOF)
    {
        fputc(c, fp2);
        c = fgetc(fp1);
    }
    fclose(fp1);
    fclose(fp2);
    return 0;
}
```

Problem 3: Write a program to check whether a given word exists in a file or not. If yes then find the number of times it occurs

Example 15:
```c
#include <string.h>

int main()
{
    FILE *fp;
    int count=0;
    char namc[100], buff[100], num[20], word[30];
    printf("Enter file name:: ");
    scanf("%s", name);
    printf("Enter search word:: ");
    scanf("%s", word);
```

```c
    fp=fopen(name,"r");
    if(fp==NULL)
    {
        return 1;
    }

    while(fscanf(fp, "%s", buff) != EOF)
    {
        if(strcmp(buff, word) == 0)
        {
            count += 1;
        }

    }
    if(count > 0)
        printf("%s exists and appears %d times.\n", word, count);
    else
        printf("%s does not exist.\n", word);

    fclose(fp);

    return 0;
}
```

Problem 4: WAP to compare the contents of two files and determine whether they are same or not.

Example 16:

```c
int main()
{
    FILE *fp1, *fp2;
    char fst[100], snd[100], c1, c2;
    int equal = 1;

    printf("Enter the first file name: ");
    scanf("%s", fst);
    printf("Enter the second file name: ");
    scanf("%s", snd);

    fp1 = fopen(fst, "r");
    fp2 = fopen(snd, "r");

    if(fp1 == NULL || fp2 == NULL)
    {
        printf("Cannot open files.");
        return 0;
    }

    c1 = fgetc(fp1);
    c2 = fgetc(fp2);
```

```c
    while(c1 != EOF && c2 != EOF)
    {
        if(c1 != c2)
        {
            equal = 0;
            break;
        }
        c1 = fgetc(fp1);
        c2 = fgetc(fp2);
    }
    if(equal == 1 && c1 == EOF && c2 == EOF)
        printf("Files content is same.");
    else
        printf("Files content is not same.");

    fclose(fp1);
    fclose(fp2);
    return 0;
}
```

Problem 5: Suppose a file contains student's records with each record containing name and age of a student. Write a C program to read these records and display them in sorted order by name.

Example 12.17:

```c
#define N 100

struct student
{
    char name[50];
    int age;
};

void main()
{
    struct student s, arr[N];
    FILE *fp;
    int i=0, count=0;

    fp=fopen("STUDENT.DAT","rb+");
    if(fp==NULL)
        exit();

    printf("List students \n");
    while(fscanf(fp, "%s%d", s.name, &s.age) != EOF)
    {
        arr[i]=s;
        count++;
        i++;
    }
    fclose(fp);
```

```c
    BubbleSort(arr,count);

    for(i=0; i<count; i++)
        printf("%s %d \n", arr[i].name, arr[i].age);
}

void BubbleSort(struct student *arr, int size)
{
    struct student temp;
    int i, j;
    for (i = 0; i < (size - 1); i++)
    {
        for (j = 0; j < (size - i - 1); j++)
        {
            if (strcmp(arr[j].name, arr[j + 1].name) > 0)
            {
                /* Swapping */
                temp = arr[j];
                arr[j] = arr[j + 1];
                arr[j + 1] = temp;
            }
        }
    }
}
```

Questions & Answers

Question 1: What are the different file opening modes in C?

Solution: Various modes of opening text file are:

Mode	Operation
r	Open a file for reading. The file must exist.
w	Create an empty file for writing. If a file with the same name already exists, its content is erased and the file is treated as a new empty file.
a	Append to a file. Writing operations append data at the end of the file. The file is created if it does not exist.
r+	File is opened at the beginning both for reading and writing.
w+	Same as "w" except both for reading and writing.
a+	Same as "a" except both for reading and writing.
rb	Open a binary file for reading.
wb	Open a binary file for writing.
ab	Open a binary file for appending.

Summary

1. The files retain their data even after the program exits.
2. There are two kinds of files, which are text files and binary files.
3. The FILE data structure is used to point and manage file streams.
4. The fopen() function is used to open a data file. fopen() opens a file stream and returns a FILE pointer.
5. The fclose() function is used to close file streams. FILE pointer is passed as argument to fclose().
6. The fputc() function is used to write a character to a file.
7. The fputs() function is used to write a null-terminated string to a file.
8. The fprintf() function is used to write a formatted string to a file.
9. The fgetc() function is used to read a character to a file.
10. The fgets() function is used to read a formatted string from a file.
11. The feof() is used to test if the file pointer is there at the end of the file.

Exercises

1. Create a file students.txt. Write a program that will take the input first name, last name and mobile number of students. Use the fprintf() function to enter each entry to the students.txt file. The first name, last name, and mobile number are separated by a single space and each student's entry is there on a separate line.

2. Write a program that will read students.txt file using fscanf() function and print the student information to the screen.

3. Create a program that will be able to modify the mobile number of any student in the students.txt file.

4. How can I send output of a program to screen as well as write it in a file.
   Sol. Implement a MyPrint() function which will do both of the jobs and call this function from all the places where you are calling printf. You can use (…) ellipsis to take a variable number of arguments.

5. Write a program to write a string to a file. Then read the file and display its content to the screen.

6. Write a c program to count the number of lines in a file.

7. Write a C program to count the number of occurrence of a word in a file

8. Write a C program to replace all occurrences of a word with another word in a given file.

9. Write a C program to append the content of two files into a third file.

CHAPTER 13: THE PREPROCESSOR

Introduction

In the compilation process when you provide a C program to a compiler. Before the compiler compiles the C program, a substitution tool called preprocessor automatically runs the program. The pre-processor replaces special statements called directives. The pre-processor does not modify the original C program but creates a new file, which contains all the substituted text. Then the compiler will take this processed file and compile it into the final executable. All preprocessor directives begin with a number sign (#) they do not require a semicolon (;) for termination.

The various uses of C Preprocessor are:
1) Preprocessor directives are used to make C code portable across different machine architectures and different operating systems.
2) Preprocessor directives help in defining constants so that you can change their value in one place and the change is reflected throughout the code.
3) Pre-processor helps in including other files, which are already written in your code.
4) Pre-processor helps in the conditional compilation and commenting code.

The various C Preprocessor directives are:
1) Using #define directive to Implement Constants or Constant Macros.
2) Using #define directives to create functional line Macros.
3) Using #include directives to read or include other files.
4) Using #if, #elif, and #else directives for conditional compilation.
5) Using #ifdef, #ifndef, and #endif directives to prevent multiple inclusion of file.

The next five sections will explain each of these preprocessor directives in detail with a proper number of examples to understand it.

#define Preprocessor Directive: Macros

A macro is defined using a #define preprocessor directive. The macro-identifier is replaced in the program with the replacement-text by the preprocessor before the program is compiled.
Macros may be defined with or without arguments.
- A macro without arguments is processed like a symbolic constant.
- A macro with arguments is processed by substituting the identifier and arguments with the replacement text.

Using #define to implement Macros as Constants

If you want to declare some constant like PI, which has a value of 3.14 then you can do it as given in the example below. The pre-processor will substitute all the instances of PI in the code with its value 3.14.

E.g.
```
#define PI 3.14
```

The syntax Macro as constant is as follows:
```
# define <constant-name>   <replacement-value>
```

It is important to take out constants out of the code and define them using #define constants. Because let us suppose that in future you want to make some changes or use a more accurate value of PI as 3.1428 so you need not have to replace all the places in the code which uses PI you just have to change it once and the work is done. This helps to keep code adaptable to changes.

Using #define to create a function like Macros

#define can also behave like functions as arguments can also pass to it (They just behave as a function both function and macros are completely different). The macros are inlined code that are substituted by the pre-processor.

The syntax of Macro with parameter is as follows:
```
# define <macro-name>   <macro-expansion>
```

You define macro sum as below:
```
#define sum(a, b)   (a+b)
```

Example 13.1: Demonstrating functions like a macro.
```c
#include<stdio.h>

#define sum(a, b) (a+b)

int main()
{
    printf("Sum of 10 & 5 is %d \n", sum(10, 5));
    return 0;
}
```

Output
```
Sum of 10 & 5 is 15
```

When the preprocessor goes through the line 5 it will replace the macro sum and when the compiler looks into it, it will see "printf("Sum of 10 & 5 is %d \n", (10+5));"

What can go wrong

If you have just forgot these parentheses and write
```
#define sum(a, b) a+b
```

The above program will work fine, but if you use it as
```
sum(10, 5)*2
```

You will expect 15*2 = 30, but the result will be 20 because the compiler will look into it as.

```
10+5*2
```

Multiplication has more precedence, so 2 will multiply by 5 and then 10 is added to 10 gives 20 Solution of this problem is using parentheses.

```
#define sum(a, b) (a+b)
```

Macros are used generally for very small operations. It is not a good practice to use Macros as there is no debug symbol generated for macros so you cannot debug macro code using a debugger.

Using #include to include other files

The #include directive has also been used to include or read the entire content of the specified file. This is generally used to read the header files of the library.

The header files generally contain the following information declaration of the functions Constants, Structure definitions, typedef declarations. There are two ways to include files:

```
#include "file"
Or
#include <file>
```

Both of these are the same except for one difference. When we use #include "file" in this, the filename is specified between double-quotes, the file is searched first in the current directory that includes the file containing the directive. If the file is not found then the pre-processor will look into the default directories where it is configured to look for the standard header files. When the file name is enclosed between angle brackets "< >" the file is searched directly where the preprocessor is configured to look for the standard header files. Standard header files are usually included in angle brackets while other specific header files are included using quotes.

Conditional Compilation using #if, #elif, #else and #endif

These directives allow including or discarding part of the C program depending on certain conditions. The #if, #else, #elif (i.e., "else if") and #endif directives include or exclude code depending upon certain conditions are true or false. The condition that follows #if or #elif can only evaluate constant expressions, including macro expressions.

Example 13.2:
```
#if SOLARIS
     printf("This is Solaris system");
     //Solaris specific code
#elif LINUX
     printf("This is Linux system");
     //Linux specific code
```

```c
#else
     printf("This is unknown OS system");
     //general OS code
#endif
```

If SOLARIS is defined, then the Solaris-specific code will be shown to the compiler, rest all will not be shown. Same in case of LINUX. If LINUX and SOLARIS are not defined, then the general OS code will be shown to the compiler.

Similarly #if and #endif is used to comment code. By giving zero to #if, the condition is always false, thus the code is commented. This is the easiest way to comment the code.

```c
#if 0
//this code will be commented as 0 is always false.
#endif
```

Conditional Compilation using #ifdef and #endif

#ifdef MACRO_NAME will return true if the MACRO_NAME is defined. It is used to control whether the given statements are part of your program.

```c
#ifdef DEBUG
printf("this is debug statement");
#endif
```

If DEBUG is not defined, using #define DEBUG then this statement will not be shown to the compiler. Therefore, if you want to print the debug information then you define the DEBUG constant and if you do not want any debug information then do not define DEBUG and the code is not compiled.

Prevent Multiple Inclusion using #ifndef, #define and #endif

C language follows the one definition rule, which means a variable, function, structure can have only one definition.
However, by accident this rule can be violated. Let us see the example below.

The file name is myBase.h
```c
typedef struct myStructure1{
     int a;
     char b;
}myStr1;
```

The file name is mySecondBase.h
```c
#include"myBase.h"

typedef struct myStructure2{
     myStr1st;
     int c;
}myStr2;
```

The file name is temp.c
```c
#include"myBase.h"
#include"mySecondBase.h"

int main()
{
    myStr1st;
    myStr2=st2;
    //rest of the code
}
```

In the above program, myBase.h file defines the structure myStr1. Since file, mySecondBase.h uses the myStr1 structure definition so it includes the myBase.h file. However, when you were writing your temp.c file you needed myStr1 so you included file myBase.h and then you needed a myStr2 structure definition so you had included mySecondBase.h, which in turn, included myBase.h file. Bang here comes the problem: the pre-processor had kept two definitions of structure myStr1 in the file and the compiler will give an error of multiple definitions. The solution of this problem is using #ifndef, #define, and #endif directives. Whenever you define an .h header file, you enclose it inside these directives. Therefore, the myBase.h should look like

The file name is myBase.h
```c
#ifndef _MY_BASE
#define _MY_BASE
typedefstructmyStructure1{
    int a;
    char b;
}myStr1;
#endif
```

When the preprocessor entered this file for the first time at that time _MY_FILE is not defined so it will go inside #ifndef and the code will be processed. Moreover, the preprocessor will define _MY_FILE. Next time when the pre-processor enters the file since _MY_FILE is defined so it will not go inside and will come out of the file hence the multiple inclusion of file is prevented.

Predefined Macros

There are some macros that are defined by the pre-processor and which cannot be redefined. Some of the predefined macros heavily used are listed below:

__DATE__	The compilation date of the current source file. The date is a string literal of the form mmddyyyy.
__FILE__	The name of the current source file.
__LINE__	The line number in the current source file.
__TIME__	The most recent compilation time of the current source file. The time is a string literal of the for mhh:mm:ss.
STDC	This identifier is defined to be 1 only in the implementations conforming to the ANSI standard.

Example 13.3: Demonstrating Predefined Macros
```
1.#include <stdio.h>
2.int main()
3.{
4.    printf("File: %s\n",  __FILE__);
5.    printf("Date: %s\n",  __DATE__);
6.    printf("Time: %s\n",  __TIME__);
7.    printf("Line: %d\n",  __LINE__);
8.    printf("ANSI: %d\n",  __STDC__);
9.    return 0;
10.}
```

Output:
```
File: Macro.c
Date: Dec222012
Time: 17:09:20
Line: 8
ANSI:1
```

#pragma Directive

#pragma preprocessor directive is used to provide the additional information to the compiler.

Syntax of #pragma directive:
```
#pragma token_name
```

#pragma startup start_function and #pragma exit end_function is used to specify the functions that are needed to run before and after main() function.

#pragma Directives	Description
#pragma startup start_function	start_function() will be called before the execution of main() function.
#pragma exit end_function	end_function() will be called after the end of main() function.

Program 13.4:
```
#include<stdio.h>
#pragma startup start
#pragma exit end

void start()
{
    printf("This is start function.\n");
}

void end()
{
    printf("This is end function.\n");
```

```c
}

int main()
{
    printf("This is main function.\n");
    return 0;
}
```

Output:
```
This is start function.
This is main function.
This is end function.
```

Analysis: start and end functions are defined and are used with #pragma start end exit. So first start() function is called then main() function is called and in the end when main() function exits then end() function is called.

#pragma warn flags directive is used to hide the warning messages which are displayed during compilation.

#pragma Directives	Description
#pragma warn -rvl	No return value warning will be ignored.
#pragma warn -par	Parameter not used warning will be ignored.
#pragma warn -rch	Unreachable code warning will be ignored.

Program 13.5: Program displaying various warnings and their #pragma to suppress these warnings.
```c
#include<stdio.h>

#pragma warn -rvl /* No return value */
#pragma warn -par /* Parameter not used */
#pragma warn -rch /* Unreachable code */

int main()
{
    int count = 1;
    printf("%d", count);
    return 0;
    count = 2;
}

int display(int a)
{
    printf("Display function.");
}
```

Analysis: Above program has three types of error. First there are few lines after return 0; statements which will never be executed. Second, the argument passed to the display() function is not used and Third the display function is supposed to return a value but does not return any value.

These three warnings are suppressed using #pragma warn directive passed with flags -par, -rch and -rvl.

Multiple line Macro (\)

Macros can be written in multiple lines
```
#define sum(a, b) (a+b)
```

Is same as
```
#define sum() \
(a+b)
```

By looking into it, the \ pre-processor will know that the macro is continuing.

Macros or Functions

Pros of using macros

1) Macros are a direct substitution of code so there is no function call overhead involved so using macros is fast.

Cons of using macros

1) Program size is increased each time a macro is used as the code is directly inserted. On the other hand, the program size will not change whether you are using function 1 time or 100 times.
2) Macros are direct substitutions so there no debug information is generated so you cannot debug macro or step into them when debugging code using a debugger like a GDB.

Solved Examples

Problem 1: Write a macro function for calculating area and perimeter of circle and rectangle.

Solution:
areaperi.h File
```
#define AREA_OF_CIRCLE(r) (3.14 * r * r)
#define PERIMETER_OF_CIRCLE(r) (3.14 * 2 * r)
#define AREA_OF_RECTANGLE(l, b) (l * b)
#define PERIMETER_OF_RECTANGLE(l, b) (2 * (l + b))
```

Main.c File
```
#include "areaperi.h"
#include <stdio.h>
int main()
{
    float radius, length, breadth;
```

```c
    printf("Enter the radius of the circle: ");
    scanf("%f", &radius);

    printf("The area of circle: %f \n", AREA_OF_CIRCLE(radius));
    printf("The perimeter of circle: %f \n", PERIMETER_OF_CIRCLE(radius));

    printf("\nEnter the length of the Rectangle: ");
    scanf("%f", &length);

    printf("Enter the breadth of the Rectangle: ");
    scanf("%f", &breadth);

    printf("The area of Rectangle: %f \n", AREA_OF_RECTANGLE(length,
breadth));
    printf("The perimeter of Rectangle: %f \n",
PERIMETER_OF_RECTANGLE(length, breadth));
}
```

Output:

```
Enter the radius of the circle: 10
The area of circle: 314.000000
The perimeter of circle: 62.800000

Enter the length of the Rectangle: 10
Enter the breadth of the Rectangle: 10
The area of Rectangle: 100.000000
The perimeter of Rectangle: 40.000000
```

Problem 2: Write a C program to swap two variables without using a temporary variable.

Solution:

```c
a ^= b ^= a ^= b;
```

or

```c
a=a+b;
b=a-b;
a=a-b;
```

Problem 3: swap macro which would swap int, float and pointers

Solution:

```c
#define Swap(A,B)\
    A=A+B;\
    B=A-B;\
    A=A-B;
```

Summary

1. All preprocessor directives begin with a number sign (#) they do not require a semicolon (;).
2. Preprocessor constants can be created using #define preprocessor directive.
3. #define can be used to implement function macros. Macros are a shortcut for frequently performing tasks.
4. The #include directive has also been used to include or read the entire content of the specified file.
5. #if, #elif, #else and #endif help in conditional compilation of the code.
6. #ifdef and #endif are also used for conditional compilation.
7. #ifndef, #define, and #endif are used to prevent multiple inclusion of a single header file. These are also called inclusion guards, which prevent same .h, file from being included more than once.
8. There are some predefined macros __DATE__, __FILE__, __LINE__, __TIME__ and _STDC_ which can be used in logging.

Questions & Answers

Question 1: What is Macros? How is it substituted? Write macro definition with arguments for calculation of area and perimeter of a circle and rectangle. Store these macro definitions in a file called "areaperi.h".

Answer: A macro is defined using a #define preprocessor directive. The macro-identifier is replaced in the program with the replacement-text by the preprocessor before the program is compiled.

Macros may be defined with or without arguments.
- A macro without arguments is processed like a symbolic constant. All occurrence of substituting identifiers is replaced with replacement text.
- A macro with arguments is processed by substituting the identifier and arguments with replacement text.

Question 2: When to use Macros and when to use Functions?

Answer: It is better to use Macros when the definition is very small.
It is better to use Functions when the definition is bigger in size

Question 3. What is the difference between the following two #include directives:
- #include "filename"
- #include <filename>

Answer: When the file is included using double-quotes " " then the pre-processor will first search the file to be included in the current directory. If the file is not found then the pre-processor will look into the default directories where it is configured to look for the standard header files.

When the file is included using angle brackets "< >" then the preprocessor will search the file directly into default directories where the preprocessor is configured to look for the standard header files.

Standard header files are usually included in angle brackets while other user-specific header files are included using double-quotes.

Question 4: What do you mean by macro? Explain types of the macro with its examples.

Answer: A macro is defined using a #define preprocessor directive. The macro-identifier is replaced in the program with the replacement-text by the preprocessor before the program is compiled.
Macros may be defined with or without arguments.
- A macro without arguments is processed like a symbolic constant.
- A macro with arguments is processed by substituting the identifier and arguments with the replacement text.

```
#define PI 3.14
int main()
{
    int radius = 10;
    printf("Area is %f", PI * radius * radius);
}
```

Question 5: What is the output of the given program?
```
#define PRODUCT(n) n* n
void main()
{
    int j;
    j = 64 / PRODUCT(4);
    printf("%d", j);
}
```

Solution: The statement will expand to. 64 / 4 * 4. The operator / and * are processed from left to right. So it will be 16 * 4. Finally the output will be "64"

Exercises

1. Write a macro to calculate the area of a rectangle. Area = length * width.
   In this program take the length and width as input from the user and give area as output.

2. Write a preprocessor macro to find the area of the circle.
   Solution: #define AREA(r) (3.14 * r * r)

3. Write a macro to find the largest among two numbers.
   Solution: #define LARGEST(a, b) (a > b ? a : b)

4. Create a.h file and add a student structure inside it. Then try to include the same file twice from a.c file. Observe the error, it should be related to the multiple inclusion errors.
   Now add the multiple inclusion guards and observe it again. Now this time it should compile fine.

5. What is "#pragma once"?

   Answer: It is a preprocessor directive, which is used to prevent multiple Inclusion. (Same use as the use of #ifndef #define, #endif explained above).

6. What is the problem when we declare two pointers using the code below?

   #define intPtr int*

   intPtr p, q;

   Answer: Only p is a pointer to int and q is an integer. We should use typedef in place of #define.

CHAPTER 14: LIBRARIES

Introduction

A library is a pre-compiled collection of code that can be readily included and used in our code. When building our program, we have already included a stdio.h file that is a header file of the library libc.a. All the standard C functions like printf and scanf are there in libc.a library.

In this chapter, I am going to explain each concept considering the Linux operating system and at the end of this chapter, I will explain what needs to be done to do the same in Windows operating systems using both Visual Studio and NetBeans.

For understanding the library, you need to understand why a library is required. Let us take an example of BubbleSort function.

We have written a sorting function BubbleSort(int a[], int count) which takes a list of integers and then sorts them in ascending order.

```
void BubbleSort(int list[], int count)
{
. . . . . . . . . . .
. . . . . . . . . . .
}
```

Modularity: Separate File for Bubble Sort

If we want to put the function BubbleSort in a separate file so that the code is organized and will be modular.
To do so we have to take this code out and put it in some separate file. BubbleSort.c and the declaration of their functions in header file BubbleSort.h.

BubbleSort.c
```
1.#include "BubbleSort.h"
2.void BubbleSort(int list[],int count)
3.{
4.    inti,j,temp;
5.    for(i=0;i<(count-1);i++)
6.    {
7.          for(j=0;j<count-i-1;j++)
8.          {
9.                if(list[j]>list[j+1])
10.               {
11.                     /*Swapping*/
12.                     temp=list[j];
13.                     list[j]=list[j+1];
14.                     list[j+1]=temp;
```

```
15.              }
16.          }
17.    }
18.}
```

BubbleSort.h
```
1.#ifndef BUBBLESORT_H
2.#define BUBBLESORT_H
3.void BubbleSort(int list[], int count);
4.#endif /*BUBBLESORT_H*/
```

Wherever we want to use this bubble sort function, we can use it by including the BubbleSort.h file.

Main.c
```
1.#include<stdio.h>
2.#include"BubbleSort.h"
3.int main()
4.{
5.    int a[]={3, 4, 6, 1, 2, 9},i;
6.    BubbleSort(a, 6);
7.    for(i=0; i<6; i++)
8.    {
9.        printf("%d", a[i]);
10.   }
11.   return 0;
12.}
```

You will be able to compile it using the following commands.

```
gcc -c BubbleSort.c -o BubbleSort.o
gcc -c main.c -o main.o
gcc main.o BubbleSort.o -o main.out
./main.out
```

We have compiled the code of BubbleSort.c file in BubbleSort.o file and compiled code of the main.c file in main.o file. Then we have linked the code of main.o and BubbleSort.o files in a final executable test. When we run the final executable main.out we will see the result " 1 2 3 4 6 9". What if I want to share my code with other programmers or I want to use my code without compiling it again. The answer for this is to create a library and put this sorting function inside it.

C Library

A library is a pre-compiled code that can be readily included in our code. Libraries are pre-compiled since libraries rarely change. It would be a waste of time to recompile the library every time you wrote a program that used them.

C library has two parts:
1) A header file that contains the information about the library which the programmer needs to know. The header file normally has a .h suffix.
2) A pre-compiled binary that contains the implementation of that library which is a collection of object files.

If you include library header files under angular braces "<" & ">" then the C compiler will look into the standard location to find the libraries. There are a bunch of standard libraries that are in the path. /usr/local/lib and /usr/lib and their corresponding header files in the path /usr/local/include and /usr/include.

E.g.
```
#include<stdio.h> //search the library under standard location.
```

If you include a library header file under the double inverted comma " & " then the compiler will look in the current directory and if it does not find the file in the current directory then it will look into the standard location.

E.g.
```
#include "MyBubbleSort.h" //search in the current directory first.
```

There are two types of libraries: static libraries and dynamic libraries.

Static Library or Archive

A static library is a collection of .o object files, which are already compiled and can directly be linked into your program. When you compile a program that uses a static library, all the functionality of the static library becomes part of your executable. Static libraries have an extension. As they are also called, Archive files.

To create an Archive / Static library, you need to compile the included files, then bundle them in the library.

The commands to do so are:
```
gcc -c BubbleSort.c -o BubbleSort.o
ar -rcs libBubbleSort.a BubbleSort.o
```

There are flags rcs given to ar command.
- r - Files will be updated if they are already there
- c - Archive will be created without any feedback.
- s - Creates an index at the start of the file.

To use a static library, you need to include its header file in the code and then need to link it to the code. This command to use the static library is

```
gcc -c main.c -o main.o
gcc main.o -lBubbleSort -o main.out
```

We have compiled mian.c into the main.o file then we have included library lib BubbleSort.a using -lBubbleSort. We do not require adding lib as prefix and .a as a suffix to BubbleSort. The compiler will add the prefix and suffix. This code will work fine as long as all the libraries are there in the same directory as our code, which is using it. What if we want to keep the include header file and library .a file in some other location. For this we use -I and -L flags with gcc. -I is used at the compilation time to tell the compiler where to look for the include header files. -L is used to tell the linker where it should look for the library files. Let us suppose that header file BubbleSort.h is in the location /home/user/hemant/include and library file libBubbleSort.a is in the location /home/user/hemant/lib. Therefore, the included code will be.

```
gcc -c main.c -o main.o
gcc main.o -I/home/user/hemant/include L/home/user/hemant/lib -lBubbleSort—
omain.out
```

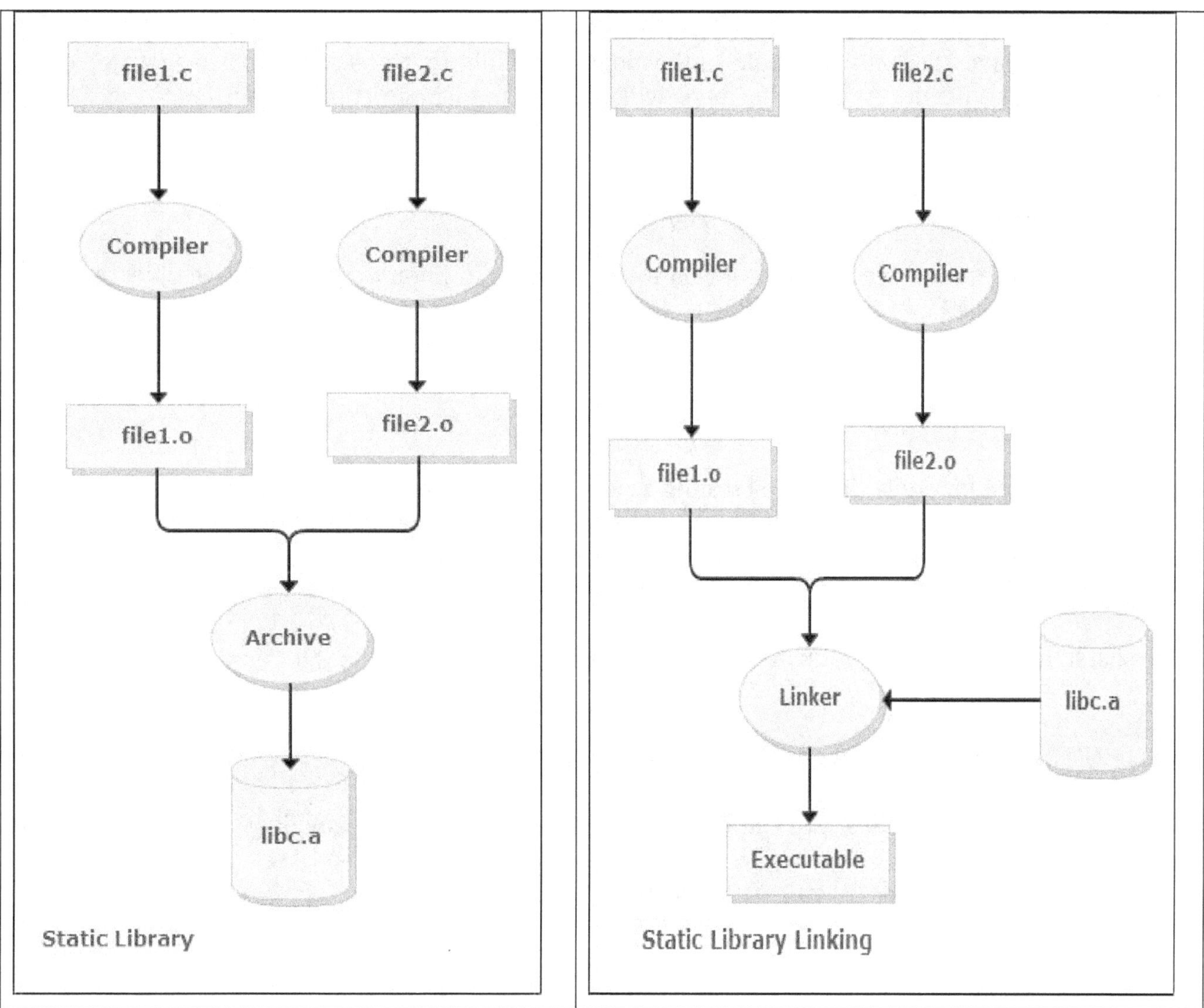

Disadvantages of Static Library

Static libraries are good, but they have following three disadvantages
- ◆ Disk space wastage: If there are n number of different code's executable, then there are n copies of the object files of the library.
- ◆ Memory space wastage: When several different programs, which are using the same library's, object files are executed at the same time. Because they hold their separate copies of the object file in virtual memory, a lot of memory will be wasted.
- ◆ Relinking problem: If there is some change in library, code (Maybe because of some bug fix) The Programs that are using this library must be re-linked in order to see changes to object modules. Because of these disadvantages, we need dynamic libraries.

Shared Library or Dynamic Library

A shared library is also a collection of object files. However, when a program is compiled with a shared library the compiler adds only the hooks of the modules and library name called so name (shared object name) to the executable. At runtime, there will be only one single copy of the library and all the applications that are running will share it.

The shared library provides the following advantages.

- ◆ Programs do not need to be re-linked to see changes in library code. (Because object modules are not copied into executable files)
- ◆ Programs are smaller, disk space and virtual memory requirements are reduced.

Creating a Shared Library

Creating a Shared library is similar to creating a static library but there are some differences.
First, while compiling the files of the library you need to provide the "-fPIC " flag to the gcc compiler. This tells the gcc compiler to generate "position independent code". We are using the same example of BubbleSort.c file and will create a libBubbleSort.so shared library.

The shared library has "lib" prefix or has ".so" extension.

For example:
```
gcc -fPIC -c BubbleSort.c -o BubbleSort.o
```

Second now you have .o files, you can link them in a shared library by providing the "-shared" option to gcc.
```
gcc -shared -o libBubbleSort.so BubbleSort.o
```

Using Shared library

Using shared library is done in two steps:
- ◆ Compile time step: We need to provide the shared library name and its location to the linker while creating an executable program. It will not add the object file to the executable, but will add hooks of the modules and library name called soname (shared object name) to the executable.
- ◆ Runtime step: We again need to provide the path of the library to the dynamic loader at the time of running the program Dynamic loader is responsible for loading the shared library at the execution time.

Compile-time linking with a Shared Library

This step is simple and is the same as linking a static library.

For example:
```
gcc -c main.c -o main.o
gcc main.o -I/home/user/hemant/include L/home/user/hemant/lib —lBubbleSort
—o main.out
```

We have provided the path of the include file"/home/user/hemant/include " using -I flag. We have provided the location of a shared library"/home/user/hemant/lib " using -L flag. We have provided a shared library name libBubbleSort.so using -l. We do not need to provide a prefix "lib" and suffix extension ".so" the compiler will add it itself. main.out is our final executable.

Runtime loading using Shared Library Paths

When you run your program, the dynamic loader will look for shared libraries in some standard directory of the system. Generally, it will look for /lib, /usr/lib,/usr/X11/lib etc. When you have created your library and it is not installed in these standard locations. You need to provide the path of the shared library using an environment variable called LD_LIBRARY_PATH so that the dynamic loader can find your shared library.

In a Bash / Sh shell, you can set the LD_LIBRARY_PATH using the following command:

```
export LD_LIBRARY_PATH=/home/user/hemant/lib:${LD_LIBRARY_PATH}
```

In a tcsh / csh shell, you can set the LD_LIBRARY_PATH using the following command:

```
setenv LD_LIBRARY_PATH/home/user/hemant/lib:${LD_LIBRARY_PATH}
```

Mention your library path in place of "/home/user/hemant/lib" which is a library path in the current example. The dynamic loader will look into the system directory like /lib, /usr/lib, /usr/X11/lib etc. Moreover, along with this it will look into the LD_LIBRARY_PATH to find the shared library.

Now you can run your executable main.out

```
./main.out
 1 2 3 4 6 9
```

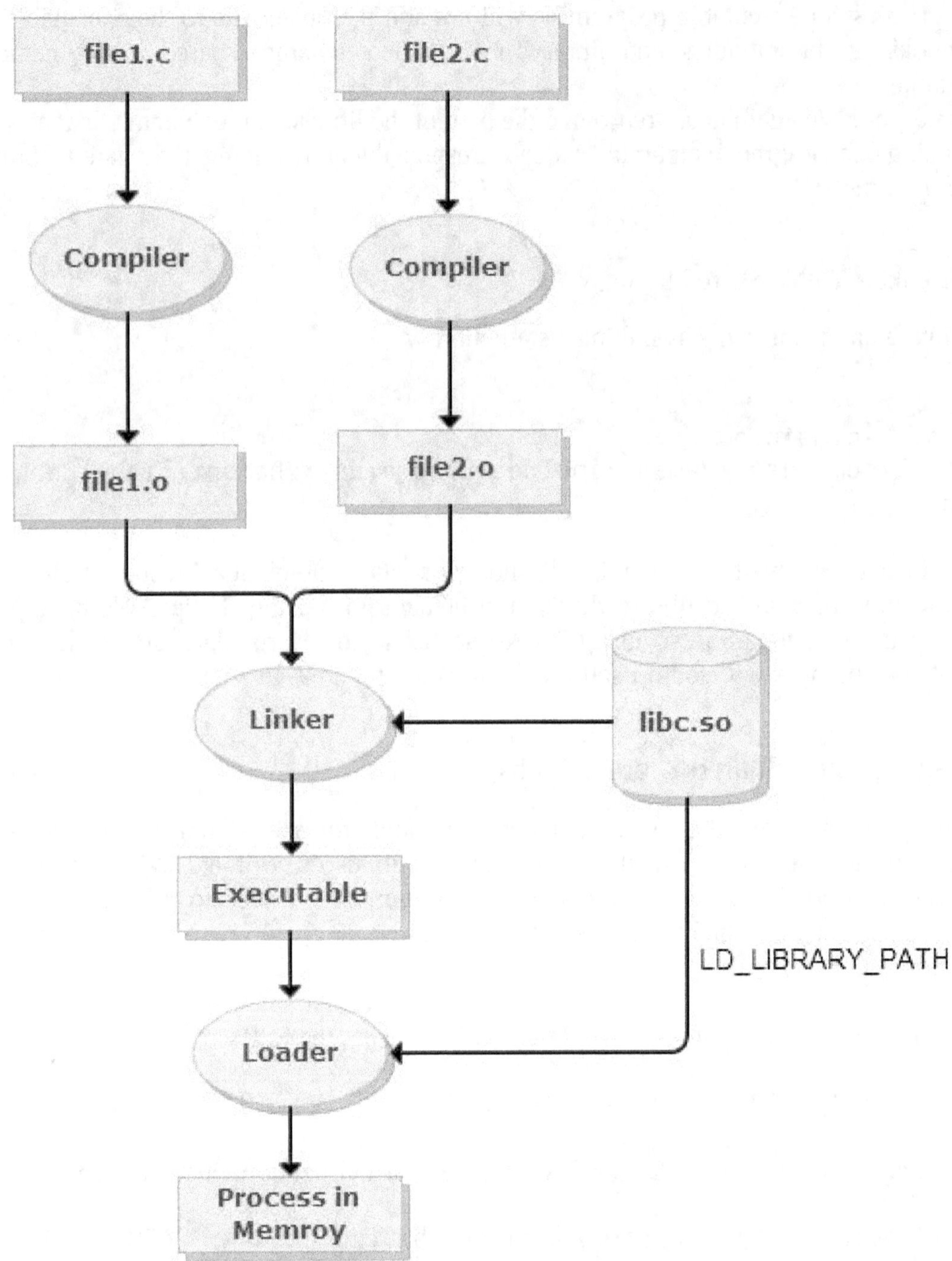

Dynamic Library Linking & Loading

Summary

1. A library is a pre-compiled code that can be readily included in our code.
2. A static library is a collection of .o object files, which are already compiled and can be directly linked into your program.
3. You can create a static library with the "ar –rcs" command.
4. Static library names start with "lib" and end with ".a". To link an archive we need to use –l compile flags.
5. A shared library is also a collection of object files. However, when a program is compiled with a shared library, then the compiler adds only the hooks of the modules and library name called soname (shared object name) to the executable.
6. Shared library name starts with "lib" and ends with ".so". The linking of Shared library is the same as the Static library.
7. -fPIC makes the object code position-independent.
8. If a shared library is not stored in a standard directory, then we need to set LD_LIBRARY_PATH.

Questions & Answers

Question 1: What are the advantages of a static library over a shared library?
Answer: Static libraries increase the overall size of the binary, but it means that you do not need to carry along a copy of the library that is being used. As the code is connected at compile time there are not any additional run-time loading costs

Exercises

1. Create a static library and add an insertion sort program inside it.

2. Create a shared library of the same insertion sort.

CHAPTER 15: BASIC ALGORITHMS

Asymptotic analysis

Asymptotic analysis is used to compare the efficiency of an algorithm independently of any particular data set or programming language.

We are generally interested in the order of growth of an algorithm and not interested in the exact time required for running an algorithm. This time is also called Asymptotic-running time.

The efficiency of the algorithm depends on:
- Time Complexity: The amount of time the algorithm is going to take.
- Space Complexity: The amount of memory that the algorithm is going to use.

Complexity analysis of algorithms

1. **Worst Case Complexity:** It is the complexity of solving the problem for the worst input of size n. It provides the upper bound for the algorithm. This is the most common analysis used.
2. **Average Case complexity**: It is the complexity of solving the problem on an average. We calculate the time for all the possible inputs and then take an average of it.
3. **Best Case complexity**: It is the complexity of solving the problem for the best input of size n.

For example, consider bubble sort algorithm complexities:
- The best case happens when the input is already sorted. Then in one single pass bubble sort will exit. So its complexity will be O(n)
- The worst case will be when the input array is reverse sorted. Then in all the iteration, we need to do the swap in each comparison. So worst-case complexity will be $O(n^2)$
- The average case will be there for some random input. In this, we will do the swap in half of the comparison. But again it will be $O(N^2)$

Asymptotic notations

Asymptotic notations are mathematical representations of time complexity and space complexity of various algorithms. Major asymptotic notations are: "Big-O Notation", "Omega-Ω Notation" and "Theta-Θ Notation".

Big-O Notation

Definition: "f(n) is big-O of g(n)" or f(n) = O(g(n)), if there are two +ve constants c and n0 such that f(n) $\leq$ c g(n) for all n $\geq$ n0,

In other words, c g(n) is an upper bound for f(n) for all n $\geq$ n0
The function f(n) growth is slower than c g(n)

We can simply say that after a sufficiently large value of input N the (c.g(n)) will always be greater than f(n).

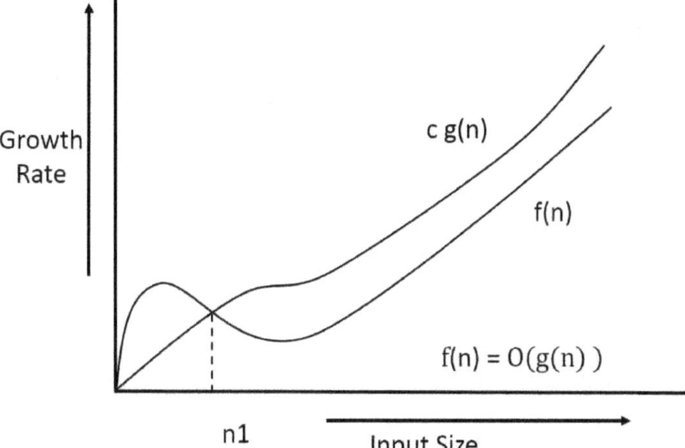

Example: $n^2 + n = O(n^2)$

Omega-Ω Notation

Definition: "f(n) is omega of g(n)." or $f(n) = \Omega(g(n))$ if there are two +ve constants c and n0 such that c g(n) ≤ f(n) for all n ≥ n0

In other words, c g(n) is lower bound for f(n)
Function f(n) growth is faster than c g(n)

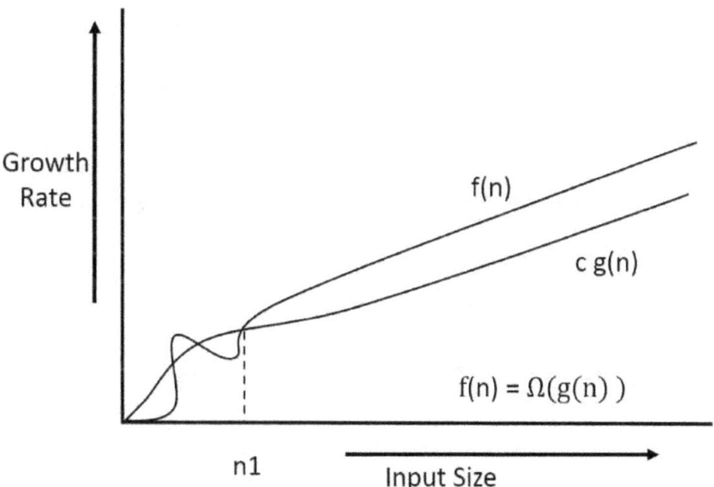

Find relationship of $f(n) = n^c$ and $g(n) = c^n$
$f(n) = \Omega(g(n))$

Theta-Θ Notation

Definition: "f(n) is theta of g(n)." or $f(n) = \Theta(g(n))$ if there are three +ve constants c1, c2 and n0 such that c1 g(n) ≤ f(n) ≤ c2 g(n) for all n ≥ n0

Function g(n) is an asymptotically tight bound on f(n). Function f(n) grows at the same rate as g(n).

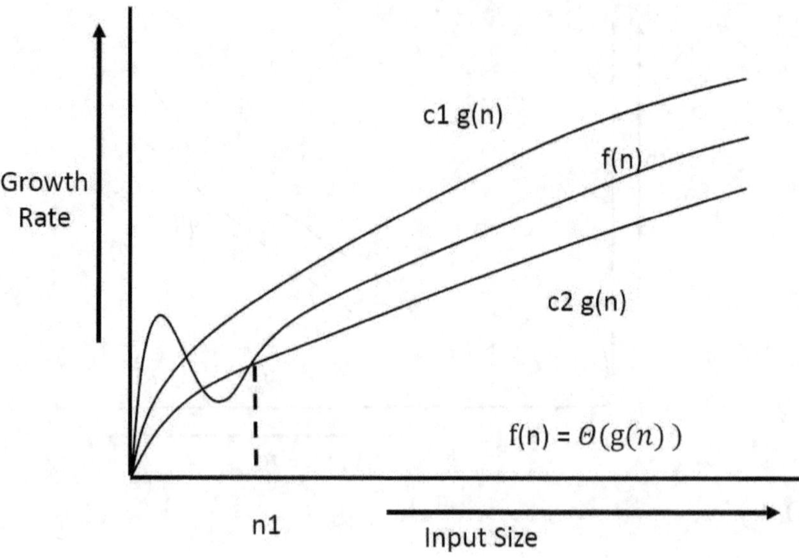

Example: $n^3 + n^2 + n = \Theta(n^3)$

Example: $n^2 + n = \Theta(n^2)$
Find relationship of $f(n) = 2n^2 + n$ and $g(n) = n^2$
$f(n) = O(g(n))$
$f(n) = \Theta(g(n))$
$f(n) = \Omega(g(n))$

Note: Asymptotic Analysis is not perfect, but that is the best way available for analyzing algorithms.

For example, say there are two sorting algorithms first take $f(n) = 10000*n*log(n)$ and second $f(n) = n^2$ time. The asymptotic analysis says that the first algorithm is better (as it ignores constants) but, actually for a small set of data when n is smaller than 10000, the first algorithm will perform better. To consider this drawback of asymptotic analysis case analysis of the algorithm is introduced.

Time Complexity Order / Growth of Complexity

A list of commonly occurring algorithm Time Complexity in increasing order:

Name	Notation
Constant	$O(1)$
Logarithmic	$O(\log n)$
Linear	$O(n)$
N-LogN	$O(n \log n)$
Quadratic	$O(n^2)$
Polynomial	$O(n^c)$ c is a constant & c>1
Exponential	$O(c^m)$ c is a constant & c>1
Factorial of N-power-N	$O(n!)$ or $O(n^n)$

The below table shows the growth rate of some of the commonly occurring complexities.

N	Function Growth Rate (Approximate)						
	O(1)	O(log n)	O(n)	O(nlog n)	O(n²)	O(n³)	O(2ⁿ)
10	1	3	10	30	10^2	10^3	10^3
10^2	1	6	10^2	6×10^2	10^4	10^6	10^{30}
10^3	1	9	10^3	9×10^3	10^6	10^9	10^{300}
10^4	1	13	10^4	13×10^4	10^8	10^{12}	10^{3000}
10^5	1	16	10^5	16×10^5	10^{10}	10^{15}	10^{30000}
10^6	1	19	10^6	19×10^6	10^{12}	10^{18}	10^{300000}

From the above table,, it is clear that the time required for completing some algorithms changes drastically with the growth rate. For the same data set, some algorithms will give results in minutes if not seconds, while other algorithms will not be able to complete in days.

Constant Time O(1)

An algorithm is said to run in constant time if the output is produced in constant time regardless of the input size.

Examples:
1. Accessing the nth element of an Array
2. Push and pop of a stack.
3. Add and remove a queue.
4. Accessing an element of Hash-Table.

Linear Time O(n)

An algorithm is said to run in linear time if the execution time of the algorithm is directly proportional to the input size.

Examples:
1. Array operations like search element, find min, find max etc.
2. Linked list operations like traversal, find min, find max etc.

Note: when we need to see/ traverse all the nodes of a data-structure for some task then complexity is no less than **O(n)**

Logarithmic Time O(logn)

An algorithm is said to run in logarithmic time if the execution time of the algorithm is proportional to the logarithm of the input size. Each step of an algorithm, a significant portion (eg. half portion) of the input is pruned/rejected out without traversing it.

Example: Binary search algorithm for searching in a sorted array.

N-LogN Time O(nlog(n))

An algorithm is said to run in logarithmic time if the execution time of an algorithm is proportional to the product of input size and logarithm of the input size. In these algorithms, each time the input is divided into half (or some proportion) and each portion is processed independently.

Example: Merge-Sort, Quick-Sort (Average case)

Note: Quicksort is a special kind of algorithm to sort an array of numbers. Its worst-case complexity is $O(n^2)$ and average-case complexity is O(n log n).

Quadratic Time $O(n^2)$

An algorithm is said to run in quadratic time if the execution time of an algorithm is proportional to the square of the input size. In these algorithms, each element is compared with all the other elements.

Examples: Bubble-Sort , Selection-Sort, Insertion-Sort

Exponential Time $O(2^n)$

In these algorithms, all possible subsets of elements of input data are generated.

Factorial Time O(n!)

In these algorithms, all possible permutations of elements of input data are generated.

Deriving the Runtime Function of an Algorithm

Constants	Each statement takes a constant time to run. Time Complexity is O(1)
Loops	The running time of a loop is a product of the running time of the statement inside a loop and the number of iterations in the loop. Time Complexity is O(n)
Nested Loop	The running time of a nested loop is a product of the running time of the statements inside the loop multiplied by a product of the size of all the loops. Time Complexity is $O(n^c)$. Where c is a number of loops. For two loops, it will be $O(n^2)$
Consecutive Statements	Just add the running times of all the consecutive statements
If-Else Statement	Consider the running time of the larger if block or else block. Moreover, ignore the other one.
Logarithmic statement	If each iteration the input size is decreased by a constant factor. Time Complexity = O(log n).

Searching

Searching is the process of finding a particular item in a collection of items. The item may be a keyword in a file, a record in a database, a node in a tree or a value in an array, etc.

Imagine you are in a library with millions of books. You want to get a specific book with a specific title. How will you find it? You will search the book in the section of the library, which contains the books whose name starts with the initial letter of the desired book. Then you continue matching with a whole book title until you find your book. (By doing this small heuristic method you have reduced the search space by a factor of 26, considering we have an equal number of books whose titles begin with a particular char.)

Similarly, computers store lots of information, and to retrieve this information efficiently, we need very efficient searching algorithms. To make searching efficient, we keep the data in some proper order. If you keep the data organized in proper order, it is easy to search for the required value or key. For example, keeping the data in sorted order is one of the ways to organize data.

Different Searching Algorithms

- ◆ Linear Search
- ◆ Binary Search (Sorted Input)

Linear Search

When elements of an array are not ordered or sorted and we want to search for a particular value, we need to scan the full list until we find the desired value. This kind of algorithm is known as an unordered linear search. The major problem with this algorithm is less performance or high Time Complexity in the worst case.

Example 15.1:

```c
int main()
{
    int arr[100], count;
    int value, i;
    printf("Enter the number of elements in array: ");
    scanf("%d", &count);
    printf("Enter the array: ");
    for(i=0; i<count ; i++)
        scanf("%d", &arr[i]);
    printf("Enter the search value: ");
    scanf("%d", &value);

    for(i = 0; i< count; i++)
    {
        if(arr[i] == value)
        {
            printf("Value found at index %d", i);
```

```c
            return 0;
        }
    }
    printf("Value not found");
    return 0;
}
```

Output:
```
Enter the number of elements in array: 9
Enter the array: 9 1 2 5 4 8 7 3 6
Enter the search value: 7
Value found at index 6
```

Time Complexity: O(n). As we need to traverse the complete list in the worst case. The worst case is when your desired element is at the last position of the array. Here, 'n' is the size of the array.

Space Complexity: O(1). No extra memory is used to allocate the array.

Binary Search

How do we search a word in a dictionary? In general, we go to some approximate page (mostly middle) and start searching from that point. If we see the word that we are searching is the same then we are done with the search. Else, if we see that alphabetically the word we are searching for is in the first half then we reject the second half and vice versa. We apply the same procedure repeatedly until we find the desired keyword.

Binary Search also works in the same way. When we want to search for some key value in a sorted list. We go to the middle point from the sorted list and start comparing it with the desired value. If the desired value is equal to the middle value then we are done. If the value is greater than the middle value then we reject the first half. If the value is less than the middle value then we reject the second half. At each comparison, we are reducing our search space by half.

Note: Binary search requires the array to be sorted otherwise binary search cannot be applied.

Example 15.2:
```c
int main()
{
    int arr[100], size;
    int value, i, low, high, mid;
    printf("Enter the number of elements in array: ");
    scanf("%d", &size);
    printf("Enter the array(sorted): ");
    for(i=0; i<size ; i++)
        scanf("%d", &arr[i]);
    printf("Enter the search value: ");
    scanf("%d", &value);

    low = 0;
    high = size - 1;
```

```c
while(low <= high)
{
    mid = (low + high) / 2;
    if (arr[mid] == value)
    {
        printf("Value found at index %d.", mid);
        return 0;
    }
    else if(arr[mid] < value)
        low = mid + 1;
    else
        high = mid - 1;
}
printf("Value not found.");
return 0;
}
```

Output:
```
Enter the number of elements in array: 6
Enter the array(sorted): 1 3 4 5 8 9
Enter the search value: 8
Value found at index 4.
```

Time Complexity: O(logn). We always take half input and throw out the other half. So the recurrence relation for binary search is T(n) = T(n/2) + c. Using master theorem (divide and conquer), we get T(n) = O(logn)

Space Complexity: O(1)

If the input array is sorted then searching the desired element can be done using recursion. Each level of recurrence half of the search space can be rejected.

Example 15.3: Binary search implementation using recursion.
```c
# Binary Search Algorithm-Recursive Way
int BinarySearch(int data[], int size, int low, int high, int value)
{
    if (low > high)
        return 0;

    int mid = (low + high) / 2;
    if (data[mid] == value)
        return 1;
    else if (data[mid] < value)
        return BinarySearch(data, size, mid + 1, high, value);
    else
        return BinarySearch(data, size, low, mid - 1, value);
}
```

```c
int main()
{
    int arr[100], size;
    int value, i, low, high, mid;
    printf("Enter the number of elements in array: ");
    scanf("%d", &size);
    printf("Enter the array(sorted): ");
    for(i=0; i<size ; i++)
        scanf("%d", &arr[i]);
    printf("Enter the search value: ");
    scanf("%d", &value);
    if (BinarySearch(arr, size, 0, size - 1, value))
        printf("Value found.");
    else
        printf("Value not found.");
    return 0;
}
```

Output:
```
Enter the number of elements in array: 6
Enter the array(sorted): 1 3 4 5 8 9
Enter the search value: 8
Value found.
```

Time Complexity: O(logn).
Space Complexity: O(logn) for system stack in recursion

Sorting

Sorting is the process of arranging elements from an array in ascending or descending order. For example, when we play cards, we sort cards according to their value so that we can find the required card easily.

When we go to some library, the books are arranged according to streams (Algorithm, Operating systems, Networking etc.). Sorting arranges data elements in order so that searching becomes easier. When books are arranged in proper indexing order, then it is easy to find a book we are looking for.

This chapter discusses algorithms for sorting an array of items. Understanding sorting algorithms is the first step towards understanding algorithm analysis. Many sorting algorithms are developed and analysed.

Type of Sorting

Some of the sorting algorithms.
1. Bubble-Sort
2. Insertion-Sort
3. Selection-Sort

Bubble-Sort

Bubble-Sort is the slowest algorithm for sorting. It is easy to implement and used when data is small.

In Bubble-Sort, we compare each pair of adjacent values. We want to sort values in increasing order so if the second value is less than the first value then we swap these two values. Otherwise, we will go to the next pair. Thus, the largest values bubble to the end of the array.

After the first pass, the largest value will be in the rightmost position. We will have N number of passes to get the array completely sorted.

First Pass

5	1	2	4	3	7	6	Swap
1	5	2	4	3	7	6	Swap
1	2	5	4	3	7	6	Swap
1	2	4	5	3	7	6	Swap
1	2	4	3	5	7	6	No Swap
1	2	4	3	5	7	6	Swap
1	2	4	3	5	6	7	

Example 15.4:

```c
void BubbleSort(int arr[], int size)
{
        int i, j, temp;
        for (i = 0; i < (size - 1); i++)
        {
                for (j = 0; j < (size - i - 1); j++)
                {
                        if (arr[j] > arr[j + 1])
                        {
                                /* Swapping */
                                temp = arr[j];
                                arr[j] = arr[j + 1];
                                arr[j + 1] = temp;
                        }
                }
        }
}

int main()
{
        int arr[100], size;
        int i, j, temp;
```

```c
    printf("Enter the number of elements in array: ");
    scanf("%d", &size);
    printf("Enter the array: ");
    for(i=0; i<size ; i++)
        scanf("%d", &arr[i]);

    BubbleSort(arr, size);
    printf("Sorted array: ");
    for(i = 0; i< size; i++)
    {
        printf("%d ", arr[i]);
    }
    return 0;
}
```

Output:
```
Enter the number of elements in array: 6
Enter the array: 5 4 7 8 3 2
Sorted array: 2 3 4 5 7 8
```

Analysis:

- The outer loop of BubbleSort() function represents the number of passes that are done for comparison of data.
- The inner loop is used to do the comparison of data. At the end of each inner loop iteration, the largest value is moved to the end of the array. In the first iteration the largest value, in the second iteration the second largest, and so on.
- Values are compared and when the value of the first argument is greater than the value of the second then a swap is performed. By this we are sorting in increasing order if we want to sort in decreasing order then we need to change this comparison.

Complexity Analysis:

The inner loop perform comparison for (n-1), (n-2), (n-3)...(n-1) + (n-2) + (n-3) + ... + 3 + 2 + 1 = n(n-1)/2

Worst-case performance	$O(n^2)$
Average case performance	$O(n^2)$
Space Complexity	$O(1)$ as we need only one temp variable
Stable Sorting	Yes

Modified / Improved Bubble-Sort

When there is, no more swap in one pass of the outer loop the array is already sorted. At this point, we should stop sorting. This sorting improvement in Bubble-Sort is extremely useful when we know that, except for a few elements, the rest of the array is already sorted.

Example 15.5:

```c
void BubbleSort2(int arr[], int size)
{
    int i, j, temp, swapped = 1;
    for (i = 0; i < (size - 1) && swapped; i++)
    {
        swapped = 0;
        for (j = 0; j < size - i - 1; j++)
        {
            if (more(arr[j], arr[j + 1]))
            {
                /* Swapping */
                temp = arr[j];
                arr[j] = arr[j + 1];
                arr[j + 1] = temp;
                swapped = 1;
            }
        }
    }
}
```

By applying this improvement, best-case performance of this algorithm is improved when an array is nearly sorted. In this case, we just need one single pass and the best-case complexity is **O(n)**

Complexity Analysis:

Worst-case performance	$O(n^2)$
Average case performance	$O(n^2)$
Space Complexity	$O(1)$
Adaptive: When the array is nearly sorted	$O(n)$
Stable Sorting	Yes

Insertion-Sort

Insertion-Sort Time Complexity is $O(n^2)$ which is the same as Bubble-Sort but performs a bit better than it. It is the way we arrange our playing cards. We keep a sorted subarray. Each value is inserted into its proper position in the sorted subarray on the left of it.

5	6	2	4	7	3	1	Insert 5
5	6	2	4	7	3	1	Insert 6
2	5	6	4	7	3	1	Insert 2
2	4	5	6	7	3	1	Insert 4
2	4	5	6	7	3	1	Insert 7
2	3	4	5	6	7	1	Insert 3
1	2	3	4	5	6	7	Insert 1

Example 15.6:

```c
void InsertionSort(int arr[], int size)
{
    int temp, i, j;
    for (i = 1; i < size; i++)
    {
        temp = arr[i];
        for (j = i; (j > 0 && arr[j-1] > temp); j--)
        {
            arr[j] = arr[j-1];
        }
        arr[j] = temp;
    }
}

int main()
{
    int arr[100], size;
    int i, j, temp;
    printf("Enter the number of elements in array: ");
    scanf("%d", &size);
    printf("Enter the array: ");
    for(i=0; i<size ; i++)
        scanf("%d", &arr[i]);

    InsertionSort(arr, size);
    printf("Sorted array: ");
    for(i = 0; i< size; i++)
    {
        printf("%d ", arr[i]);
    }
    return 0;
}
```

Output:
```
Enter the number of elements in the array: 10
Enter the array: 4 5 3 2 6 7 1 8 9 10
Sorted array: 1 2 3 4 5 6 7 8 9 10
```

Analysis:

- The outer loop is used to pick the value we want to insert into the sorted array on the left.
- The value we want to insert we have picked and saved in a temp variable.
- The inner loop is doing the comparison of the selected value with the array elements. The values are shifted to the right until we find the proper position of the temp value for which we are doing this iteration.
- Finally, the value is placed in the proper position. In each iteration of the outer loop, the length of the sorted array increases by one. When we exit the outer loop, the whole array is sorted.

Complexity Analysis:

Worst-case Time Complexity	$O(n^2)$
Best case Time Complexity	$O(n)$
Average case Time Complexity	$O(n^2)$
Space Complexity	$O(1)$
Stable sorting	Yes

Selection-Sort

Selection-Sort searches traverse the unsorted array and put the largest value at the end of it. This process is repeated (n-1) number to times. This algorithm also has quadratic time complexity. but performs better than both bubble and Insertion-Sort as a smaller number of comparisons required. The sorted array is created backward in Selection-Sort.

5	6	2	4	7	3	1	Swap
5	6	2	4	1	3	7	Swap
5	3	2	4	1	6	7	Swap
1	3	2	4	5	6	7	No Swap
1	3	2	4	5	6	7	Swap
1	2	3	4	5	6	7	No Swap
1	2	3	4	5	6	7	

Example 15.7:

```
void SelectionSort(int arr[], int size)
{
    int i, j, max, temp;
    for (i = 0; i < size - 1; i++)
    {
        max = 0;
```

```c
            for (j = 1; j < (size - i); j++)
            {
                if (arr[j] > arr[max])
                {
                    max = j;
                }
            }
            temp = arr[size-1-i];
            arr[size-1-i] = arr[max];
            arr[max] = temp;
        }
}

int main()
{
    int arr[100], size;
    int i, j, temp;
    printf("Enter the number of elements in array: ");
    scanf("%d", &size);
    printf("Enter the array: ");
    for(i=0; i<size ; i++)
        scanf("%d", &arr[i]);
    SelectionSort(arr, size);
    printf("Sorted array: ");
    for(i = 0; i< size; i++)
    {
        printf("%d ", arr[i]);
    }
    return 0;
}
```

Output:
```
Enter the number of elements in array: 10
Enter the array: 4 5 3 2 6 7 1 8 9 10
Sorted array: 1 2 3 4 5 6 7 8 9 10
```

Analysis:
♦ The outer loop decides the number of times the inner loop will iterate. For an input of N elements, the inner loop will iterate N number of times.

♦ In each iteration of the inner loop, the largest value is calculated and is placed at the end of the array.

♦ This is the final replacement of the maximum value to the proper location. The sorted array is created backward.

Complexity Analysis:

Worst Case Time Complexity	$O(n^2)$
Best Case Time Complexity	$O(n^2)$
Average case Time Complexity	$O(n^2)$
Space Complexity	$O(1)$
Stable Sorting	No

Problem 1: Write a program to find roots of a quadratic equation.

Roots of quadratic equations can be real or complex depending upon the value of determinant. The determinant is calculated by formula (b^2-4ac).

1. If determinant is greater than 0, the roots are real and are (-b + sqrt(determinant))/2a and (-b − sqrt(determinant))/2a.
2. If the determinant is 0 then both the roots are real and equal with value (-b/2a).
3. If the determinant is negative then the roots are complex with values (-b/2a + i sqrt(-determinant)/2a) and (-b/2a − i sqrt(- determinant)/2a).

Example 15.8:

```c
int main()
{
    double a, b, c, desc, root1, root2, real, img;
    printf("Please enter coefficient A,B & C in equation AX2+BX+C=0 :: ");
    scanf("%lf%lf%lf", &a, &b, &c);
    desc = b*b - 4*a*c;

    if(desc > 0)
    {
        root1 = (-b + sqrt(desc))/2*a ;
        root2 = (-b - sqrt(desc))/2*a ;
        printf("Roots are : %.2lf & %.2lf", root1, root2);
    }
    else if(desc == 0)
    {
        root1 = root2 = -b/(2*a);
        printf("Roots are : %.2lf & %.2lf", root1, root2);
    }
    else
    {
        real = -b/(2*a);
        img = sqrt(-1*desc)/2*a;
        printf("Roots are: %.2lf+%.2lfi & %.2lf-%.2lfi",real,img,real,img);
    }
    return 0;
}
```

Output:

```
Please enter coefficient of A,B & C in equation AX2+BX+C=0 :: 2 4 5
Roots are : -1.00+4.90i & -1.00-4.90i
```

Problem 2: What do you mean by sorting. Write a program in C to sort the given n positive integers. Also, give the flowchart for the same.

Solution: A Sorting Algorithm is used to rearrange a given array element according to a comparison operator on the elements.

Example 15.9: Complete bubble sort algorithm with its use.

```c
void BubbleSort(int arr[], int size)
{
    int i, j, temp;
    for (i = 0; i < (size - 1); i++)
    {
        for (j = 0; j < (size - i - 1); j++)
        {
            if (arr[j] > arr[j + 1])
            {
                /* Swapping */
                temp = arr[j];
                arr[j] = arr[j + 1];
                arr[j + 1] = temp;
            }
        }
    }
}

int main()
{
    int arr[100], size;
    int i, j, temp;
    printf("Enter the number of elements in array: ");
    scanf("%d", &size);

    BubbleSort(arr, size);
    printf("Sorted array: ");
    for(i = 0; i< size; i++)
    {
        printf("%d ", arr[i]);
    }
    return 0;
}
```

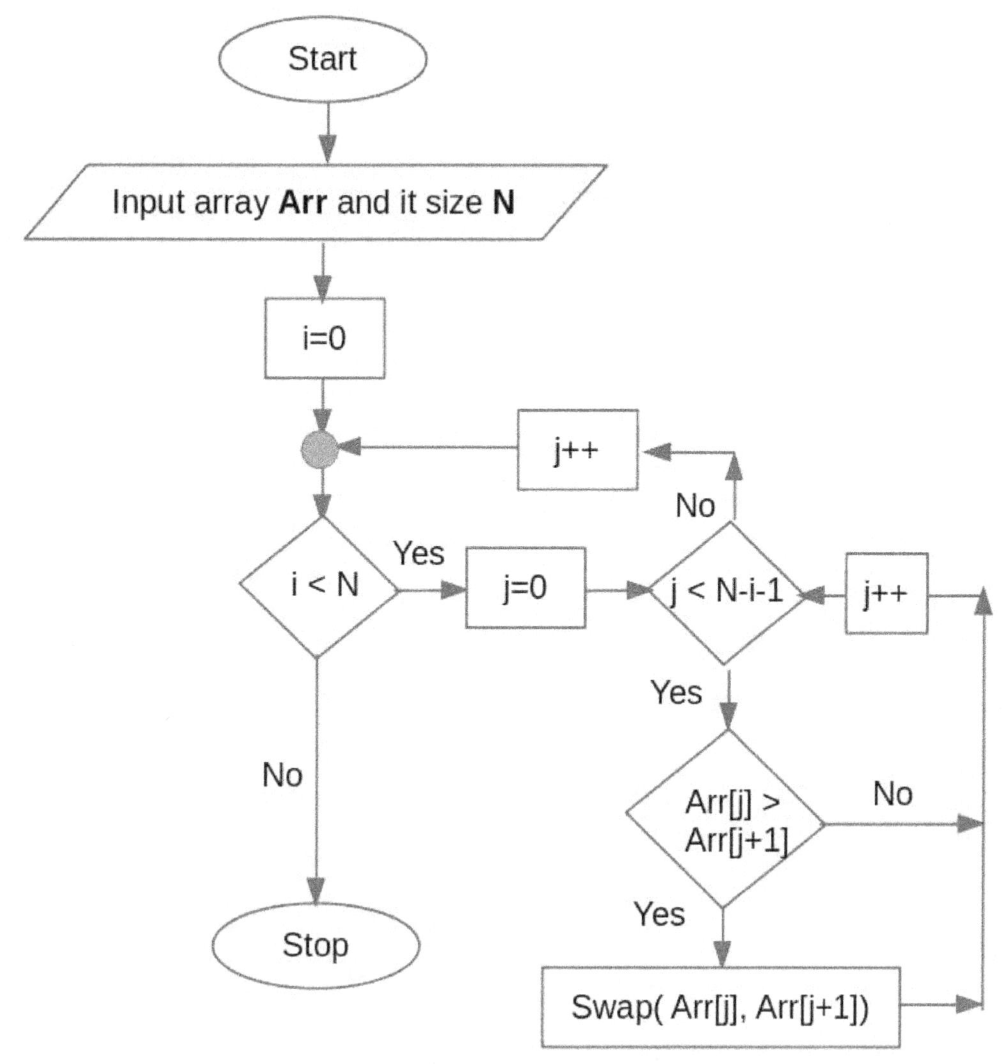

Problem 3: Find time complexity of the following programs.

Example 15.10:
```
int fun1(int n)
{
      int m = 0;
      for (int i = 0; i < n; i++)
      {
            m += 1;
      }
      return m;
}
```

Solution: Time Complexity: O(n)

Example 15.11:

```c
int fun2(int n)
{
    int i, j, m = 0;
    for (i = 0; i < n; i++)
    {
        for (j = 0; j < n; j++)
        {
            m += 1;
        }
    }
    return m;
}
```

Solution: Time Complexity: $O(n^2)$

Example 15.12:

```c
int fun3(int n)
{
    int i, j, m = 0;
    for (i = 0; i < n; i++)
    {
        for (j = 0; j < i; j++)
        {
            m += 1;
        }
    }
    return m;
}
```

Solution: Time Complexity: $O(N+(N-1)+(N-2)+...) == O(N(N+1)/2) == O(n^2)$

Example 15.13:

```c
int fun4(int n)
{
    int i, m = 0;
    i = 1;
    while (i < n)
    {
        m += 1;
        i = i * 2;
    }
    return m;
}
```

Solution: Each time problem space is divided into half.
Time Complexity: $O(\log(n))$

Example 15.14:
```c
int fun5(int n)
{
    int i, m = 0;
    i = n;
    while (i > 0)
    {
        m += 1;
        i = i / 2;
    }
    return m;
}
```

Solution: Same as above each time problem space is divided into half.
Time Complexity: O(log(n))

Example 15.15:
```c
int fun6(int n)
{
    int i, j, k, m = 0;
    for (i = 0; i < n; i++)
    {
        for (j = 0; j < n; j++)
        {
            for (k = 0; k < n; k++)
            {
                m += 1;
            }
        }
    }
    return m;
}
```

Solution: Outer loop will run for n number of iterations. In each iteration of the outer loop, the inner loop will run for n iterations of its own. Final complexity is n*n*n.
Time Complexity: $O(n^3)$

Example 15.16:
```c
int fun7(int n)
{
    int i, j, k, m = 0;
    for (i = 0; i < n; i++)
    {
        for (j = 0; j < n; j++)
        {
            m += 1;
        }
    }
```

```c
for (i = 0; i < n; i++)
{
        for (k = 0; k < n; k++)
        {
                m += 1;
        }
}
    return m;
}
```

Solution: These two groups of loops are in consecutive so their complexity will add up to form the final complexity of the program.
Time Complexity: $O(n^2) + O(n^2) = O(n^2)$

Example 15.17:
```c
int fun8(int n)
{
    int i, j, m = 0;
    for (i = 0; i < n; i++)
    {
        for (j = 0; j < sqrt(n); j++)
        {
                m += 1;
        }
    }
    return m;
}
```

Solution: Time Complexity: $O(n * \sqrt{n}) = O(n^{3/2})$

Example 15.18:
```c
int fun9(int n)
{
    int i, j, m = 0;
    for (i = n; i > 0; i /= 2)
    {
        for (j = 0; j < i; j++)
        {
                m += 1;
        }
    }
    return m;
}
```

Solution: For nested loops look for inner loop iterations. Time complexity is calculated by looking into the inner loop. First, it will run for several times then n/2, and so on. (n+n/2 +n/4+n/8+n/16 ......)
Time Complexity: $O(n)$

Example 15.19:

```
int fun10(int n)
{
      int i, j, m = 0;
      for (i = 0; i < n; i++)
      {
            for (j = i; j > 0; j--)
            {
                  m += 1;
            }
      }
      return m;
}
```

Solution: O(N+(N-1)+(N-2)+...) = O(N(N+1)/2) // arithmetic progression.
Time Complexity: $O(n^2)$

Example 15.20:

```
int fun11(int n)
{
      int i, j, k, m = 0;
      for (i = 0; i < n; i++)
      {
            for (j = i; j < n; j++)
            {
                  for (k = j + 1; k < n; k++)
                  {
                        m += 1;
                  }
            }
      }
      return m;
}
```

Solution: Time Complexity: $O(n^3)$

Example 15.21:

```
int fun12(int n)
{
      int i, j = 0, m = 0;
      for (i = 0; i < n; i++)
      {
            for (; j < n; j++)
            {
                  m += 1;
            }
      }
      return m;
}
```

Solution: Think carefully once again before finding a solution, j value is not reset at each iteration.
Time Complexity: O(n)

Example 15.22:
```c
int fun13(int n)
{
    int i, j, m = 0;
    for (i = 1; i <= n; i *= 2)
    {
        for (j = 0; j <= i; j++)
        {
            m += 1;
        }
    }
    return m;
}
```

Solution: The inner loop will run for 1, 2, 4, 8,... n times in successive iteration of the outer loop.
Time Complexity: T(n) = O(1+ 2+ 4+ ....+n/2+n) = O(n)

Exercise

1. Write a program to implement Binary search using the function, implement iterative using loops. Function definition mentioned below:
   int BinarySearch(int data[], int size, int value)

2. Write a program to take an input list of students in a list of structures. Students should have names and marks as two fields. Then sort the list of structures according to the students' names.

   Hint: Structure chapter has code to implement a list of students. Use bubble sort algorithms to sort the structure list. Use function strlen() to compare two student names.

   ```c
   if(strlen(arr[j].name, arr[j+1].name))
   {
       temp = arr[j];
       arr[j] = arr[j+1];
       arr[j+1] = temp;
   }
   ```

3. Write a program to take an input list of students in a list of structures. Students should have names and marks as two fields. Then sort the list of structures according to the marks.

   Hint: Structure chapter has code to implement a list of students. Use bubble sort algorithms to sort the structure list.

```
if(arr[j].marks, arr[j+1].marks)
{
    temp = arr[j];
    arr[j] = arr[j+1];
    arr[j+1] = temp;
}
```

4. Write a program to take an input list of students in a list of structures. Students should have names and marks as two fields. Marks can have value from 0 to 100. Then print all the students who score more than 60 marks.

   Hint: Take input from all the students in an array of structure. Then traverse the array using a loop and print the students name whose marks are greater than 60.

5. Write a Selection sort algorithm to sort a given array. Also draw a flowchart of the same.

6. Write Insertion sort algorithm to sort a given array. Also draw a flowchart of the same.

CHAPTER 16: BASIC DATA STRUCTURES

Data-Structure

Data structures are concrete representations of data and is defined as a programmer point of view of data. Data-structure represents how data will be stored in memory. All data-structures have their own pros and cons. Depending upon the type of problem we pick a data-structure that is best suited for it.

For example, we can store data in an array, a linked-list, stack, queue, tree, etc.

Linear and Non-linear data structures.

In a linear data structure, data elements are arranged in a linear order where each and every element is attached to its previous and next adjacent. Linear data structures are easy to implement. Array, Queue, Stack, Linked List are linear data structures.

In Non-linear data structure, the data elements can be attached to more than one element exhibiting the hierarchical relationship. Implementation of non-linear data structures is complex. Trees and graphs are non-linear data structures.

Array

The array represents a collection of multiple elements of the same data types.

Array Operations

Below is the API of array:
- Adds an element at kth position. Value can be stored in an array at Kth position in **O(1)** constant time. We just need to store value at arr[k].
- Reading the value stored in the kth position. Accessing the value stored at some index in the array is also **O(1)** constant time. We just need to read the value stored at arr[k].
- Substitution of value stored in kth position with a new value. Time complexity: **O(1)** constant time.

Arrays are of fixed size so it is not possible to store values more than the array capacity. If we want to add more values then we need to create a new array that has sufficient space to store these values and copy the old array to the new array. Reallocation and copy operations are slow. We have the option to allocate a larger size array but this creates wastage of memory. The solution to this problem is to use Linked-List.

Linked List

Linked lists are a dynamic data structure and memory is allocated at run time. The concept of linked lists is not to store data contiguously. Use links that point to the next elements.

The linked list is a list of items, called nodes. Nodes have two parts, the value part, and the linked part. The value part is used to store the data. Either the value part of the node can be a basic data-type like an integer or it can be some other data-type like a structure. The link part is a pointer, which is used to store addresses of the next element in the list.

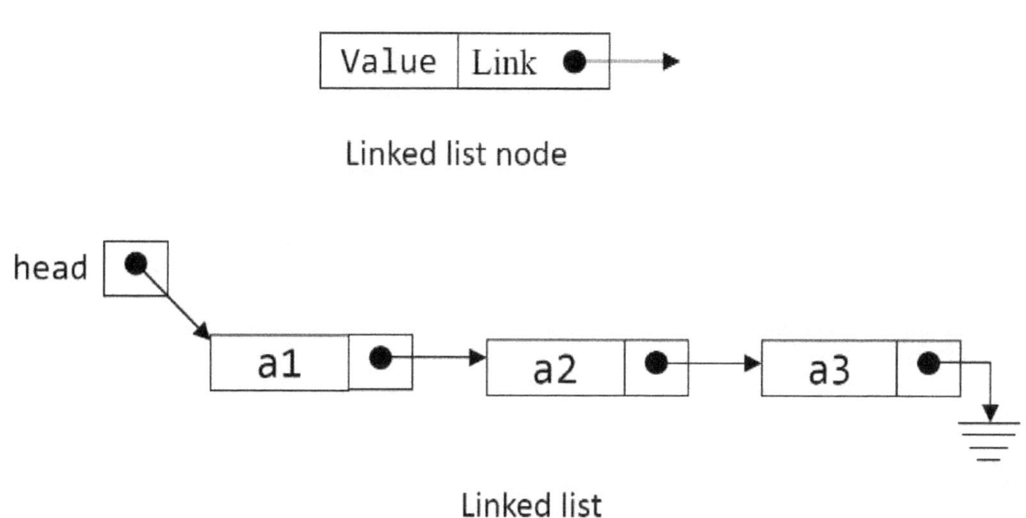

The various parts of the linked list:
- **Head**: Head is a pointer that holds the address of the first node in the linked list.
- **Nodes**: Items in the linked list are called nodes.
- **Value**: The data that is stored in each node of the linked list.
- **Link**: The link part of the node is used to store the reference of other nodes.

Performance-wise linked lists are slower than arrays because there is no direct access to linked list elements. A linked list is a useful data structure when we do not know the number of elements to be stored ahead of time. There are many types of linked list: linear, circular, doubly, doubly circular etc.

Linked list Operations:
- **Insert(k):** adds k to the start of the list
- **Delete():** delete the element at the start of the list
- **PrintList():** display all the elements of the list.
- **Find(k):** find the position of the element with value k
- **FindKth(k):** find element at position k
- **IsEmpty():** check if the number of elements in the list are zero.

Linked List

Each node (Except the last node) has a reference to the next node in the linked list. The link portion of node contains the address of the next node. The link portion of the last node contains the value null.

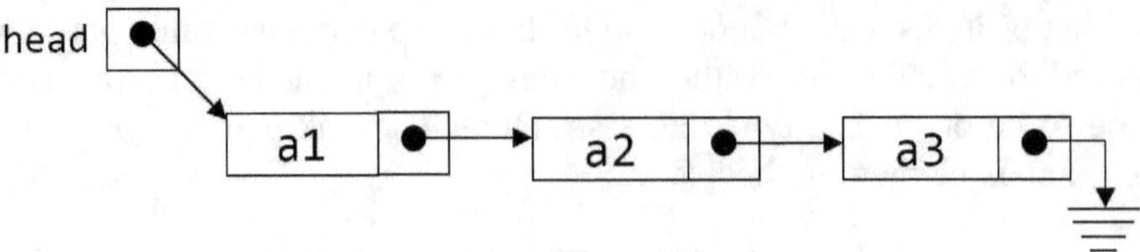

Let us look at the Node. The Value part of the node is of type integer, but it can be some other data-type. The link part of the node is named as Pointer in the diagram below.

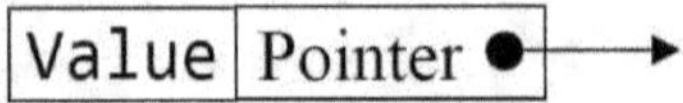

Example 16.1: Linked List node struct
```
typedef struct Node
{
    int value;
    struct Node *next;
} ListNode;
```

For a singly linked, we should always test these three test cases:
1. Zero element / Empty linked list.
2. One element / Single node case.
3. General case.

One node and zero node case are used to test boundary cases. It is always mandatory to take care of these cases before submitting code.

Problem 1: Insert an element at the start of the linked list.

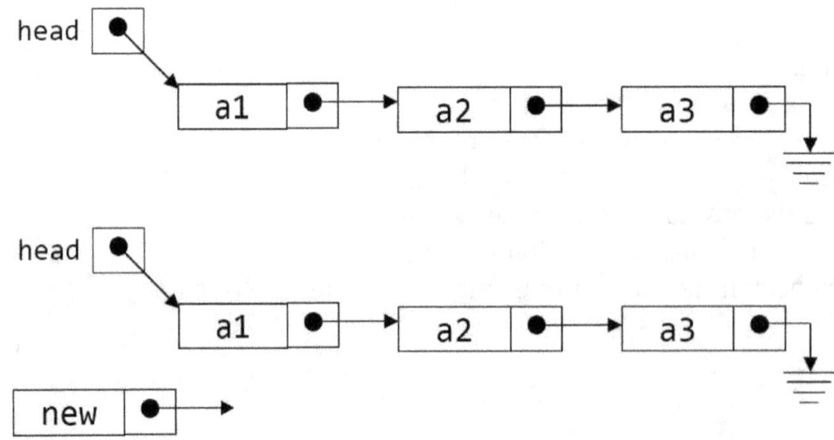

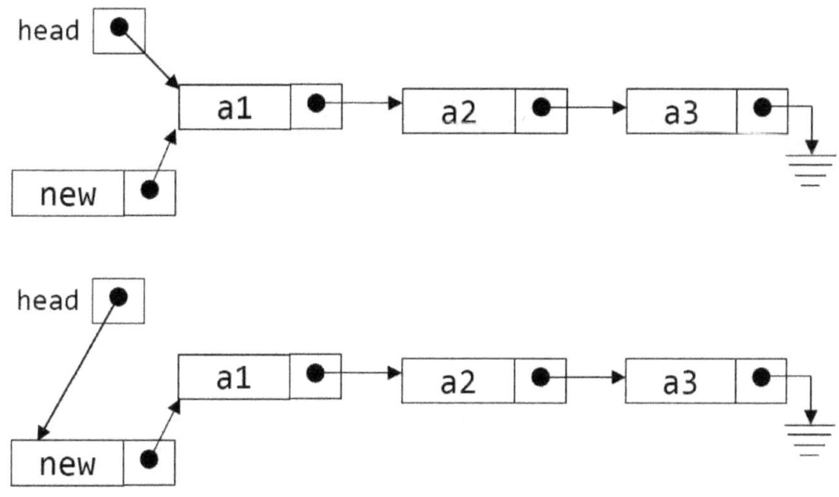

Example 16.2:

```c
int insertNode(ListNode **ptrHead, int value)
{
    ListNode *tempNode = (ListNode *)malloc(sizeof(ListNode));
    if (!tempNode)
        return -1;
    tempNode->value = value;
    tempNode->next = *ptrHead;
    *ptrHead = tempNode;
    return 1;
}
```

Analysis:

- We need to create a new node with the value passed to the function as an argument.
- The next pointer of the new node will point to the head of the linked list or null in the case when the list is empty.
- The newly created node will become the head of the linked list.

Time Complexity: O(1).

Problem 2: Insertion of an element at the end of the linked list

Example 16.3:

```c
int insertAtEnd(ListNode** ptrHead, int value)
{
    ListNode* head = *ptrHead;
    ListNode* tempNode = (ListNode* )malloc(sizeof(ListNode));

    if (!tempNode)
        return -1;

    tempNode->value = value;
```

```c
        tempNode->next = NULL;

        if (head == NULL)
        {
                tempNode->next = *ptrHead;
                *ptrHead = tempNode;
                return 1;
        }
        while (head->next != NULL)
        {
                head = head->next;
        }
        tempNode->next = head->next;
        head->next = tempNode;
        return 1;
}
```

Analysis:
- A new node is created and the value is stored inside it and stores null value to its next pointer.
- If the list is empty then this new node will become head of the linked list.
- If the list is not empty then we have to traverse to the end of the list.
- Finally, a new node is added to the end of the list.

Time Complexity: O(n).

Note: This operation is un-efficient as each time you want to insert an element you have to traverse to the end of the list. Therefore, the complexity of the creation of the list is $O(n^2)$. So to make it efficient we have to keep track of the last element by keeping a tail pointer. Therefore, if it is required to insert the element at the end of the linked list, then we will keep track of the tail reference also.

Problem 3: Print various elements of a linked list

Example 16.4:
```c
void printList(ListNode* head)
{
        printf("PrintLIst: ");
        while (head)
        {
                printf(" %d ", head->value);
                head = head->next;
        }
        printf("\n");
}
```

Analysis: We will traverse the list and print the value stored in nodes. The list is traversed by making head pointing to its next.

Time Complexity: O(n).

Example 16.5: Test code for linked list creation, adding value at the head, and printing elements.

```c
int main()
{
        ListNode* head = NULL;
        InsertNode(&head, 1);
        InsertNode(&head, 2);
        InsertNode(&head, 3);
        PrintList(head);
}
```

Analysis:

- ◆ A new instance of the linked list is created. Various elements are added to the list by calling the InsertNode() method.
- ◆ Finally, all the content of the list is printed to the screen by calling PrintList() method.

Problem 4: Search element in the linked list. Given a head pointer and value. Returns 1 if the value found in the list else returns 0.

Example 16.6:

```c
int searchList(ListNode* head, int value)
{
        while (head)
        {
                if (head->value == value)
                {
                        printf("\nThe value is found\n");
                        return 1;
                }
                head = head->next;
        }
        printf("\nThe value not found\n");
        return 0;
}
```

Analysis:

- ◆ Using a while loop we will iterate through the list.
- ◆ The value of each element of the list is compared with the given value. If the value is found, then the function will return 1.
- ◆ If the value is not found, then false will be returned from the function in the end.

Time Complexity: O(n).

Note: Search in a single linked list can only be done in one direction. Since all elements in the list have reference to the next item in the list. Therefore, the traversal of the linked list is linear.

Problem 5: Delete element at the head of the linked list.

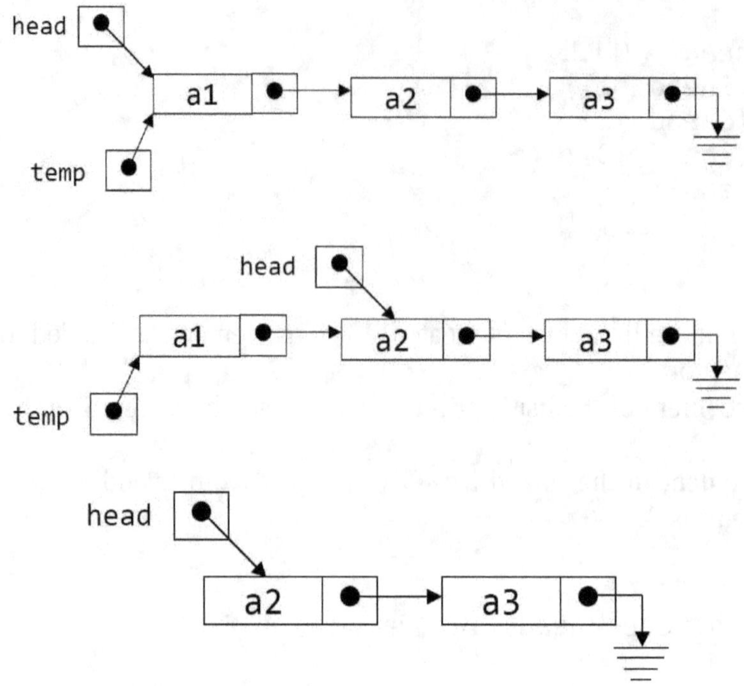

Example 16.7:
```c
void deleteFirstNodes(ListNode** ptrHead)
{
    ListNode* currNode = *ptrHead;
    ListNode* nextNode;

    if (currNode == NULL)
        return;

    nextNode = currNode->next;
    free(currNode);

    *ptrHead = nextNode;
}
```

Analysis:
- First, we need to check if the list is already empty. If empty then return.
- If the list is not empty then store the head node in a temporary variable currNode.
- Find the second node in the list and store it in the nextNode variable.
- Free memory of the first node of the linked list by calling free() function.
- Store address stored in pointer nextNode as head of the linked list.

Time Complexity: O(1).

Problem 6: Delete the first node whose value is equal to the given value.

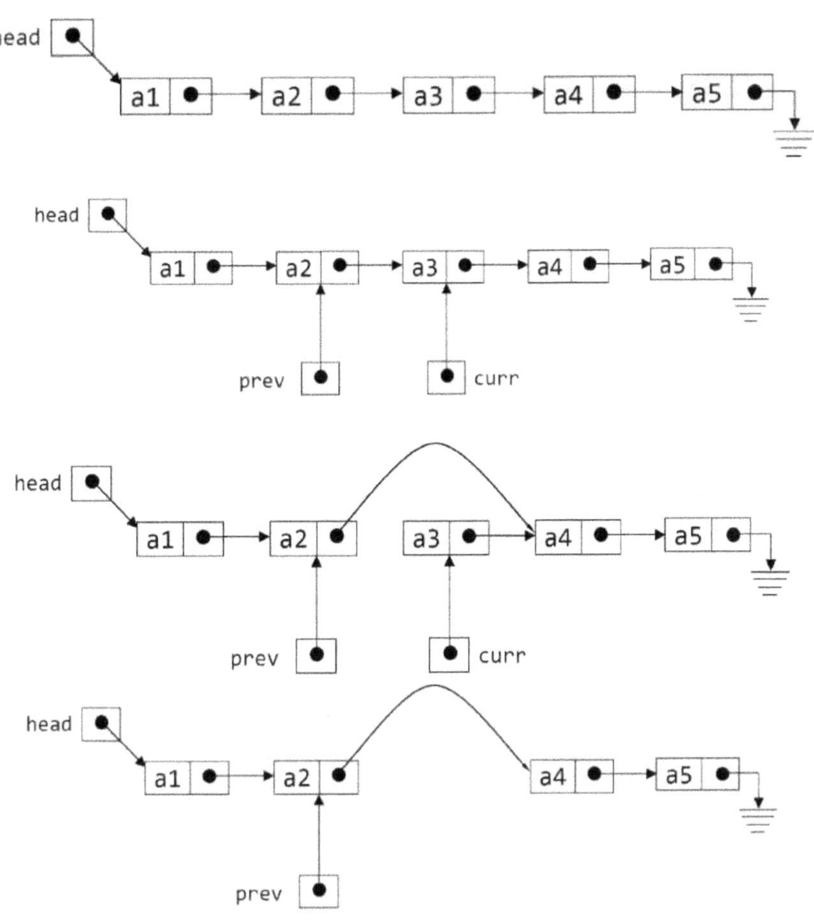

Example 16.8:
```c
void deleteNode(ListNode** ptrHead, int delValue)
{
        printf("\nDelete Node \n");
        ListNode* currNode = *ptrHead;
        ListNode* nextNode;

        if (currNode && currNode->value == delValue) /*first node */
        {
                *ptrHead = currNode->next;
                free(currNode);
                return;
        }

        while (currNode != NULL)
        {
                nextNode = currNode->next;
                if (nextNode && nextNode->value == delValue)
                {
                        currNode->next = nextNode->next;
                        free(nextNode);
```

```
            return;
        }
        else
        {
            currNode = nextNode;
        }
    }
}
```

Analysis:
- There are two cases when the node that needs to be deleted is the first node or is some other node in the list. When the node that needs to be deleted is the first node then the head of the linked list will be modified. In other cases, it will not modify.
- First, we check if the first node is the node with the value we are searching for, then we delete the first node and the head pointer is modified and point to the next node.
- In a while loop, we will traverse the link list and try to find the node that needs to be deleted. If the node is found then, we will point its previous node next point to the node next to the one we want to delete.
- Finally, we delete the node with the value which we are searching for by calling the free() function.

Time Complexity: O(n).

Stack

A stack is a basic data structure that organizes items in a last-in-first-out (LIFO) manner. The last element inserted in a stack will be the first to be removed from it.

The real-life analogy of the stack is "stack of plates". Imagine a stack of plates in a dining area everybody takes a plate at the top of the stack, thereby uncovering the next plate for the next person.

Stack allows you to only access the top element. The elements that are at the bottom of the stack are the one that is going to stay in the stack for the longest time.

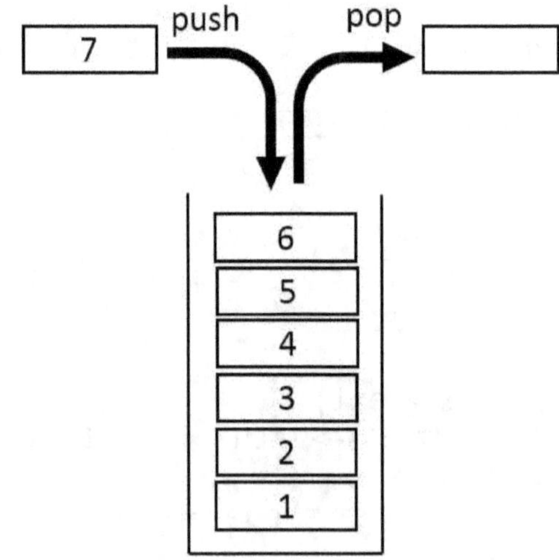

The various applications of stack are:
- ◆ Recursion: recursive calls are performed using system stack.
- ◆ Postfix evaluation of expression.
- ◆ Backtracking implemented using stack.
- ◆ Depth-first search of trees and graphs.
- ◆ Converting a decimal number into a binary number etc

Stack Operations:
- ◆ **Push(k):** Adds value k to the top of the stack
- ◆ **Pop():** Remove an element from the top of the stack and return its value.
- ◆ **Top():** Returns the value of the element at the top of the stack
- ◆ **Size():** Returns the number of elements in the stack
- ◆ **IsEmpty():** determines whether the stack is empty. It returns 1 if the stack is empty otherwise return 0.

Note: All the above stack operations are implemented in **O(1)** Time Complexity.

Push: Add value to the top of a stack

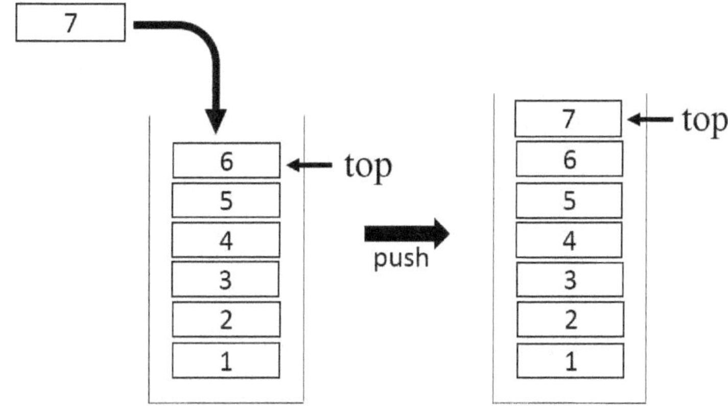

Pop: Remove the top element of the stack and return it to the caller function.

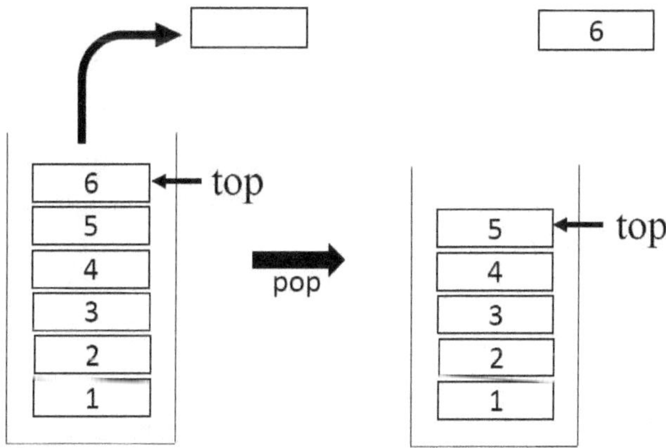

Problem 7: Implement a stack using a fixed-length array.

Example 16.9: Stack implementation using the array

```c
typedef struct stack
{
     int top;
     int data[MAX_CAPACITY];
} Stack;

void StackInitialize(Stack *stk)
{
     stk->top = -1;
}

int StackIsEmpty(Stack *stk) // returns 1 if the stack is empty or 0 in all
other cases.
{
     return (stk->top == -1);
}

int StackSize(Stack stk) // Returns the number of elements in the stack.
{
     return (stk->top + 1);
}

void StackPrint(Stack stk) //Print function to print elements of the array.
{
     printf("Stack :: ");
     for (int i = stk->top; i >= 0; i--)
     {
          printf("%d ", stk->data[i]);
     }
     printf("\n");
}

void StackPush(Stack *stk, int value) //Append value to the stack.
{
     if (stk->top < MAX_CAPACITY - 1)
     {
          stk->top++;
          stk->data[stk->top] = value;
     }
     else
     {
          printf("stack overflow\n");
     }
}
```

In the StackPop() function, first it will check that the stack is not empty. Then it will pop the value from the data array and return it.

```c
int StackPop(Stack *stk)
{
        if (stk->top >= 0)
        {
                int value = stk->data[stk->top];
                stk->top--;
                return value;
        }
        printf("stack empty\n");
        return ERROR_VALUE;
}
```

StackTop() function returns the value of stored in the top element of stack (does not remove it).

```c
int StackTop(Stack *stk)
{
        int value = stk->data[stk->top];
        return value;
}
```

Test code for the stack.

```c
int main()
{
        Stack stk;
        StackInitialize(&stk);
        StackPush(&stk, 1);
        StackPush(&stk, 2);
        StackPush(&stk, 3);
        StackPush(&stk, 4);
        StackPush(&stk, 5);
        StackPrint(&stk);
        return 0;
}
```

Analysis:
- The stack is initialized using StackInitialize() function.
- Use StackPush() and StackPop() functions to add / remove variables to the stack.
- Read the top element using the StackTop() function call.
- Query regarding the size of the stack using StackSize() function call
- Query if stack is empty using StackIsEmpty() function call

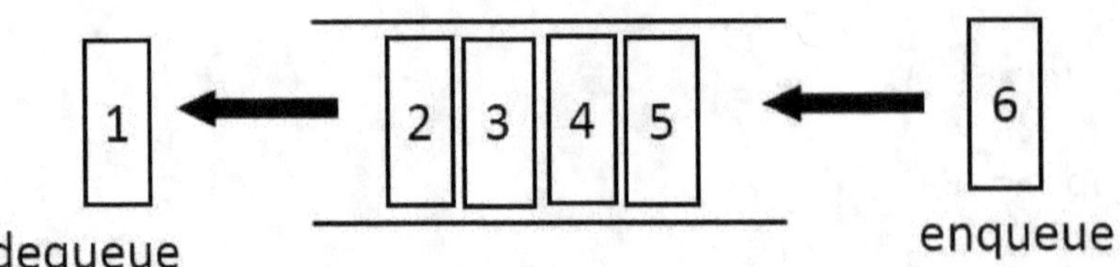

A queue is a basic data structure that organizes items in a first-in-first-out (FIFO) manner. The first element, inserted into a queue, will be the first to be removed. It is also known as "first-come-first-served".

The real-life analogy of queue is typical lines in which we all participate from time to time.
- We wait in a line at the railway reservation counter.
- We wait in the cafeteria line.
- We wait in a queue when we call some customer-care.

The elements, which are at the front of the queue, are the ones that stayed in the queue for the longest time.

Computer science also has many common examples of queues. We issue a print command from our office to a single printer per floor. The print task is lined up in a printer queue. The print command that is issued first will be printed before the next commands in line.

In addition to printing queues, the operating system is also using different queues to control process scheduling. Processes are added to the processing queue, which is used by an operating system for various scheduling algorithms.

A queue is a First-In-First-Out (FIFO) kind of data structure. The element that is added to the queue first will be the first to be removed and so on.

A queue has the following application uses:
- Access to shared resources (e.g., printer)
- Multiprogramming
- Message queue
- BFS, breadth-first traversal of graph or tree is implemented using the queue.

Queue Operations:
- **Add(K):** Adds a new element k to the back of the queue.
- **Remove():** Removes an element from the front of the queue and returns its value.
- **Front():** Returns the value of the element at the front of the queue.
- **Size():** Returns the number of elements inside the queue.
- **IsEmpty():** Returns 1 if the queue is empty otherwise returns 0

Note: All the above queue operations are implemented in **O(1)** Time Complexity.

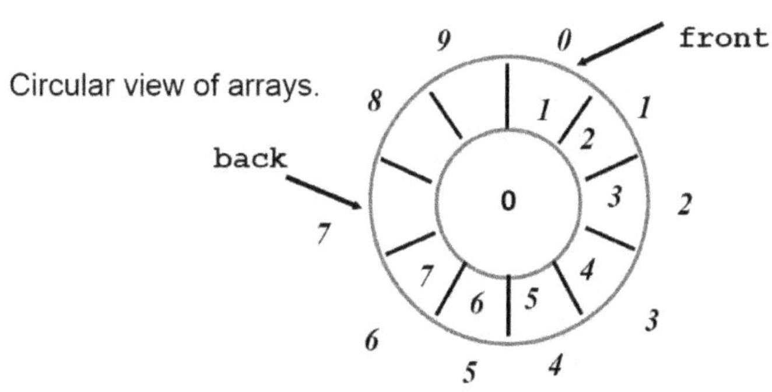

Example 16.10:

```c
typedef struct Queue_t
{
     int front;
     int back;
     int size;
     int data[MAX_CAPACITY];
} Queue;

void QueueInitialize(Queue *que)
{
     que->back = 0;
     que->front = 0;
     que->size = 0;
}

void QueueAdd(Queue *que, int value)
{
     if (que->size >= MAX_CAPACITY)
     {
          printf("\n Queue is full.");
          return;
     }
     else
     {
          que->size++;
          que->data[que->back] = value;
          que->back = (++(que->back)) % (MAX_CAPACITY - 1);
     }
}
```

```c
int QueueRemove(Queue *que)
{
    int value;
    if (que->size <= 0)
    {
        printf("\n Queue is empty.");
        return ERROR_VALUE;
    }
    else
    {
        que->size--;
        value = que->data[que->front];
        que->front = (++(que->front)) % (MAX_CAPACITY - 1);
    }
    return value;
}

int QueueFront(Queue *que)
{
    return que->data[que->front];
}

int QueueBack(Queue *que)
{
    return que->data[que->back - 1];
}

int QueueRemoveBack(Queue *que)
{
    int value;
    if (que->size <= 0)
    {
        printf("\n Queue is empty.");
        return ERROR_VALUE;
    }
    else
    {
        que->size--;
        value = que->data[que->back - 1];
        que->back = (que->front - 1) % (MAX_CAPACITY - 1);
    }
    return value;
}

int QueueIsEmpty(Queue *que)
{
    return que->size == 0;
}
```

```c
int QueueSize(Queue *que)
{
        return que->size;
}
```

Analysis:

- ◆ Hear queue is created using Array.
- ◆ QueueInitialize() is used to initialize queue.
- ◆ QueueAdd() to insert one element at the back of the queue.
- ◆ QueueRemove() to delete one element from the front of the queue.
- ◆ QueueFront() and QueueBack() is used to read front or back element of the queue.
- ◆ QueueRemoveBack() is used to remove the last element of the queue.
- ◆ QueueIsEmpty() is used to check if queue is empty.
- ◆ QueueSize() is used to find the number of elements in the queue.

Tree

Tree is a non-linear and hierarchical data structure. The top element of a tree is called the root of the tree. Except the root element, every element in a tree has a parent element, and zero or more child elements. The tree is the most useful data structure when you have hierarchical information to store.

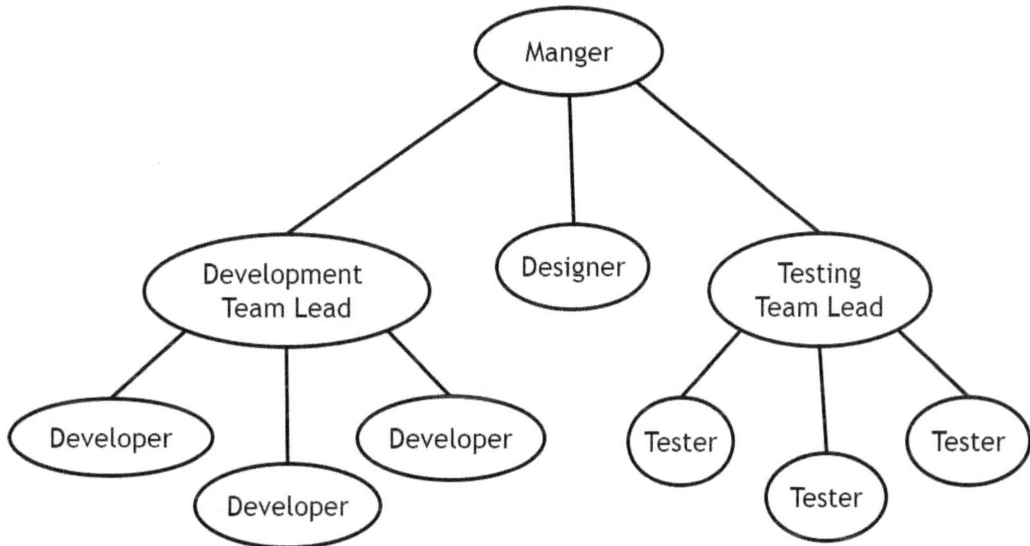

There are many types of trees, for example, binary-tree, Red-black tree, AVL tree, etc.

Exercise

1. Difference between linear and non-linear data-structure.

2. Give examples of linear and non-linear data-structure.

3. Compare array and linked list.

4. Implement a stack using a linked list.

5. Implement a queue using a linked list.